ADVANCES IN SOCIAL COGNITION, VOLUME I

A Dual Process Model of Impression Formation

ADVANCES IN SOCIAL COGNITION, Volume I

A Dual Process Model of Impression Formation

Edited by
THOMAS K. SRULL
ROBERT S. WYER, JR.
University of Illinois, Urbana-Champaign

LEA LAWRENCE ERLBAUM ASSOCIATES, PUBLISHERS
1988   Hillsdale, New Jersey   Hove and London

Lawrence Erlbaum Associates, Inc., Publishers
365 Broadway
Hillsdale, New Jersey 07642

ISBN 0-89859-888-5
ISBN 0-89859-673-4
ISSN 0898-2007

Printed in the United States of America
10 9 8 7 6 5 4 3 2 1

Contents

Preface

The present volume initiates a new series in *Advances in Social Cognition*. The purpose of the series is to present and evaluate new theoretical advances in social cognition and information processing. An entire volume will be devoted to each theory. This will allow it to be evaluated from a variety of perspectives and its implications for a wide range of issues to be considered.

The series reflects the two major characteristics of social cognition: the high level of activity in the field and the interstitial nature of the work. Each volume will contain a target article that is timely in its application, novel in its approach, and precise in its explication. The target article will then be followed by a set of critical commentaries that represent different theoretical persuasions, different subdisciplines within psychology, and occasionally separate disciplines. We believe that the dialogue created by such a format is highly unusual but, if done with care, extremely beneficial to the field.

Public debates are interesting and informative but they require a special group of people if they are to be productive. In this respect, we want to thank all of the contributors. Marilynn Brewer developed a theory of impression formation that is perspicacious and intrepid. She took a number of firm theoretical stands that were sure to provoke controversy. However, she worked with such diligence and élan that she made a long and difficult project enjoyable for all concerned. We truly admire her scholarship and we owe her a debt of gratitude that will probably never be repaid in full.

The commentators have played an equally important and difficult role. They were asked to prepare chapters that were critical but fair, and ones that were detailed but well reasoned. Readers will find that each of them is insightful, thought provoking, and an important contribution in its own right. We want to extend our sincere appreciation to each of the commentators for being so analytical and clear.

We also want to acknowledge the help of Larry Erlbaum in launching this new series. His encouragement was necessary and his suggestions were invariably helpful. Larry's wit and sense of humor always seem to appear at just the right time. We noticed. We will not forget.

Thomas K. Srull
Robert S. Wyer, Jr.

1 A Dual Process Model of Impression Formation

Marilynn B. Brewer
*University of California,
Los Angeles*

Broadly speaking, social cognition is the study of the interaction between internal knowledge structures—our mental representations of social objects and events—and new information about a specific person or social occasion. As a subfield of social psychology, social cognition draws liberally from theory and methods of cognitive psychology, but considerable attention is given to differences between social cognition and nonsocial cognition. Most often the distinction is made in terms of the nature of the *object* of perception. Ordinary cognition becomes social when the target of interest is a "social object," usually another person or group of persons.

Social objects are distinguished from other objects along a number of dimensions. In particular, persons are likely to be dynamic rather than static, active rather than passive, and to be perceived as causal agents—sources, rather than objects (Ostrom, 1984). In comparison to object categories, social categories have been postulated to be overlapping rather than hierarchically organized (Holyoak & Gordon, 1984; Lingle, Altom, & Medin, 1984), disjunctively rather than conjunctively defined (Wyer & Podeschi, 1978), and more susceptible to accessibility effects (Lingle et al., 1984).

The differences between social and nonsocial cognition may derive as much from differences in research focus and method as from any intrinsic differences in psychological processes. The study of object perception is generally concerned with the structure, format, and utilization of object categories or concepts. Once an adequate set of object categories has been acquired by the perceiver, individual objects are rarely encoded except as instances of some class. Such "top-down" processing assures stability of perception against recoding the same or equivalent objects across different occasions (Grossberg, 1976).

1

In contrast to the above, the study of person perception can best be characterized as the study of concept *formation* rather than concept utilization. Impression formation processes are assumed to be bottom-up, or data-driven, with an integrated representation of the individual person as the final product. The present paper challenges this prevailing view of the person perception process by proposing an alternative model of social cognition that incorporates top down processing as well as data-driven constructions. In the sections that follow, the differences between these two modes of impression formation are elaborated, and the implications for how and when social cognition differs from object perception are discussed.

TWO MODES OF PERSON PERCEPTION

Though they differ in their conceptualization of the integration processes involved, the classic impression formation theories of Asch (1946) and Anderson (1965) both conceive of the person perception process as the formation of an integrated impression derived from the stimulus information provided. Asch (1946), for instance, was convinced that the ability to form impressions of individual persons is a critical human skill:

> This remarkable capacity we possess to understand something of the character of another person, to form a conception of him as a human being . . . with particular characteristics *forming a distinct individuality,* is a precondition of social life. (p. 258, italics added)

These earlier theories of impression formation pretty much ignored information overload and cognitive capacity limitations in their conceptualizations of the person perception process. It was assumed (implicitly, at least) that when a perceiver is presented with information about a previously unfamiliar person, a kind of "mental slot" is created to receive and process data about that person. As individual pieces of information are encountered, they are integrated, on-line, with previously received information to form (or modify) a unified impression of the person as a single unit.

More recent social cognition models (e.g., Asch & Zukier, 1984; Burnstein & Schul, 1982; Hamilton, 1981; Hartwick, 1979; Srull, Lichtenstein, & Rothbart, 1985) place greater emphasis on the interaction between incoming stimulus information and prior knowledge (schemas), but still postulate a single process of selection, abstraction, interpretation, and integration (Alba & Hasher, 1983) that culminates in a person-based representation of the information provided. Once an integrated representation has been formed, further information processing and judgments about the target individual may be guided by the integrated impression as much or more than the original trait or behavior information on which it was based (Carlston, 1980; Lingle, 1983; Lingle & Ostrom, 1979; Schul, 1983). However, stimulus-based, on-line concept formation is clearly assumed to be prior to these memory-based impression effects (Hastie & Park, 1986).

Recent research casts doubt on the assumption that individual persons—more than any other object—automatically serve as the basis for organizing information in a complex stimulus array (cf. Pryor & Ostrom, 1981). Instead, social information processing may be organized around available social categories, which include mental representations of social attributes and classes of social events, social roles, and social groups. One reason that earlier research on impression formation failed to recognize this is that the typical research paradigm presented information to subjects about *one person at a time,* with all information pertinent to a particular stimulus person provided in a single block (either successively or simultaneously). Hence, impressions that were person-based could not be distinguished from category-based organization of the same information.

Based on a series of studies utilizing stimulus situations in which a variety of social information is presented about each of several persons, Pryor and Ostrom (1981; Ostrom Pryor, & Simpson, 1981) have suggested that person-based encoding is the exception rather than the rule in such complex information settings. Person-based organization in recall of information is found only for previously familiar persons (Pryor & Ostrom, 1981), when there is a substantial overlap between person information and prior social categories (Pryor, Kott, & Bovee, 1984), or when future interaction with individual stimulus persons is anticipated (Srull & Brand, 1983). Even the addition of pictorial information was not found to enhance person-based clustering in memory, although such visual cues did improve overall recall for social information (Lynn, Shavitt, & Ostrom, 1985).

Pryor and Ostrom's conclusions are supported by other research on the effects of memory load on person memory and on the differences between memory for persons as individuals versus persons in groups. Rothbart, Fulero, Jensen, Howard, and Birrell (1978) demonstrated that under low memory load conditions (i.e., few instances of person-trait pairings), subjects organized their impressions of a group around the characteristics of its individual members. When the amount of person-trait information increased, however, subjects organized trait information in an undifferentiated way around the group as a whole, failing to distinguish between repeated occurrences of a particular trait in the same individual and comparable repeated occurrences of that trait in different individuals.

If individuals are observed in a group context, the ability of a perceiver to remember which individuals were associated with specific traits or behaviors is apparently dependent on categorization processes. Category identity (such as race or gender) can either facilitate or interfere with accuracy of person recognition, depending on the nature of the group composition. When the categorical identity of an individual in a group is distinctive, person-based memory is enhanced (McCann, Ostrom, Tyner, & Mitchell, 1985; Taylor, Fiske, Etcoff, &

Ruderman, 1978). When groups or subgroups of individuals are homogeneous with respect to such category identity, however, recognition errors are enhanced and person-based organization in recall is decreased (Arcuri, 1982; Brewer, Dull, & Lui, 1981; Frable & Bem, 1985; Taylor et al., 1978).

Further research along these lines suggests that the way new information is integrated with previous impressions differs for perceptions of individual persons and persons in groups or aggregates. With impressions of single individuals, information that is inconsistent with previously established expectancies is processed more elaborately, and recalled better, than new information that is consistent or irrelevant to prior impressions (Hastie, 1980; Srull, 1981; Srull et al., 1985). When the same information is dispersed among members of a social category, however, items that are inconsistent with category stereotypes are remembered less than congruent items (Carney, DeWitt, & Davis, 1986; Stern, Marrs, Millar, & Cole, 1984; Wyer, Bodenhausen, & Srull, 1984).

Because high information load and input from multiple stimulus persons are certainly characteristic of many real-life social settings, research on impression formation in groups casts doubt on the ecological validity of person-centered views of social perception. In contrast to perspectives that emphasize the unique aspects of social cognition, I propose an alternative position based on the following two contentions: (1) The majority of the time, perception of social objects does not differ from nonsocial perception in either structure or process. (2) When it does differ, it is determined by the *perceiver's* purposes and processing goals, not by the characteristics of the target of perception. The same social information can be processed in a top-down manner that results in category-based cognitions, or in a bottom-up fashion that results in person-based representations, with implications for how new information is received, incorporated into existing knowledge structures, and used in making social judgments.

Both these premises are incorporated in the processing model represented in Fig. 1.1. This representation should not be considered a comprehensive processing model of the level of generality proposed, for instance, by Wyer and Srull (1986). Rather, it should be viewed as representing that portion of social information processing in which incoming information about a new stimulus person (or set of persons) is integrated with prior knowledge drawn from long-term memory. The model postulates two different routes by which such integration can take place. Which route is taken ultimately affects the form in which the new information is transferred to permanent storage.

The rectangles in the figure represent processing stages, each involving different types of knowledge structures and rules of inference. The processing modes are stages in the sense that they are assumed to occur sequentially; stages later in the sequence will not be activated until prior processing stages have been completed. Consistent with the "cognitive miser" perspective on social cognition (Fiske & Taylor, 1984), it is assumed that the individual perceiver resists moving to processing stages that require elaboration or modification of existing cognitive structures, unless it is required by certain decision rules. These decision rules

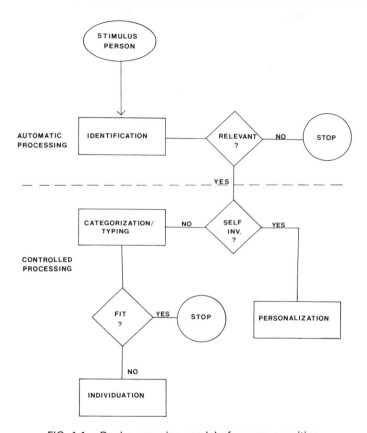

FIG. 1.1.   Dual processing model of person cognition.

(represented by diamonds in Fig. 1.1) reflect the demands of the stimulus configuration and the perceiver's goals or motives. If a satisfactory resolution of the stimulus information is achieved at an early stage, no further processing will be undertaken (as represented by the ''stop'' symbols in Fig. 1.1).

The process begins with the recognition that the stimulus environment contains a person or group of persons. Information about the stimulus person may be apprehended directly, or indirectly through verbal description. In either case, the model assumes that the mere presentation of a stimulus person activates certain classification processes (the *identification* stage in Fig. 1.1) that occur automatically and without conscious intent. This stage is common to all person perception. It is only in later stages, which are subject to conscious control, that significant differences in modes of processing take place.

The primary distinction drawn in the model is that between processing stages that are category-based (those depicted in the left-most pathway in Fig. 1.1) and processing that is person-based (personalized). The two types of processing result in different representations of the same social information. Category-based representations are assumed to result from processing that is primarily top-down, while personalized representations result from bottom-up processing.

This distinction parallels that made by Fiske and Pavelchak (1986) between category-based and "piecemeal-based" affect. The present model differs in its emphasis on cognitive representations rather than evaluative judgments of social objects, and in its incorporation of a levels of processing approach. Fiske and Pavelchak focus on stimulus properties as the primary determinant of the type of processing that will be activated. Trait information that fits an available category label is assumed to elicit category-based affect, while traits that are not congruent with an accessible category require piecemeal processing. The present model gives greater emphasis to perceiver motives and objectives as the primary determinant of processing mode. The same stimulus information may be processed in either way, depending on decisions made by the processor. The present model also expands on the basic distinction between category-based and piecemeal processing by postulating different stages of category-based processing.

One important distinction between the two processing modes is the level of abstraction or generality at which encoding of new information is likely to be stopped. Category-based processing proceeds from global to specific (Navon, 1977, 1981) and is expected to stop at the highest level of abstraction that will suffice. Bottom-up encoding begins with information at the most concrete level and stops at the lowest level of abstraction required by the prevailing processing objectives (Wyer & Srull, 1986). (The implications of this difference in level of encoding for order of recall of information at different levels are discussed later.)

The postulated differences in the nature of the knowledge structures that are accessed and the cognitive processes that are engaged in each of the stages represented in Fig. 1.1 are summarized in Table 1.1. The following sections are more detailed, emphasizing the points of distinction between stages and indicating some research results that lend credence to the meaningfulness of the hypothesized distinctions.

IDENTIFICATION: AUTOMATIC PROCESSING

Whenever a novel social object is encountered, an initial identification stage is postulated to precede any conscious, goal-driven information processing. In part, this identification is automatic in the sense of being stimulus controlled and not attentionally mediated (Bargh, 1984; McArthur & Baron, 1983). This is the stage that Bruner (1957) referred to as "primitive categorization," involving those dimensions of information about persons that are used so frequently and consistently as to become automatic, processed unconsciously and without intention. The process is one of "placing" the individual social object along well-established stimulus dimensions such as gender, age, and skin color.

TABLE 1.1
Comparison of Processing Stages

STAGE	KNOWLEDGE STRUCTURE	COGNITIVE PROCESSING
IDENTIFICATION	MULTIDIMENSIONAL SPACE	AUTOMATIC/ NONCONSCIOUS
TYPING	PICTOLITERAL PROTOTYPES	WHOLISTIC, NONVERBAL PATTERN-MATCHING
INDIVIDUATION	CATEGORY SUBTYPE OR EXEMPLAR	FEATURE DIFFERENTIATION
PERSONALIZATION	INDIVIDUAL SCHEMA, PROPOSITIONAL NETWORK	INTEGRATION AND ELABORATION

Evidence that some social information is processed automatically comes from studies of (a) the ease and speed with which some judgments are made, and (b) the difficulty of suppressing some stimulus information that is irrelevant to the processing task at hand. Research from the depth-of-processing tradition indicates that sex or gender of a stimulus person is identified at a much shallower level of processing than other judgments, such as "honesty" or "likeableness." Bower and Karlin (1974) had subjects review a series of 72 slides of male and female faces. For each slide they were asked to judge, as quickly as possible, whether the face was either (a) male or female, (b) honest or dishonest, or (c) likeable or not likeable. Later, subjects were given an unexpected recognition test to determine whether they could distinguish the faces they had seen from matched slides of previously unpresented faces. Faces that had been judged on the honesty and likeableness dimensions were correctly recognized 78% of the time, whereas faces that had been judged for gender were correctly recognized on only 60% of the test trials, suggesting that the gender judgments (though 100% accurate) required significantly less information processing or encoding than the former.

Further evidence for the automatic processing of gender information comes from preliminary research applying the "Stroop effect" to social judgments. The effect is demonstrated when an asymmetry appears in the relationship between two stimulus dimensions such that values on one dimension either facilitate or interfere with judgments on the second dimension, but not vice versa (Stroop, 1935). This effect is taken as evidence that the first dimension is attended to automatically, even when it is not relevant to the judgment task at hand. To illustrate this effect in the social domain, my colleagues and I have designed a set of stimulus pictures containing clear cues as to gender and occupation of the stimulus person depicted. On each of a series of trials, subjects are shown a selected pair of stimulus pictures and asked to indicate as quickly as possible whether the pictures were *the same* or *different* in either (a) sex, or (b) occupation. The same–different judgment task requires that subjects match the two pictures on cues relevant to the specified category while ignoring similarities or differences on irrelevant dimensions.

Preliminary results from one reaction time study employing these stimulus pictures support the predicted asymmetry of cross-dimension effects on response time. Gender information had significant effects on subjects' ability to make judgments of occupational match, but not vice versa. When stimulus pictures were of different sex, for instance, it took longer to make a correct judgment that they were the same in occupation than to make the judgment that they were different in occupation. The occupation of the two pictures, however, had no differential effects on speed of same–different judgments with regard to sex. Subjects apparently could not avoid processing irrelevant information regarding gender match vs. mismatch when making occupation judgments, but were able to ignore occupational cues when making gender decisions.

We assume that initial identification of a social stimulus is based on a limited number of stimulus dimensions that are processed simultaneously. In addition to those dimensions that are accessed frequently and consistently across social situations, the initial classification includes a global judgment along the dimension of relevance–irrelevance to the perceiver's immediate needs and goals. If, for instance, the perceiver is a traveler lost in a foreign city, a judgment as to whether a passing stranger is a "local" as opposed to another foreigner will be made prior to any further information seeking. Judgments at this stage may also include classification along primary affective dimensions such as hostile–friendly and strong–weak (Zajonc, 1980).

The primary outcome of the initial classification stage is a decision as to whether further processing is necessary. If, relative to the perceiver's current needs and immediate goals, the other is judged to be incompatible or irrelevant, he or she can be disregarded and no additional processing or information seeking will be undertaken. (It is possible, in fact, that no information about the other will be consciously recognized or referred to long-term memory.) If the other does not fall below this threshold, however, further efforts will be made to process information about the individual. It is at this point that a critical choice is made between two alternative processing modes. To the extent that the situation or characteristics of the stimulus person engage *self-involvement* (i.e., the perceiver feels closely related to or interdependent with the target person, or feels ego-involved in the judgment task), processing will be person-based and data-driven. Some of the specific factors that promote such person-based processing are discussed later. In the absence of such attentional involvement, however, processing will be directed toward categorizing the stimulus information at some appropriate level of specificity within a prior category structure.

TYPING: STRUCTURE AND FORMAT
OF PERSON CATEGORIES

In considering what kinds of knowledge structures are accessed when a stimulus person is being classified, the present model differs from most prior conceptualizations in its emphasis on social categories or person "types," rather than trait dimensions. Although some set theoretic models have been advanced previously (e.g., Rosenberg & Gara, 1985), theories of "implicit personality theory" have usually depicted the individual's social knowledge structure as a multidimensional trait space (Passini & Norman, 1966; Rosenberg & Sedlak, 1972; Schneider, 1973). According to Gangestad and Snyder (1985), there is a prevailing assumption among personologists that the units of personality are continuous dimensions, and a concomitant "prejudice" against discrete class variables.

Recent studies that have compared the adequacy of multidimensional scaling representations of proximity among social stimuli to discrete clustering representations of the same data (Dull, 1982; Powell & Juhnke, 1983; Tversky & Hutchinson, 1986) challenge the assumption that similarity judgments among social objects can be mapped by geometric models. One reason that multidimensional models prove inadequate is that individuals are able to process stimuli along a limited number of dimensions at one time. Prinz and Scheerer-Neumann (1974) demonstrated that when the number of dimensions relevant to a multiattribute stimulus classification task exceeds two or three, subjects abandon dimensional discriminations in favor of a feature detection strategy. That is, they do not attempt to localize the target stimulus within the total multidimensional space but represent it instead in terms of the presence of discriminating features.

Most attributes can be represented either as features or as points along a stimulus dimension, but which representation is chosen can have important implications for category structure and processing (Lingle et al., 1984). Dimensions allow for sensitive discriminations between stimuli but feature analysis implies all-or-nothing judgments. Dimensional versus feature representations also affect how similarity judgments are made. Similarity in multidimensional space is a Euclidian distance measure, and the degree of similarity between any pair of objects is assumed to be symmetric. With feature representations, similarity is based on the relative number of common features between two objects or categories and judgments of similarity need not be symmetric, depending on which object is the standard of comparison (Tversky, 1977).

Results of a social judgment experiment by Dull (1982) illustrate the difference in processing of the same social stimuli when analyzed in terms of dimensions versus features. Subjects were given descriptions of 14 different women, each characterized by a set of behavioral statements, and were asked to sort the stimulus persons either in terms of a trait dimension (active-passive) or a categorical judgment (career woman vs. housewife). Following the initial sortings, subjects rated each stimulus on the degree to which they possessed the trait or fit the category. Stimuli had been constructed of differing numbers of statements that were relevant or irrelevant (neutral) with respect to the target judgment. Regression analyses of ratings indicated that the extremity of categorical judgments was affected only by the number of relevant statements contained in the stimulus description, and was insensitive to the number of irrelevant features, thus fitting a summative model of impression formation. Dimensional ratings, on the other hand, were affected positively by the number of relevant statements and negatively by the number of irrelevant, or neutral, items, thus fitting an averaging model of stimulus integration.

Dull (1982) also found that the structure of similarity ratings among behavior descriptions differed depending on whether they were being sorted according to semantic similarity or as category features. Semantic ratings were best represented by mulidimensional scaling analyses, but category-based judgments were best represented by cluster analysis. Schneider and Blankmeyer (1983) also demonstrated that ratings of trait associations are altered when particular social categories are made salient.

In line with these research findings, the present model is based on the assumption that the mental structures against which we evaluate social objects are categories rather than dimensions, and this assumption is reflected in the structural and processing descriptions associated with the second stage in Table 1.1. Drawing largely from Rosch's (1978) theory of natural categories, social categories are assumed to be "fuzzy sets," represented in the form of prototypic *images* rather than verbal trait lists. A schematic representation of this mental structure is provided in Fig. 1.2, which illustrates both the structure and format of the postulated social category system.

The model is hierarchical in the sense that social categories (person "types") are nested within superordinate sets defined by *partitionings* along a few primary dimensions. These dimensions are those used so frequently as to be processed automatically in the initial identification stage of social perception. (Two such

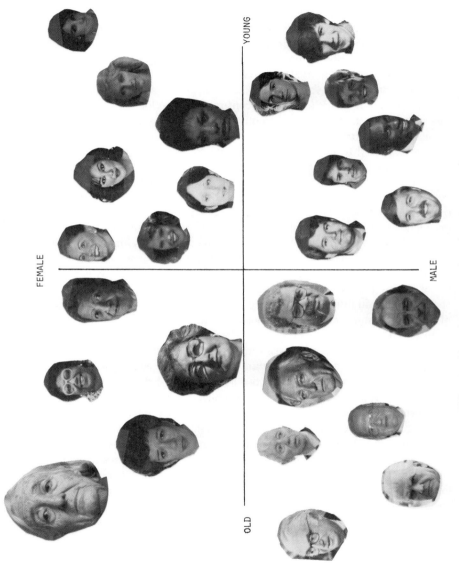

FIG. 1.2. Mental representation of person types.

dimensions—age and sex—are represented in the figure for illustrative purposes. In actuality, most perceivers probably utilize three or four dimensions of classification, but consistent with the earlier research, it is assumed that the number of primary dimensions is limited.)

Apart from the primary partitionings, social categories are defined by features rather than by location in multidimensional space. From personal and shared social experience, the individual perceiver derives a set of person ''types'' that are represented in the form of abstract images or interrelated features. The primary partitionings are assumed to constrain the development of social categories in the sense that further differentiations among classes of social stimuli are made after this primary classification has taken place. Hence, all social categories are expected to be clustered within quadrants of the primary dimensional space and categories are not expected to cross-cut partition boundaries. One interesting implication of this assumption is the relationship that is expected between the representation of social roles (such as occupation) and primary dimensions such as gender. Many social roles are not exclusively associated with one gender. However, social roles are among the features that define person types, which are presumed to be nested within gender. This implies that *different* representations of the same social role are developed, depending on whether the role occupant is male or female. In other words, the concept of ''woman doctor'' is not simply the intersection of the categories ''woman'' and ''doctor,'' but a specific type within the general category of women, and part of a configuration of traits and features distinct from those associated with ''man doctor'' (or, more simply, ''doctor'').

The same is expected to be true for age-related distinctions. ''Businessmen,'' for instance may be a category within ''young men'' and within ''older men,'' but the features associated with ''businessman'' will differ depending on the hierarchy in which it is contained. This conceptualization has implications for interpretation of the sex–occupation judgment study cited previously. If the mental representation of occupations is differentiated by age and gender, then a male and female figure who represent the same occupation do not ''match'' on occupation in the same sense that two males occupying the same role would.

The model depicted in Fig. 1.2 also assumes that category types exist at different levels of generality—from the highly abstract to the more concrete and specific. For instance, within the partition of ''older men,'' there may be a relatively abstract image of the general subcategory ''businessmen'' and more specific subtypes such as ''uptight authoritarian boss who is a tightwad and a stickler for detail.'' As this illustration suggests, the specific (lower level) subtypes are assumed to be represented in richer and more vivid detail than the more generalized categories. The existence of distinct category subtypes that differ in level of concreteness and detail from more general category representations has been demonstrated in research on gender stereotypes (Ashmore, DelBoca, &

Titus, 1984), stereotypes of the elderly (Brewer et al., 1981), and personality types (Cantor & Mischel, 1979).

Person Types: Words or Images?

Person categories are represented in Fig. 1.2 by faces to reflect the assumption (in its strongest form) that such person types are *pictoliteral* representations (Klatzky, 1984). Pictoliteral representations differ from nonvisual or conceptual representations in both content and form. In comparison to nonvisual concepts, images are more specific, configural, and *unmediated by verbal description.* Traits, and other semantic features, are assumed to be *inferred* from the category representation at the time judgments are made, rather than represented directly in the mental image.

Pictoliteral representations are also analogue rather than propositional in form; spatial information is retained in memory in a form that preserves continuity of information. As Kosslyn (1980) states it, visual representations *depict* the stimulus rather than describe it. The resulting representation is a point-by-point mapping of the stimulus that can be operated on in a manner analogous to the processing of external stimuli.

The issue of whether mental representations of social constructs are literally images rather than propositional in format may be empirically unresolveable (see Anderson, 1978), but there are a number of advantages to conceptualizing category prototypes as "picture-like" in format. First, as Medin has convincingly pointed out (Medin, 1983; Murphy & Medin, 1985), definitions of categories based on constituent attributes or feature correlations are inadequate for a number of reasons. Categories contain not only attributes but operations, transformations, and relations among attributes (Murphy & Medin, 1985, p. 295). Basic categories are *configurations of parts,* with parts being simultaneously functional and perceptual (Tversky & Hemenway, 1984). Pictoliteral representations have the advantage of preserving these temporal, spatial, and configural relations among category features and thus function more like schemas than do associative networks (Wyer & Gordon, 1984).

A second reason for emphasizing the image-like nature of category prototypes is that visual information has been generally underrepresented in person perception research. Although image formats have been included in some social memory models (e.g., Lord, 1980; Swann & Miller, 1982; Wyer & Srull, 1986), the stimulus information presented in most social perception experiments has been in the verbal form of trait lists or descriptive sentences. This is true despite evidence that our perceptions of people's character and personality is strongly affected by facial appearance (Berry & McArthur, 1986; McArthur, 1982). Early research on impression formation by Secord and his associates (e.g., Secord, Dukes, & Bevan, 1954; Secord & Muthard, 1955) found that with facial photographs as stimuli, physiognomic features tend to be associated with personality impressions. Persons who were categorized as similar in physical appearance were perceived as similar in personality, and those who looked different were seen as having different personalities.

In his work on the relationship between facial characteristics and impressions, Secord also attempted to determine whether particular physical features were strongly associated with specific personality traits (e.g., "wearing glasses" is equated with "intelligence"). He found for the most part that such relationships are complex, with the effect of any given facial feature depending upon the other facial features with which it appeared. He also found that impressions were formed quickly (with high interrater agreement), whereas judgments of physiognomic features took longer and appeared to be more labored. These results accord well with findings from research on facial recognition from which it appears that faces are encoded and remembered as "gestalts" rather than as assortments of discrete features.

The strength and rapidity with which social inferences are drawn from facial information suggests that individuals maintain visual "templates" corresponding to important social experiences. When features of a new social stimulus match those of a preexisting template, corresponding inferences are made. Based on an ecological approach to social perception (McArthur & Baron, 1983), Berry and McArthur (1986) have suggested that facial characteristics influence impressions if they *reveal* psychological attributes whose detection has adaptive significance. Individuals become attuned to detect specific features or feature configurations that connote functional distinctions between persons. Although the association between facial features and psychological characteristics may have some ecological validity, such associations may also become overgeneralized. For instance, the facial features associated with "babyishness" are highly represented in infant faces and strongly connote helplessness. The inference of helplessness is also made, however, to adults whose facial characteristics include any of these features (Berry & McArthur, 1986).

Recent research on the content of social stereotypes also indicates that stereotypes have a visual component. Ashmore and his colleagues (e.g., Ashmore et al., 1984) have demonstrated in their research that the labels associated with gender types can elicit rich visual images of the kind of person represented by the label. Research on gender stereotypes by Deaux and Lewis (1984) also indicates that physical characteristics associated with sex differences are highly linked to trait and role inferences. In fact, the implicational associations from physical features to gender-related traits and roles were stronger in general than the linkages between other components of the gender stereotype.

Experimental evidence that category labels generate implicit visual images comes from studies conducted by Klatzky, Martin, and Kane (1982) on occupational stereotypes. Subjects were presented with a visual discrimination task in which they had to decide whether slides containing split facial images were actual faces (i.e., two sides of the same face) or "nonfaces" (i.e., two halves of different faces). Some of the decision trials were preceded by a verbal "prime" in the form of an occupational label (e.g., judge, truckdriver, hairdresser). Faces used to construct the visual stimuli had been previously scaled for association with the occupational categories. On those trials in which an actual face was preceded by an occupational prime *different from* its stereotypic associate, reaction time to identify the stimulus correctly as a face was significantly greater than on trials in which no prime had been provided. These results indicate that the occupational label automatically elicited a mental image which then interfered with the processing of a visual stimulus that was incongruent with that image.

These studies suggest that verbal labels for social categories and visual images of members of those categories are associatively linked. Labels elicit visual characteristics and visual information generates trait inferences. Results from our own research on the visual representation of social categories (Brewer & Lui, 1983) suggests, in fact, that many more shared person types are available than have corresponding verbal labels. When given sets of photographs representing different person types, subjects tend to show high agreement on which photos go together as a category, and to agree on the personality and behavioral attributes that characterize members of the category. Yet when asked to provide a verbal label for these person types, they often find the task difficult and come up with lengthy, idiosyncratic descriptions rather than brief, agreed upon labels. Thus it seems that person labels are consistently able to elicit mental images, but images do not always have corresponding labels.

The methods we have used in our research to elicit person types differ in a number of ways from studies that rely on verbal labels to delineate category subtypes. First and foremost, we start from visual stimuli rather than verbal descriptions. From a variety of sources we have collected a set of 140 facial photographs, containing an equal number of males and females (all Caucasian), ranging in apparent age from 20 to 70+. The entire set of photos is given to subjects (with no mention of superordinate features such as age or gender) who are asked to sort the photos into separate stacks that "contain pictures of people that you feel are similar in character or personality type."

From the free sortings obtained from 20 college student subjects we generated a matrix of cooccurrences for all pairings of the 140 stimulus photos. Such a cooccurrence matrix represents a similarity matrix for the photos based on the degree of intersubject agreement that the pairs of photos do or do not go together (i.e., a consensual measure of interitem similarity or dissimilarity). This similarity matrix was then subjected to cluster analysis to identify subclusters of photos that were associated by a significant proportion of our subjects. A representation of the results of the cluster analysis is provided in Fig. 1.3, where individual photos (identified by ID numbers in the figure) are arranged by age and gender and optimal clusterings indicated by closed circles.

Note that relatively few of the clusters cross age-sex boundaries, except at the

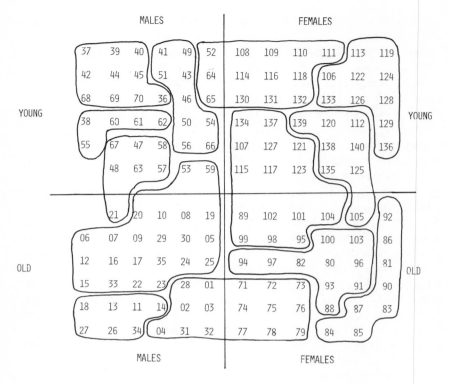

FIG. 1.3.   Cluster analysis of photo sorts.

extremes on the age dimension (where some young, long-haired males are categorized with young females, and very elderly men and women are categorized in a common cluster). Thus, our empirically derived categories are consistent with the hypothesized partitionings represented in Fig. 1.2. These partitions, however, are apparently implicit rather than consciously recognized. When subjects were asked to provide brief verbal descriptions for the categories they had generated, age or sex were rarely explicitly mentioned as category features. Instead, descriptions tended to be a combination of roles, trait descriptors, and behavioral characteristics, such as the following:

"serious professionals with I-dare-you-to-challenge-my-opinion attitudes"
"elderly but happy people who seem to enjoy life although possibly they are faking it"
"businessmen who sit behind a desk dealing with money, which is important to them"
"white collar workers who are uptight about their jobs"

"people who are persistent talkers and don't pay attention to their listeners' reactions"

"people who have lived a harsh life or experienced a trauma and never fully recovered"

"Barbara Walters-types, gossipers, nosey, yet sly and slightly snobbish"

"secretaries who are happy that it is lunchtime!"

(One possible interpretation of our findings is that our subjects sorted photographs on the basis of specific physical features and then inferred personality traits from those features rather than from preexisting mental images. In a separate version of the sorting study, however, in which subjects were explicitly instructed to sort the photos according to shared physical features, the resulting clusters overlapped only partially with those based on character types. In addition, when subjects in the physical feature sorting condition were asked to describe the categories they had generated, their descriptions tended to depart from simple physical attributes and to include personality and behavioral information much like that generated in the character type sorting condition. Further, subjects in the physical sorting condition found the task more difficult than subjects asked to use personality types, and generated significantly more categories on average.)

Impression Formation as Category Matching

What do these data on the structural characteristics of person types as represented in memory imply about how we form impressions of new individuals that we encounter? Returning to Table 1.1, the model assumes that impressions are based on an active categorization process in which available "person types" are matched to the information given about the new person. The search is presumed to continue as an iterative, pattern-matching process, starting at the most general level of categorization and progressing to more specific subtypes, until an adequate fit is achieved. The level of specificity needed for an adequate categorization will be determined primarily by the amount and degree of detail available about the target person that is attended to. Thus, level of categorization is affected both by stimulus characteristics and by task demands that influence motivation and attention.

Category activation.   How a particular stimulus person is categorized will depend a great deal on where in the perceiver's available category system the search for a category match begins. The structural model represented in Fig. 1.2 implies that the search will be delimited by the initial classification of the stimulus along the primary dimensions of classification. Beyond that, category selection will be determined by (1) category accessibility, (2) contextual cues, and (3) the processing goals of the perceiver.

The likelihood that a particular category will be accessed in the process of categorizing a new stimulus person will depend in part on the frequency and recency with which that category has been activiated in the past (Higgins & King, 1981; Wyer & Srull, 1981). (Although most of the research on category priming effects has been done utilizing trait concepts rather than person types, we can assume that the same factors that increase the accessibility of traits also affect the utilization of particular person types.) In a series of experiments, Higgins, Rholes, and Jones (1977) and Wyer and Srull (1981) have demonstrated that the activation of a particular trait construct in one task context affects subjects' judgments of a stimulus person in a subsequent, unrelated person perception task. Construct accessibility can also be enhanced by its prominence or distinctiveness in memory and by the activation of closely related constructs (Higgins & King, 1981).

Category activation is also affected by salient cues and labels in the stimulus environment. If one meets a new person on the tennis court, categorization in terms of some athletic person type is much more likely than if the same individual was first encountered in a work setting. Similarly, if the perceiver is told that Dr. Smith teaches at the local university, she is more likely to be matched against a professorial subtype than if that role information had not been provided. Category salience can also be affected by group composition. Gender-related categories are more likely to be activated, for instance, in social contexts involving mixed-sex groups than in same-sex groups, particularly if one sex is a distinctive minority (Higgins & King, 1981).

Finally, categorization is influenced by the current or chronic processing goals of the perceiver. In his classic paper on construct accessibility, Bruner (1957) hypothesized that a primary determinant of category activation is the search requirements imposed by the perceiver's needs, objectives, and task goals. The perceiver being asked to make a psychiatric diagnosis of a new individual is going to start from a different set of categories than a perceiver trying to decide who to ask out for next Saturday night. Srull and Wyer (1986) have provided a recent review of processing goals induced by personal concerns, values, and task requirements and their role in the encoding and retrieval of social information.

Consequences of category activation. Once a particular category has been activated, the threshold for identifying a match between the category prototype and incoming stimulus information is lowered (Higgins & King, 1981). If the initial fit is not adequate, however, the search for an appropriate categorization will be directed downward, among subtypes of the original category, rather than horizontally among alternative categories at the same level of abstraction. If, for instance, the stimulus person does not match the perceiver's prototypic image of a "businessman," the perceiver will search for more concrete, specific types of businessmen (e.g., the "young whiz-kid") that provide a better fit. It is unlikely that the perceiver would instead start the categorization process over with a different general category. Thus, initial category activation sets in motion an iterative process that constrains the final category selection.

Once a satisfactory categorization of a stimulus person has been achieved in this iterative fashion, further information processing will be organized around that category. Additional attributes of the person will be inferred from category content and new information will be assimilated to category expectations. Further, affective reactions to the individual will be category-based in the sense that the evaluation associated with the category type will be "transferred" directly to the person, irrespective of the specific information available about the individual (Fiske & Pavelchak, 1986).

A number of lines of research support the role of category activation in selection, interpretation, and memory for information about individual persons. Most of these reveal biases that favor the encoding and retrieval of information that is consistent with or confirms prior category expectancies or knowledge. Such biases have been demonstrated in (1) selective retrieval from memory of category consistent information, (2) selective attention to category relevant cues, and (3) selective encoding of ambiguous stimulus information in category consistent ways.

Category effects on memory for social information are well established. Research on illusory correlations (Chapman & Chapman, 1967; Hamilton & Rose, 1980) demonstrates expectancy-confirming biases in that the remembered frequence of person-trait pairings that fit prior expectations is high relative to recall for the frequency of pairings that are not stereotype consistent. Cohen (1981) demonstrated that knowledge of an individual's occupational categorization strongly influenced memory for behavioral details from a videotaped presentation. Brewer et al., (1981) further demonstrated that such category-based memory effects are especially strong for information that fits category prototypes that are highly concrete and specific.

Social category information also affects the search for information, prior to encoding and recall. Carver and de la Garza (1984), for instance, found that subjects requested different types of information regarding possible causes of a traffic accident when they had been told that the driver was an elderly person than when they were told he was young.

Some of the more interesting research on effects of categorization on information processing is that demonstrating that category labels in combination with behavioral information about an individual produce more category-biased judgments than category labels alone. Darley and Gross (1983) suggest that this effect occurs because category information generates hypotheses about person characteristics which are not expressed in confident judgments about that person until they have been tested against behavioral data. However, since hypothesis-guided information search is biased in the direction of confirming prior expectancies, additional information is likely to lead to category-consistent judgments, particularly if it is ambiguous or nondiagnostic with respect to the judgment to be made. These effects were confirmed in research by Clark and Rutter (1985) who found that visual cues had little effect on social judgments when subjects had prior social categorical knowledge about the targets, but the presence of visual information significantly enhanced subjects' confidence in their category-based judgments. Such studies strongly support a top-down processing model in which prior categorical knowledge is fit to incoming information about a novel social object, as opposed to a data-driven process in which a person impression is "built" from available stimulus information.

INDIVIDUATION: INTRACATEGORY DIFFERENTIATION

Although ambiguous information can readily be assimilated to preexisting category attributes, what happens when information about a stimulus person is clearly incongruent with category prototypes, either because some feature of the individual is blatantly inconsistent with aspects of the most appropriate category, or because much more information is available about the new person than can be fit into a single category? Tracing the effects of exposure to disconfirming information on the structure and content of social categories is one of the more intriguing problems of social cognition research.

Once an individual has been identified with a particular social category, new information that is inconsistent with category expectations can be handled in a number of ways. For one thing, such information may simply be ignored or discounted. We have already cited evidence indicating that in a group context, information that is inconsistent with group stereotypes may be less well attended to than inconsistent information processed at the individual level.

When information that is discrepant with category membership is either highly salient or frequently encountered, it may be attended to but still not affect the content of category stereotypes (Weber & Crocker, 1983). If several category members share the same distinguishing features, these instances may be differentiated into a category subtype, with the distinctive features constituting the prototypic characteristics of the new social type. Such differentiation leads to what Quattrone (1986) refers to as "taxonomic variability" of category stereotypes. This refers to the extent to which the general category is differentiated into distinctive subtypes, each subtype being represented by a unique configuration of characteristic features. The formation of category subtypes preserves the dynamic aspect of social category systems, in the face of conservative tendencies to resist category change.

When category-discrepant features are associated with a single person rather than a subgroup, that particular person may be individuated as a member of the general category. Such individuated category members may become the basis for the formation of a category subtype. For example, the first anchorwoman that appeared on a national television news program was no doubt highly individuated as a member of the category of news broadcasters. However, once the distinguishing features of a successful anchorwoman had been identified, women with similar characteristics appeared in newsrooms all over the country, thus generating a new cultural prototype.

Individuation refers to encoding a specific object as a *special instance* of a more general type. This is the process that Billig (1985) refers to as "particularization." Although differentiating features are attached directly to the individual and not to the category as a whole (e.g., the U.S. President who was an alcoholic; the Sunday School teacher who swears when she is angry), the process is still category-based in that the distinguishing features are defined with reference to the more general category or person type. Information about the individual that is not inconsistent with category expectations is not incorporated into the individuated representation. This model of individuation is thus similar to Graesser's schema-pointer-plus-tag model of memory for atypical features of social events or scripts (Graesser, Gordon, & Sawyer, 1979; Smith & Graesser, 1981).

Individuation of memory for category inconsistent information is illustrated by the results of a recognition experiment conducted by Lui and Brewer (1983). In the impression formation phase of this experiment, college student subjects were presented with photographs of elderly women who were prototypic representatives of specific person types. Each photograph was described by a set of behavior statements all of which were consistent with prototypic attributes, or by a set that contained a combination of consistent and inconsistent statements. Subjects were subsequently given a recognition task in which they were provided with one descriptive statement as a cue and asked to decide which of two photographs had been originally associated with that particular statement.

When the two photographs in a recognition trial were both representatives of the same social category (type), correct recognition was generally low for items that were consistent with category prototypes. In other words, when information that was category consistent was presented, subjects could not remember which particular member of that category had been paired with that statement. Such information was apparently remembered as representative of the social category rather than as a feature of specific individuals. On the other hand, for items that had been incongruent with category prototypes, recognition of the correct individual was very high, regardless of whether the distractor photograph was a member of the same or a different social category from that of the correct photo. However, category-consistent items that had been presented with the same photo were correctly recognized with only chance accuracy. Thus, it was only the distinctive, inconsistent pieces of information that were directly linked with the specific individual, while consistent information was more strongly linked to the social category.

PERSONALIZATION: THE FORMATION OF PERSON-BASED IMPRESSIONS

Although individuation and differentiation involve elaborations of the structure and content of social categories as a function of new social information, both processes still result in category-based impressions of the target individual. Thus both are the product of top-down processing in which the representation of the individual person is subordinate to that of the social category. Category-based processing of person information produces little difference between social and nonsocial cognition. Nonsocial objects such as tables, automobiles, snakes, and swingsets, are rarely cognized outside of the context of the basic object categories they represent. Most of the time members of object categories are treated as essentially equivalent, but some are remembered distinctively, such as the apple I bit into when I was 12 years old that had a worm in it. Although specific instances of nonsocial object categories may be individuated, however, it is rarely the case that such objects would be represented in a way that is highly personalized.

Personalization refers to the formation of a different type of cognitive structure in which the individual becomes the basis for organization of all relevant information. The new organizational structure is sort of a mental flip-flop of the category-based structure we have been describing. Consider, for example, the statement "Janet is a nurse." This description can be psychologically represented in one of two ways. It could mean that Janet is subordinate to (i.e., a specific instance of) the general category of nurses. Or, alternatively, it could mean that being a nurse is subordinate to (i.e., a particular feature of) the concept of Janet. The former interpretation is an example of category-based individuation, while the latter is an example of personalization.

In category-based cognition, the individual is attached to a category node and most information about the individual (with the exception of individuating features that would be attached directly to the specific object) is associated with the category. When information is personalized, however, category membership is stored as a feature of the individual, to be integrated with other information about that person in a way that prevents confusion with other individuals who may share any particular attribute. The concept of "nurse" as a feature of Janet would contain only those aspects of nursing that are characteristic of Janet in that role, and would be disassociated from the prototypic representation of nurse as a general category, which may contain many features not applicable to Janet personally.

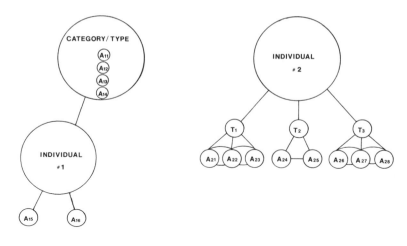

a. CATEGORY-BASED REPRESENTATION   b. PERSON-BASED REPRESENTATION

FIG. 1.4.   Organization of social knowledge: Individuated vs. person-alized.

Figure 1.4 presents a schematic representation of the difference between the organization of social information (attributes) in a category-based structure and a personalized structure. The person-based organizational structure is differenti-ated into traits and roles that are in turn associated with specific attributes and behaviors. This implies that a personalized representation of an individual is more complex and differentiated than an individuated representation in which attributes are organized with reference to a single category identity.

The structural differences between category-based and person-based cognitive representations have implications for how new information is processed and incorporated into the existing knowledge structure. As discussed previously, with category-based processing, new information that is inconsistent with cate-gory stereotypes will either be ignored or differentiated from the category pro-totype. When information is personalized, however, attributes or behaviors that are inconsistent with previously established expectancies will be processed ex-tensively and incorporated into the person representation. Because such exten-sive processing increases the number and strength of associative pathways among attributes within the cognitive network, the incorporation of inconsistent information may have the effect of strengthening memory for expectancy-con-gruent information as well (Srull, 1981; Srull et al., 1985).

The level of abstraction at which new information is initially encoded is also expected to be different for category-based and person-based processing. The processing model represented in Fig. 1.1 assumes that categorization at higher levels of abstraction precedes differentiation into subtypes or recognition of individuating features. When information processing is person-based, however, specific behaviors are first encoded as discrete occurrences at a relatively concrete level and result in trait attributions only at later, inferential stages of processing (cf. Trope, 1986).

Assuming a recency effect in retrieval, whereby the last representation encoded is most accessibile and retrieved first (Wyer & Srull, 1986), the above processing differences imply that category-based representations can be distinguished from personalized representations in terms of the order of recall for information at different levels of abstraction. Recall of information about an individual in a category-based structure should begin with specific individuating features and progress to subtype identification, with superordinate categorization occurring last and with lowest probability. Free recall for characteristics of personalized individuals, however, should begin with superordinate traits and progress to more specific attributes or behaviors with additional retrieval effort. These predictions regarding order of recall are consistent with findings that the preference for trait terms in free descriptions of other individuals increases with familiarity with the other person (Hampson, 1983).

Our processing assumptions also have implications for what can be remembered, as well as the order in which it will be recalled. Memory-based judgments can be influenced both by trait and behavior memory when the representation of the individual has been personalized (Carlston & Skowronski, 1986; Lingle, 1983). However, when information has been processed in a category-based mode, the perceiver should be unable to retrieve the specific category-consistent information on which the categorization of the individual was initially based. Thus, later judgments of that individual will be based solely on category inferences and not on the amount or content of information originally provided about that specific person.

Data consistent with this last hypothesis were obtained by Dull (1982) in her studies of the differential effects of dimensional and categorical encoding of person information. She found that after subjects had been asked to classify descriptions of eight stimulus persons into one of four categories ("grandmother," "housewife," "career woman," or "sorority girl"), they were unable later to recall accurately which descriptive statements had been presented for each individual, or to rank order the eight persons along specific trait dimensions (even for traits judged relevant to the initial categorization task). Control subjects, who read the descriptions without making categorical judgments, showed significantly better recall for specific item information but were not significantly better at the rank ordering task (again suggesting that subjects' spontaneous impressions are categorical rather than dimensional).

The Form of Person-Based Representations

The dual processing model assumes that personalized knowledge differs from category-based knowledge in format as well as in organizational structure. As depicted in Fig. 1.4, person-based knowledge is represented in memory as a *propositional network* rather than a pictoliteral image. This difference is similar to that hypothesized by Lord (1980) to distinguish self-knowledge from knowledge about other persons. In the present model, the propositional format is assumed to characterize not only self-knowledge, but all person-based representations of social information. Little data directly relevant to this hypothesis are available, but some support is available from results of research indicating that the cognitive organization of information about highly familiar others is more differentiated in cluster space (Powell & Juhnke, 1983) and more likely to be person-based in recall (Ostrom et al., 1981) than information about unfamiliar others.

Although the outcomes of category-based and person-based processing modes are distinctly different, they are not necessarily mutually exclusive, and it is possible that information about a particular individual may be coded in both ways. Evidence for such dual coding was obtained by Wyer and Martin (1986). In their experiments, subjects were first given information about a particular individual's category membership (i.e., Nazi or Nobel prizewinner) and also provided with three trait adjectives descriptive of that individual. This initial information was followed by 32 behavioral statements, with each statement referring either to the individual by name (person-referent) or by category label (group-referent). When expectancies about the individual based on trait inferences were in conflict with expectancies based on category membership, subjects' recall for behavioral information showed evidence of dual-concept encoding. Correct recall was found to be a function of the consistency of the behavior with its particular referent, regardless of its relevance to the other referent. These results suggest that subjects organized the information in memory separately in terms of the category or person referent with which it was most immediately associated, and did not attempt to form a single integrated impression of the target person.

Determinants of Personalized Processing

The level of specificity at which category-based encoding is stopped is determined primarily by characteristics of the stimulus person and by task demands imposed by the environment. The decision to engage personalized information processing, on the other hand, is determined more by the needs and goals of the perceiver than by factors in the stimulus environment. Personalization implies some degree of *affective* investment on the part of the perceiver, either because of the target person's relationship to the perceiver's personal or social identity, or because of the target's relevance to the perceiver's personal goals.

Effect of similarity. Other things being equal, we are more likely to form person-based representations of individuals who are similar to ourselves than of those who are distinctly different. A number of lines of research support the hypothesis that perceivers form more complex and differentiated impressions of members of ingroup categories than they do of outgroup category members (Jones, Wood, & Quattrone, 1981; Linville, 1982; Linville & Jones, 1980; Park & Rothbart, 1982). This in-group complexity effect is manifest in a number of different ways. More individuating features are remembered about ingroup members than about outgroup members (Park & Rothbart, 1982), judgments about ingroup members are less evaluatively extreme than judgments about members of outgroup categories (Linville & Jones, 1980), and ingroup members are perceived as varying more along specific trait dimensions than are outgroupers (Jones et al., 1981; Park & Rothbart, 1982). Further, these differences in perceived variability are apparently determined by differences in *attention* to available information about category members rather than by differential exposure to members of ingroup and outgroup categories (Jones et al., 1981; Quattrone, 1986).

All of these findings are consistent with the conclusion that personalized representations are more likely to be formed for individuals who belong to the same social categories as the perceiver than for members of other categories. Brewer and Lui (1985), however, report evidence that such ingroup effects are limited to ingroups defined at the subtype rather than superordinate category level. These researchers had young college students and older women make judgments of similarity and personality ratings of photographs of elderly women and men. In comparison to college students, older subjects showed greater differentiation and complexity in their judgments of the stimulus persons who were categorized as "grandmotherly" types. In their judgments of other representatives of the general category of elderly persons, however, the older subjects responded in accord with the same stereotypes as the younger subjects. Since the elderly women in this study generally perceived themselves to be more similar to target persons that were classified as grandmothers than to other targets in the same age category, Brewer and Lui concluded that the complexity effect is more a function of perceived similarity to the self than of shared category membership per se.

Effect of perceiver goals.   Although it seems intuitively obvious that the processing of information about a target person will vary depending on the importance of that individual to the perceiver's needs or goals, relatively little research has been done to test this hypothesis directly. Erber and Fiske (1984) found that perceivers were more attentive to expectancy-inconsistent information when they interacted with another individual under conditions of *outcome interdependency* than when outcomes of the two individuals were made independent. In that extensive processing of inconsistent information is characteristic of person-based impression formation, this experiment supports the hypothesis that goal-relevance promotes personalized processing, but considerably more research is needed on the relationship between interdependence and cognitive representations of persons.

IMPLICATIONS OF THE DUAL PROCESS MODEL

Potential differences in the ways in which person information may be encoded and organized in memory are of interest to social psychologists only to the extent that such differences have implications for social behavior. Thus far, the distinction between category-based and person-based representations of social information has been applied to two areas of general social concern—the impact of desegregation on intergroup attitudes, and the validity of social judgments in decision-making contexts.

Categorization and the Effects of Intergroup Contact

The fact that individual persons can be encoded either as representatives of a social type or apart from any category identity creates an interesting dilemma for social programs designed to reduce intergroup prejudice and stereotyping through contact and familiarity. The rationale underlying the contact hypothesis is that extended interpersonal experience with members of the outgroup will disconfirm stereotypes and change intergroup attitudes. Such outcomes require that positive experiences with individual outgroup members are generalized to the group as a whole. But, as Rothbart and John (1985) have pointed out, generalization will occur only if those experiences are encoded and stored with information about the social category. According to the present model, if interpersonal experiences are encoded in a person-based network, they will be dissociated from category-based representations. Personalization involves, in effect, a "decategorization" of the target individual and reduces the probability that experiences with that individual will be generalized in any form to more inclusive social categories.

It was for this reason that Brewer and Miller (1984) sought to specify those conditions under which intergroup contact could be expected to result in category-based information processing and what conditions would promote personalized interactions. Their general conclusion is that the encoding of contact experiences will be category-based to the extent that the contact situation promotes task-oriented interaction and when the basis for assignment of roles, status, functions, or subgroup membership in the setting is in any way correlated with category membership. When interactions are personalized and category membership is not relevant to social goals, person-based impressions are more likely to be formed.

The paradox in this is that the more successful the contact environment is in producing positive interpersonal relationships, the less likely it is to generalize to category stereotypes. If the interaction is processed in a category-based manner, those aspects of the experience that are incongruent with category expectations will be differentiated from the category prototype through subtype formation and individuation (Lord, Lepper, & Mackie, 1984; Weber & Crocker, 1983). As a result, the overall category structure may become more complex, but the dominant category stereotype is not likely to be changed. (In new situations, it is the prototypic category image that is most likely to be activated, rather than the subtype representation.) On the other hand, if contact experiences are personalized, inconsistent information will be processed and incorporated in the representation of that individual, but in isolation from category representations.

Despite this dilemma, Brewer and Miller (1984) argue that contact promoting personalized interactions is the best strategy in the long run for reducing intergroup prejudice. The more frequently outgroup members are encountered under conditions in which they are "decategorized," the less salient or accessible that particular category will be in future encounters (Higgins & King, 1981). The cumulative effect of personalized experiences result in the atrophying of superordinate category representations. Data consistent with this hypothesis are reported by Miller, Brewer, and Edwards (1985) from experiments employing a laboratory analogue of desegregation. After subjects had been differentiated into two experimentally created social categories, members of both categories were placed together in a cooperative work situation. Subsequently, subjects viewed a videotape in which other representatives of the two social categories were depicted working together. When the conditions of intergroup contact had been manipulated to promote person-based interactions, subjects showed less category-based differentiation in their perceptions of the videotaped stimulus persons than when the contact experience had taken place under conditions that promoted a task focus. Although single interpersonal contact experiences cannot be expected to alter long-standing category representations in any significant way, repeated experiences across a variety of settings and persons can have meaningful effects in the long run.

The Validity of Category-based Impressions

Issues such as prejudice and intergroup hostility make salient the social problems associated with category-based person perception. Apart from the affective consequences of classifying individuals as outgroup members, category-based encoding is problematic to the extent that relevant information about an individual is either lost or misrepresented in the categorization process. Because all category prototypes represent simplifications of the stimulus variability that actually exists among objects in the same general category, any typing of individuals is bound to lose much of the complexity and richness of detail that a more personalized representation of that individual would contain. Some oversimplification is, however, a cognitive necessity and becomes problematic only when functionally important interpersonal distinctions are being missed. The validity of category-based social cognition depends first on how adequately the perceiver's system of social categories and subtypes captures meaningful distinctions between individuals in the real world, and second, on how thorough the category-matching process is in each case.

Research on the formation of natural categories (e.g., Medin, 1983; Shweder, 1977) suggests that categories are defined not on the basis of specific differentiating features but on the basis of perceived *patterns* of cooccurring attributes. That is, the individual cognizer appears to be particularly sensitive to natural combinations of object features (e.g., the cooccurrence of wings and feathers) and it is these redundant features that are represented in category prototypes. When the same feature appears in a different attribute context (e.g., the combination of wings and engines), a completely different category is formed.

Eleanor Rosch's (1978) theory of natural categories assumes that the disposition to build categories around feature cooccurrences parallels the distribution of attributes in the real world of objects. In nature, trait dimensions are not entirely independent, and discrete, physical objects are not distributed evenly across all trait combinations. If an object is living and has feathers, it is more likely also to have wings than living objects without feathers because both are associated with the ability to fly. Inanimate objects that have handles are more likely to be hollow than solid because both these features are associated with carrying, and so forth. When categories are based on such natural redundancies, the larger the number of features associated with a particular category, the more *distinctive* it is likely to be, even though each of those features considered singly might be associated with a large number of other categories. (E.g., the feature "has wings" is part of the prototypic insect, bird, and airplane, yet each of these categories are highly distinct from each other and are rarely considered as having common attributes—except perhaps in the context of an artificial task such as "name all the objects you can think of that have wings".)

The strategy of category formation represented above is both efficient and functional, so long as the real world it is intended to represent is characterized by natural discontinuities in feature patterns. But the question remains as to how true this is of the world of social objects. Gangestad and Snyder (1985) have argued that there is evidence for the validity of some typological representations of personality, at least at the genotypic (rather than phenotypic) level. Years of research comparing perceived personality trait associations with objective data on trait intercorrelations, however, suggest that social perceivers generally exaggerate the degree of association between trait dimensions that are actually orthogonal (D'Andrade, 1965; Schneider, 1973; Shweder & D'Andrade, 1980). According to Shweder and D'Andrade's (1980) "systematic distortion hypothesis," the covariation among traits in memory-based ratings of people's behavior is determined more by the semantic relations between trait terms than by actual cooccurrence as measured by observer frequency counts. Other research indicates that perceived cooccurrence of traits is based not only on semantic associations but on shared stereotypes and implicit theories of personality as well (Bourne, 1977; DeSoto, Hamilton, & Taylor, 1985; Gara & Rosenberg, 1981; Semin & Greenslade, 1985; Weiss & Mendelsohn, 1986). Further, the cooccurrence of distinctive traits or features is exaggerated in memory relative to actual covariation (Hamilton & Gifford, 1976).

Studies of the validity of personality judgments suggest that the actual distribution of characteristics across persons is more multidimensional than our implicit categorical representations reflect. Yet, in decision-making situations ranging from clinical diagnosis (Cantor, Smith, French, & Mezzich, 1980) to graduate admissions (Dawes, 1971), human judges apparently rely heavily on prototypic representations of diagnostic categories in classifying and evaluating individual cases. Empirical studies (e.g., Goldberg, 1968; Meehl, 1954; Sawyer, 1966) consistently reveal the inferiority of predictions based on such clinical judgments to statistical predictions based on linear combination rules. But despite the preponderance of evidence favoring statistical prediction over "holistic" judgments, we tend to have a strong, intuitive preference for the latter in decision-making settings.

When making judgments based on our cognitive representations of individuals, we tend to be overconfident of the validity of those representations. This overconfidence may stem, in part, from a failure to recognize just how "shallow" our social information processing is in most cases (Dawes, 1976). Once an individual has been matched to a person type, the generic representation associated with that type is merged with information about the specific person with little, if any, discrimination between the two sources. As a consequence, the perceiver's memory for that individual is characterized by an "illusion of richness," because it is based on a cognitive representation more detailed than what has actually been extracted from incoming information about that person.

The above analysis implies that when cognitive representations are utilized to make judgments or decisions about a particular individual, the judges are not aware whether they are drawing on category-based or person-based representations, particularly if the category-based processing has resulted in a typing of that individual at a relatively concrete level. The failure to discriminate between the two processing modes occurs whether judgments are based on memory for past events or made at the time information is first encoded. When impressions are formed quickly or under conditions of stimulus overload, the amount of time between encoding and judgment should make relatively little difference. On-line judgments afford more opportunity for revision in light of incoming information, but do not guarantee that new information will be incorporated. In contexts where such judgments have important implications, human decision makers may need to be trained to recognize the difference between categorization of social objects and the cognition of persons.

REFERENCES

Alba, J. W., & Hasher, L. (1983). Is memory schematic?. *Psychological Bulletin, 93,* 203–231.
Anderson, J. R. (1978). Arguments concerning representations for mental imagery. *Psychological Review, 85,* 249–277.

Anderson, N. (1965). Averaging vs. adding as a stimulus-combination rule in impression formation. *Journal of Experimental Psychology, 70*, 394–400.

Arcuri, L. (1982). Three patterns of social categorization in attribution memory. *European Journal of Social Psychology, 12*, 271–282.

Asch, S. E. (1946). Forming impressions of personality. *Journal of Abnormal and Social Psychology, 41*, 258–290.

Asch, S. E., & Zukier, H. (1984). Thinking about persons. *Journal of Personality and Social Psychology, 46*, 1230–1240.

Ashmore, R. D., DelBoca, F. K., & Titus, D. (1984, August). *Types of women and men: Yours, mine, and ours.* Paper presented at annual meeting of American Psychological Association, Toronto.

Bargh, J. A. (1984). Automatic and conscious processing of social information. In R. Wyer & T. Srull (Eds.), *Handbook of social cognition* (Vol. 3, pp. 1–43). Hillsdale, NJ: Lawrence Erlbaum Associates.

Berry, D. S., & McArthur, L. Z. (1986). Perceiving character in faces: The impact of age-related craniofacial changes on social perception. *Psychological Bulletin, 100*, 3–18.

Billig, M. (1985). Prejudice, categorization and particularization: From a perceptual to a rhetorical approach. *European Journal of Social Psychology, 15*, 79–103.

Bourne, E. (1977). Can we describe an individual's personality? Agreement on stereotype versus individual attributes. *Journal of Personality and Social Psychology, 35*, 863–872.

Bower, G. H., & Karlin, M. B. (1974). Depth of processing pictures of faces and recognition memory. *Journal of Experimental Psychology, 103*, 751–757.

Brewer, M. B., Dull, V., & Lui, L. (1981). Perceptions of the elderly: Stereotypes as prototypes. *Journal of Personality and Social Psychology, 41*, 656–670.

Brewer, M. B., & Lui, L. (1983, August). *The visual representation of social categories.* Paper presented at the annual meeting of the American Psychological Association, Anaheim, CA.

Brewer, M. B., & Lui, L. (1985). Categorization of the elderly by the elderly: Effects of perceiver category membership. *Personality and Social Psychology Bulletin, 10*, 585–595.

Brewer, M. B., & Miller, N. (1984). Beyond the contact hypothesis: Theoretical perspectives on desegregation. In N. Miller & M. Brewer (Eds.), *Groups in contact: The psychology of desegregation* (pp. 281–302). New York: Academic Press.

Bruner, J. S. (1957). On perceptual readiness. *Psychological Review, 64*, 123–152.

Burnstein, E., & Schul, Y. (1982). The informational basis of social judgments: Operations in forming an impression of another person. *Journal of Experimental Social Psychology, 18*, 217–234.

Cantor, N., & Mischel, W. (1979). Prototypes in person perception. In L. Berkowtiz (Ed.), *Advances in experimental social psychology* (Vol. 12, pp. 3–52). New York: Academic Press.

Cantor, N., Smith, E., French, R., & Mezzich, J. (1980). Psychiatric diagnosis as prototype categorization. *Journal of Abnormal Psychology, 72*, 193–204.

Carlston, D. E. (1980). The recall and use of traits and events in social inference processes. *Journal of Experimental Social Psychology, 16*, 303–328.

Carlston, D. E., & Skowronski, J. J. (1986). Trait memory and behavior memory: The effects of alternative pathways on impression judgment response times. *Journal of Personality and Social Psychology, 50*, 5–13.

Carney, A., DeWitt, J. S., & Davis, D. (1986, May). *Effects of stereotypes, presentation order, and familiarity on person memory.* Paper presented at annual meeting of the Western Psychological Association, Seattle, Washington.

Carver, C. S., & de la Garza, N. H. (1984). Schema-guided information search in stereotyping of the elderly. *Journal of Applied Social Psychology, 14*, 69–81.

Chapman, L. J., & Chapman, J. F. (1967). Genesis of popular but erroneous psychodiagnostic observations. *Journal of Abnormal Psychology, 72*, 193–204.

Clark, N. K., & Rutter, D. H. (1985). Social categorization, visual cues, and social judgments. *European Journal of Social Psychology, 15,* 105–119.

Cohen, C. E. (1981). Person categories and social perception: Testing some boundaries of the processing effects of prior knowledge. *Journal of Personality and Social Psychology, 40,* 441–452.

D'Andrade, R. G. (1965). Trait psychology and component analysis. *American Anthropologist, 67,* 215–228.

Darley, J. M., & Gross, P. H. (1983). A hypothesis-confirming bias in labeling effects. *Journal of Personality and Social Psychology, 44,* 20–33.

Dawes, R. M. (1971). A case study of graduate admissions: Application of three principles of human decision making. *American Psychologist, 26,* 181–188.

Dawes, R. M. (1976). Shallow psychology. In J. Carroll & J. Payne (Eds.), *Cognition and social behavior* (pp. 3–11). Hillsdale, NJ: Lawrence Erlbaum Associates.

Deaux, K., & Lewis, L. L. (1984). The structure of gender stereotypes: Interrelationships among components and gender label. *Journal of Personality and Social Psychology, 46,* 991–1004.

DeSoto, C. B., Hamilton, M. M., & Taylor, R. B. (1985). Words, people, and implicit personality theory. *Social Cognition, 3,* 369–382.

Dull, V. T. (1982). *Two strategies of social classification.* Unpublished dissertation, University of California, Santa Barbara.

Erber, R., & Fiske, S. T. (1984). Outcome dependency and attention to inconsistent information. *Journal of Personality and Social Psychology, 47,* 709–726.

Fiske, S. T., & Pavelchak, M. A. (1986). Category-based versus piecemeal-based affective responses: Developments in schema-triggered affect. In R. Sorrentino & E. T. Higgins (Eds.), *Handbook of motivation and cognition: Foundations of social behavior* (pp. 167–203). New York: Guilford Press.

Fiske, S. T., & Taylor, S. E. (1984). *Social cognition.* Reading, MA: Addison-Wesley.

Frable, D. E. S., & Bem, S. L. (1985). If you are gender schematic, all members of the opposite sex look alike. *Journal of Personality and Social Psychology, 49,* 459–468.

Gangestad, S., & Snyder, M. (1985). "To carve nature at its joints"; On the existence of discrete classes in personality. *Psychological Review, 92,* 317–349.

Gara, M. A., & Rosenberg, S. (1981). Linguistic factors in implicit personality theory. *Journal of Personality and Social Psychology, 41,* 450–457.

Goldberg, L. R. (1968). Simple models or simple processes? Some research on clinical judgment. *American Psychologist, 23,* 483–496.

Graesser, A. C., Gordon, S. E., & Sawyer, J. D. (1979). Recognition memory for typical and atypical actions in scripted activities: Tests of a script pointer and tag hypothesis. *Journal of Verbal Learning and Verbal Behavior, 18,* 319–332.

Grossberg, S. (1976). Adaptive pattern classification and universal recoding: II. Feedback, expectation, olfaction, and illusions. *Biological Cybernetics, 23,* 187–202.

Hamilton, D. L. (1981). Cognitive representations of persons. In E. T. Higgins, C. P. Herman, & M. Zanna (Eds.), *Social cognition: The Ontario symposium* (Vol. 1, pp. 135–160). Hillsdale, NJ: Lawrence Erlbaum Associates.

Hamilton, D. L., & Gifford, R. K. (1976). Illusory correlation in interpersonal perception: A cognitive basis of stereotypic judgments. *Journal of Personality and Social Psychology, 12,* 392–407.

Hamilton, D. L., & Rose, T. L. (1980). Illusory correlation and the maintenance of stereotypic beliefs. *Journal of Personality and Social Psychology, 39,* 832–845.

Hampson, S. E. (1983). Trait ascription and depth of acquaintance: The preference for traits in personality descriptions and its relation to target familiarity. *Journal of Research in Personality, 17,* 398–411.

Hartwick, J. (1979). Memory for trait information: A signal detection analysis. *Journal of Experimental Social Psychology, 15,* 533–552.

Hastie, R. (1980). Memory for behavioral information that confirms or contradicts a personality impression. In R. Hastie, T. Ostrom, E. Ebbesen, R. Wyer, D. Hamilton, & D. Carlston (Eds.), *Person memory: The cognitive basis of social perception* (pp. 155–177). Hillsdale, NJ: Lawrence Erlbaum Associates.

Hastie, R., & Park, B. (1986). The relationship between memory and judgment depends on whether the judgment task is memory-based or on-line. *Psychological Review, 93,* 258–268.

Higgins, E. T., & King, G. (1981). Accessibility of social constructs: Information-processing consequences of individual and contextual variability. In N. Cantor & J. Kihlstrom (Eds.), *Personality, cognition, and social interaction* (pp. 69–122). Hillsdale, NJ: Lawrence Erlbaum Associates.

Higgins, E. T., Rholes, W. S., & Jones, C. R. (1977). Category accessibility and impression formation. *Journal of Experimental Social Psychology, 13,* 141–154.

Holyoak, K. J., & Gordon, P. C. (1984). Information processing and social cognition. In R. Wyer & T. Srull (Eds.), *Handbook of social cognition* (Vol. 1, pp. 39–70). Hillsdale, NJ: Lawrence Erlbaum Associates.

Jones, E. E., Wood, G. C., & Quattrone, G. A. (1981). Perceived variability of personal characteristics in in-groups and out-groups: The role of knowledge and evaluation. *Personality and Social Psychology Bulletin, 7,* 523–528.

Klatzky, R. L. (1984). Visual memory: Definitions and functions. In R. Wyer & T. Srull (Eds.), *Handbook of social cognition* (Vol. 2, pp. 233–270). Hillsdale, NJ: Lawrence Erlbaum Associates.

Klatzky, R. L., Martin, G. L., & Kane, R. A. (1982). Influence of social-category activation on processing of visual information. *Social Cognition, 1,* 95–109.

Kosslyn, S. M. (1980). *Images and mind.* Cambridge, MA: Harvard University Press.

Lingle, J. H. (1983). Tracing memory-structure activation during person judgments. *Journal of Experimental Social Psychology, 19,* 480–496.

Lingle, J. H., Altom, M. W., & Medin, D. L. (1984). Of cabbages and kings: Assessing the extendibility of natural object concept models to social things. In R. Wyer & T. Srull (Eds.), *Handbook of social cognition* (Vol. 1, pp. 71–117). Hillsdale, NJ: Lawrence Erlbaum Associates.

Lingle, J. H., & Ostrom, T. M. (1979). Retrieval selectivity in memory-based impression judgments. *Journal of Personality and Social Psychology, 37,* 180–194.

Linville, P. W. (1982). The complexity-extremity effect and age-based stereotyping. *Journal of Personality and Social Psychology, 42,* 193–211.

Linville, P. W., & Jones, E. E. (1980). Polarized appraisals of out-group members. *Journal of Personality and Social Psychology, 38,* 689–703.

Lord, C. G. (1980). Schemas and images as memory aids: Two modes of processing social information. *Journal of Personality and Social Psychology, 38,* 257–269.

Lord, C. G., Lepper, M. R., & Mackie, D. (1984). Attitude prototypes as determinants of attitude-behavior consistency. *Journal of Personality and Social Psychology, 46,* 1254–1266.

Lui, L., & Brewer, M. B. (1983). Recognition accuracy as evidence of category consistency effects in person memory. *Social Cognition, 2,* 89–107.

Lynn, M., Shavitt, S., & Ostrom, T. (1985). Effects of pictures on the organization and recall of social information. *Journal of Personality and Social Psychology, 49,* 1160–1168.

McArthur, L. Z. (1982). Judging a book by its cover: A cognitive analysis of the relationship between physical appearance and stereotyping. In A. Hastorf & A. Isen (Eds.), *Cognitive social psychology* (pp. 149–211). New York: Elsevier.

McArthur, L. Z., & Baron, R. M. (1983). Toward an ecological theory of social perception. *Psychological Review, 90,* 215–238.

McCann, C. D., Ostrom, T. M., Tyner, L. K., & Mitchell, M. L. (1985). Person perception in heterogeneous groups. *Journal of Personality and Social Psychology, 49,* 1449–1459.

Medin, D. L. (1983). Structural principles in categorization. In T. Tighe, B. Shepp, & H. Pick

(Eds.), *Interactions: Perception, cognition, and development* (pp. 203–230). Hillsdale, NJ: Lawrence Erlbaum Associates.

Meehl, P. E. (1954). *Clinical versus statistical prediction: A theoretical analysis and review of the evidence.* Minneapolis: University of Minnesota Press.

Miller, N., Brewer, M. B., & Edwards, K. (1985). Cooperative interaction in desegregated settings: A laboratory analogue. *Journal of Social Issues, 41*(3), 63–79.

Murphy, G. L., & Medin, D. L. (1985). The role of theories in conceptual coherence. *Psychological Review, 92,* 289–316.

Navon, D. (1977). Forest before trees: The precedence of global features in visual perception. *Cognitive Psychology, 9,* 353–383.

Navon, D. (1981). The forest revisited: More on global precedence. *Psychological Research, 43,* 1–32.

Ostrom, T. M. (1984). The sovereignty of social cognition. In R. Wyer & T. Srull (Eds.), *Handbook of social cognition* (Vol. 1, pp. 1–38). Hillsdale, NJ: Lawrence Erlbaum Associates.

Ostrom, T. M., Pryor, J. B., & Simpson, D. D. (1981). The organization of social information. In E. T. Higgins, C. P. Herman, & M. Zanna (Eds.), *Social cognition: The Ontario symposium* (Vol. 1, pp. 3–38). Hillsdale, NJ: Lawrence Erlbaum Associates.

Park, B., & Rothbart, M. (1982). Perception of out-group homogeneity and levels of social categorization: Memory for the subordinate attributes of in-group and out-group members. *Journal of Personality and Social Psychology, 42,* 1051–1068.

Passini, F. T., & Norman, W. T. (1966). A universal conception of personality structure?. *Journal of Personality and Social Psychology, 4,* 44–49.

Powell, R. S., & Juhnke, R. G. (1983). Statistical models of implicit personality theory: A comparison. *Journal of Personality and Social Psychology, 44,* 911–922.

Prinz, W., & Scheerer-Neumann, G. (1974). Component processes in multiattribute stimulus classification. *Psychological Research, 37,* 25–50.

Pryor, J. B., Kott, T. L., & Bovee, G. R. (1984). The influence of information redundancy upon the use of traits and persons as organizing categories. *Journal of Experimental Social Psychology, 20,* 246–262.

Pryor, J. B., & Ostrom, T. M. (1981). The cognitive organization of social information: A converging operations approach. *Journal of Personality and Social Psychology, 41,* 628–641.

Quattrone, G. A. (1986). On the perception of a group's variability. In S. Worchel & W. Austin (Eds.), *Psychology of intergroup relations* (pp. 25–48). Chicago: Nelson-Hall.

Rosch, E. (1978). Principles of categorization. In E. Rosch & B. B. Lloyd (Eds.), *Cognition and categorization* (pp. 27–48). Hillsdale, NJ: Lawrence Erlbaum Associates.

Rosenberg, S., & Gara, M. A. (1985). The multiplicity of personal identity. In P. Shaver (Ed.), *Review of personality and social psychology* (Vol. 6, pp. 87–113). Beverly Hills, CA: Sage.

Rosenberg, S., & Sedlak, A. (1972). Structural representations of implicit personality theory. In L. Berkowitz (Ed.), *Advances in experimental social psychology* (Vol. 6, pp. 235–297). New York: Academic Press.

Rothbart, M., Fulero, S., Jensen, C., Howard, J., & Birrell, P. (1978). From individual to group impressions: Availability heuristics in stereotype formation. *Journal of Experimental Social Psychology, 14,* 237–255.

Rothbart, M., & John, O. P. (1985). Social categorization and behavioral episodes: A cognitive analysis of the effects of intergroup contact. *Journal of Social Issues, 41*(3), 81–104.

Sawyer, J. (1966). Measurement and prediction: Clinical and statistical. *Psychological Bulletin, 66,* 178–206.

Schneider, D. J. (1973). Implicit personality theory: A review. *Psychological Bulletin, 79,* 294–309.

Schneider, D. J., & Blankmeyer, B. L. (1983). Prototype salience and implicit personality theories. *Journal of Personality and Social Psychology, 44,* 712–722.

Schul, Y. (1983). Integration and abstraction in impression formation. *Journal of Personality and Social Psychology, 44,* 45–54.

Secord, P. F., Dukes, W. F., & Bevan, W. (1954). Personalities in faces: I. An experiment in social perceiving. *Genetic Psychology Monographs, 49,* 231–279.

Secord, P. F., & Muthard, J. E. (1955). Personalities in faces: IV. A descriptive analysis of the perception of women's faces and the identification of physiognomic determinants. *Journal of Psychology, 39,* 261–278.

Semin, G. R., & Greenslade, L. (1985). Differential contributions of linguistic factors to memory-based ratings: Systematizing the systematic distortion hypothesis. *Journal of Personality and Social Psychology, 49,* 1713–1723.

Shweder, R. A. (1977). Likeness and likelihood in everyday thought: Magical thinking in judgments about personality. *Current Anthropology, 18,* 637–658.

Shweder, R. A., & D'Andrade, R. G. (1980). The systematic distortion hypothesis. In R. Shweder (Ed.), *Fallible judgment in behavioral research. New directions for methodology of social and behavioral science* (pp. 3–38). San Francisco: Jossey-Bass.

Smith, D. A., & Graesser, A. C. (1981). Memory for actions in scripted activities as a function of typicality, retention interval, and retrieval task. *Memory and Cognition, 9,* 550–559.

Srull, T. K. (1981). Person memory: Some tests of associative storage and retrieval models. *Journal of Experimental Psychology: Human Learning and Memory, 7,* 440–463.

Srull, T. K., & Brand, J. F. (1983). Memory for information about persons: The effect of encoding operations on subsequent retrieval. *Journal of Verbal Learning and Verbal Behavior, 22,* 219–230.

Srull, T. K., Lichtenstein, M., & Rothbart, M. (1985). Associative storage and retrieval processes in person memory. *Journal of Experimental Psychology: Learning, Memory, and Cognition, 11,* 316–345.

Srull, T. K., & Wyer, R. S. (1986). The role of chronic and temporary goals in social information processing. In R. Sorrentino & E. T. Higgins (Eds.), *Handbook of motivation and cognition. Foundations of social behavior* (pp. 503–549). New York: Guilford Press.

Stern, L. D., Marrs, S., Millar, M. G., & Cole, E. (1984). Processing time and the recall of inconsistent and consistent behaviors of individuals and groups. *Journal of Personality and Social Psychology, 47,* 253–262.

Stroop, J. R. (1935). Studies of interference in serial verbal reactions. *Journal of Experimental Psychology, 18,* 643–662.

Swann, W. E., & Miller, L. C. (1982). Why never forgetting a face matters: Visual imagery and social memory. *Journal of Personality and Social Psychology, 43,* 475–480.

Taylor, S. E., Fiske, S. T., Etcoff, N. L., & Ruderman, A. J. (1978). Categorical and contextual bases of person memory and stereotyping. *Journal of Personality and Social Psychology, 36,* 778–793.

Trope, Y. (1986). Identification and inferential processes in dispositional attribution. *Psychological Review, 93,* 239–257.

Tversky, A. (1977). Features of similarity. *Psychological Review, 84,* 327–352.

Tversky, A., & Hutchinson, J. W. (1986). Nearest neighbor analysis of psychological spaces. *Psychological Review, 93,* 3–22.

Tversky, B., & Hemenway, K. (1984). Objects, parts, and categories. *Journal of Experimental Psychology: General, 113,* 169–191.

Weber, R., & Crocker, J. (1983). Cognitive processes in the revision of stereotypic beliefs. *Journal of Personality and Social Psychology, 45,* 961–977.

Weiss, D., & Mendelsohn, G. (1986). An empirical demonstration of the implausibility of the semantic similarity explanation of how trait ratings are made and what they mean. *Journal of Personality and Social Psychology, 50,* 595–601.

Wyer, R. S., Bodenhausen, G. V., & Srull, T. K. (1984). The cognitive representation of persons and groups and its effect on recall and recognition memory. *Journal of Experimental Social Psychology, 20,* 445–469.

Wyer, R. S., & Gordon, S. E. (1984). The cognitive representation of social information. In R. Wyer & T. Srull (Eds.), *Handbook of social cognition* (Vol. 2, pp. 73–150). Hillsdale, NJ: Lawrence Erlbaum Associates.

Wyer, R. S., & Martin, L. L. (1986). Person memory: The role of traits, group stereotypes, and specific behaviors in the cognitive representation of persons. *Journal of Personality and Social Psychology, 50,* 661–675.

Wyer, R. S., & Podeschi, D. M. (1978). The acceptance of generalizations about persons, objects, and events. In R. Revlin & R. Mayer (Eds.), *Human reasoning* (pp. 101–137). Washington, DC: V. H. Winston.

Wyer, R. S., & Srull, T. K. (1981). Category accessibility: Some theoretical and empirical issues concerning the processing of social stimulus information. In E. T. Higgins, C. P. Herman, & M. Zanna (Eds.), *Social cognition: The Ontario symposium* (Vol. 1, pp. 161–198). Hillsdale, NJ: Lawrence Erlbaum Associates.

Wyer, R. S., & Srull, T. K. (1986). Human cognition in its social context. *Psychological Review, 93,* 322–359.

Zajonc, R. B. (1980). Feeling and thinking: Preferences need no inferences. *American Psychologist, 35,* 151–175.

2 A Functional Approach to Person Cognition

Norman H. Anderson
University of California, San Diego

As Brewer presents her position, it "challenges" prevailing views of person perception and presents an "alternative position" that allows either top-down or bottom-up processing. The theory of information integration, however, has long allowed for both modes of processing. Although Brewer refers to integration theory as a "classic theory," she cites only a 1965 experimental report that had little bearing on modes of processing. Her comments about integration theory are thus wide of the mark.

To relate her position to integration theory, accordingly, requires a brief overview of *functional memory,* which is done in the first part of this commentary. The next two sections take up similarities with and differences from Brewer's position, while the final section considers some theoretical issues raised by her discussion.

FUNCTIONAL MEMORY

A functional perspective is basic to information integration theory (IIT). This reflects its focus on judgment and action, which are goal-oriented in character. Interpersonal interaction, in particular, involves approaching others, avoiding them, doing things for them, getting them to do things for us, and so on. Such interpersonal goals are a major determinant of person cognition. This goal-oriented perspective entails a corresponding conception of functional memory, which relates to the concepts of knowledge systems and of memory assemblage.

Knowledge Systems

The present conceptualization of knowledge systems may be illustrated in the distinction between attitudes and attitudinal responses (Anderson, 1976a, Section 3.4, 1976b, Section 7.2.1, 1981a, 1981b). Attitudes are considered knowledge systems that underlie and partially determine overt attitudinal responses. This view of attitudes as systems differs from the predominant view, which treats attitudes as one-dimensional reactions (see, e.g., Berscheid, 1982, pp. 38ff; Cacioppo, Harkins, & Petty, 1981, pp. 32, 53; Fazio, 1986, p. 214). Such evaluative reactions are here considered only one kind of attitudinal response, derivative and qualitatively different from the attitude as a knowledge system.

The traditional emphasis on evaluative reactions does, however, bring out an important property of attitudes: they contain affect. This reflects their functional role as guides towards positive goals and away from negative goals. In the present view, affect and emotion are integral components of cognition, for they provide signal information for goal-directed action; that is their biosocial function (Anderson, in press).

Social stereotypes form one class of attitudes. The functional approach looks for the usefulness of stereotypes and finds it in their cognitive economy and stability. Stereotypes provide a readily accessible memory store that can guide judgment and action in diverse situations. This virtue of stereotypes, together with their much-belabored limitations, were noted long ago by Walter Lippmann and are discussed more extensively in Anderson (1983a).

Functional Conception of Memory

The functional perspective entails a functional conception of memory, as it subserves judgment and action. This departs from the traditional conception of reproductive memory, which emphasizes recall, to study how memory is used in judgment and action.

The concept of functional memory originated from a study that planned to relate the impression of a person based on a serial list of trait adjectives to the serial curve of adjective recall (Anderson & Hubert, 1963). A natural hypothesis was that the impression would be based on the verbal memory, so that recall probabilities could serve as weighting factors in the impression response. This verbal memory hypothesis, however, was not supported. Instead, the results revealed the existence of separate memories for the person impression and for the verbal materials from which it was constructed. This two-memory hypothesis has been confirmed and extended (see Anderson, 1981a, Sections 4.2 and 4.5.4; Hastie, 1981).

The theoretical interpretation of the two-memory hypothesis reflected the functional perspective. Each adjective was assumed to be processed for goal-relevant information as it was received, with this information being integrated into the developing impression. The adjective itself was no longer essential and in fact had different memory storage.

This functional processing mirrors everyday life. Impressions and opinions often, if not typically, develop by serial integration over periods of time. The serial integration model, moreover, has a natural place for affective and other continuous response measures, which are awkward to handle with other information processing theories. And it is useful for limited-capacity cognition, for it does not require storage and retrieval of all the original material from which the impression was constructed.

This initial two-memory hypothesis has been broadened to a multiform conception of memory. If the subject were required to judge the person on a different, unexpected dimension after the assigned judgment had been made, this would be expected to make use of both memory systems. Even for the assigned judgment, long-term memory is necessary in valuation processing of each single adjective, for valuation is a constructive process that depends on the operative goal (Anderson, 1974, pp. 88–90).

In everyday life, moreover, person cognition is usually about familiar persons, so functional memory may include assorted episodic information as well as previously processed impressions and judgments, both affective and nonaffective (e.g., Anderson 1976a, p. 21, 1981b). "The operative memory may include present behavior, diverse recollected behaviors, and general attitudes about the person whose informational basis has been lost. It may include contributions from both episodic and semantic memory. And it may include diverse forms of nonverbal stimulation, including affect and emotion, that lack expressible form" (Anderson, 1983c, p. 39).

Assemblage

The functional approach entails a concept of assemblage. The operating memory for any judgment or action is typically assembled from diverse forms of memory storage, as already indicated, as well as from situational stimuli. Assemblage is not a simple matter of memory retrieval, but an active process of construction. Assemblage thus combines both top-down and bottom-up processing.

The necessity for an assemblage concept appears in the multiplicity of possible goals. A spouse, for example, may figure in many different motivations and goals. Even when a general goal is fixed, moreover, its particular realization may evolve and change over time. The contents of operating memory can hardly be based on simple memory retrieval, for this would require individuated storage for each possible and potential goal. Assemblage provides a base for goal-oriented judgment and action that is realistic in storage requirements as well as sensitive to social context.

Although assemblages function as operating memory, they may themselves be stored, in whole or in part. An example of partial storage appears in Shanteau's (in press) functional measurement analysis of reaction times (see Anderson, 1981a, Section 1.5.7). Goals and goal plans, in particular, may be stored in this manner, as part of social learning. Recurrent interaction with another person will thus lead to development of a corresponding knowledge system that will be utilized in future assemblage.

SIMILARITIES

Two primary themes in Brewer's article concern the operation of top-down and bottom-up processing and the relation between social perception and object perception. In both cases, the position adopted by Brewer has substantial similarities with IIT.

Top-Down and Bottom-Up

Brewer "challenges" the view that person perception is bottom-up processing and discusses an alternative mode of top-down, categorical processing. Both modes of processing are included in IIT.

The operation of both kinds of processing may be illustrated with a study of judgments of persons described by occupational category and trait adjectives (Anderson & Lopes, 1974; see Anderson, 1981a, Section 4.4.4, Note 3.5.1a). The occupation acts as a stereotype or category, which is processed in top-down fashion, in a manner not unlike that discussed by Brewer, to yield information about the person. The trait adjectives undergo similar processing that yields additional information. This complex of information constitutes a person assemblage, and it is often, although not always processed in a bottom-up mode to arrive at particular judgments or decisions about the person.

There is, however, a basic difference between the present dual process formulation and that of Brewer. Brewer takes an either-or view, as illustrated in her Fig. 1.1 and in her statement that "It is at this point that a critical choice is made between the two alternative processing modes" (p. 9). In IIT, in contrast, top-down and bottom-up processing operate jointly.

This difference stems in part from the theoretical distinction between valuation and integration. Valuation is often top-down, as in the foregoing example of stereotypes. Integration, as its name indicates, typically has something of a bottom-up nature. This distinction in turn relates to the concept of assemblage, which may embody both processing modes together.

Categories seem basic to social cognition, as Brewer emphasizes. In the present view, however, many social categories are more properly considered knowledge systems, as with attitudes and roles. Brewer's either-or position does not seem capable of representing categories in social cognition.

Object Perception and Social Perception

Information integration theory provides a unified approach that covers a number of domains, from social cognition to psychophysics. Object perception and social perception are thus treated within the same conceptual framework. Brewer adopts a similar position in her primary contention that "The majority of the time, perception of social objects does not differ from nonsocial perception in either structure or process" (p. 4).

The respective conceptualizations of structure and process, however, exhibit one basic difference. IIT considers the object-social equivalence to have a primary locus in common processing operators, especially operators for valuation and integration. Brewer, in contrast, is largely silent on these operations. Instead, she considers the similarity to reside in a common process of top-down categorical classification. This assumption involves the further assumption that object perception is basically categorical. "Individual objects are rarely encoded except as instances of some class" (p. 1) and "Nonsocial objects . . . are rarely cognized outside of the context of the basic object categories they represent. Most of the time members of object categories are treated as essentially equivalent . . ." (p. 22).

In the functional view, in contrast, perception of individual objects commonly involves assemblage that includes more than object classification. We interact with individual objects, not with categories of objects. We drive particular cars, eat particular meals, and see particular TV shows. Even selecting tomatoes from the supermarket bin involves individual inspection for size, color, spots, and firmness. Interaction with each individual object involves an assemblage that goes beyond the object category to bottom-up processing that includes characteristics of the individual object as well as its context.

This difference stems from the functional concern with goal-oriented judgment and action. Brewer's view of object perception seems to derive from laboratory studies of classification, in which individuating object information is often an irrelevant hindrance to the assigned goal of classification. In everyday life, however, classification, although certainly important, is typically functional in the pursuit of further goals. Brewer's claims that object perception is basically categorical fails to recognize the functions of objects in everyday life.

DIFFERENCES

Some implications of the functional perspective have already appeared in the foregoing discussion of similarities between the two approaches to person cognition. Other implications appear in the following discussion of differences.

Assemblage Theory

In the functional view, ongoing person cognition involves constructive processes of assemblage. This assemblage view applies to new or hypothetical persons as well as to friends, acquaintances, and public figures. Brewer, in contrast, claims that impressions of new individuals result from activation of already existing categories, that is, a "categorization process in which available 'person types' are matched to the information given about the new person" (p. 17). Impression formation thus involves identifying which person category in memory best fits the given information. This does not take cognizance of the multiplicity of possible goals, each of which may lead to a different assemblage. Brewer's position thus seems inadequate for functional theory.

Social categories may be components of an assemblage. Brewer is right in emphasizing the importance of categories in forming impressions of new persons. A primary function of social categories, such as stereotypes, is to guide action with limited information or limited processing resources. Categorical information will become less important with known persons simply because more individual information is available from memory. For both new and old, however, assemblage will generally contain noncategorical information as well. Assemblage thus involves both top-down and bottom-up processing.

Brewer's own data seem to support the assemblage view rather than her categorical view. Subjects asked for brief verbal descriptions following a face sorting task rarely mentioned the sorting categories of age and sex, on which Brewer based her interpretation (her Fig. 1.2). Instead, as Brewer acknowledges, their descriptions combined roles, traits, and behaviors. Similar results have been found with written paragraphs in integration studies based on adjective descriptions. Such verbal descriptions evidently involve considerable idiosyncratic problem solving, which hardly fits the category view but accords well with assemblage theory.

An empirical test between the two formulations appears in the analysis of individuating personal information. Brewer requires that "the process is still category-based" and hence that "Information about the individual that is not inconsistent with category expectations is not incorporated into the individuated impression" (p. 21). Assemblage, in contrast, is not limited to the category representation. Hence additional information that is not inconsistent with the category may nevertheless be included in the individuated representation. This differential prediction is readily testable.

Representation

Within IIT, a social group and its individual members generally have different kinds of cognitive representations (Anderson, 1983a, pp. 32–35). This differs from customary views of groups as categories, defined by the properties of their members. Instead, the group is cognitively distinct from the class of its members. Brewer adopts a similar view for bottom-up processing, but retains the standard categorical view for top-down processing.

One base for the present view lies in the two-memory hypothesis, which suggests that memory storage for a group concept will generally be qualitatively distinct from memory storage for individual members from which the group concept was formed. A second base lies in the fact that many categories are not even formed from experience with individuals, but from sociocultural information.

The standard categorical conception embodies a classificational view of knowledge. This class-instance conceptualization assumes that the properties of a class are the properties of its members. Such categorical thinking may be seen in the puzzlement, mentioned by Brewer, over the resistance of group stereotypes to change through experience with group members. In the present interpretation, this puzzlement reflects the grip of an insufficient conception of knowledge as categorical or classificational. Brewer's conception of categorical knowledge seems inadequate for functional social cognition.

Similarity as Averaging

A different aspect of the problem of representation arises with similarity. Similarity judgments between given stimuli and long-term memory are basic to the constructive valuation process in IIT. The usual approach to similarity judgments, of course, has been through multidimensional scaling, which favors dimensional representations.

IIT, in contrast, favors a more complex representation as already indicated in the discussion of functional memory. IIT also suggests a different rule for similarity integration. Whereas multidimensional scaling has postulated an addition of dissimilarities, IIT suggests an averaging of similarities. This similarity averaging hypothesis originated in a thought experiment that common features should increase similarity whereas noncommon features should decrease similarity (see Anderson, 1981a, Section 5.6.5).

Results that might seem to differ from the similarity averaging model are claimed by Brewer, who cites an unpublished dissertation by Dull (1982). In this study, women described by behavioral sentences were rated on two scales, an *active-passive* scale and a scale whose endpoints were defined by the categories *housewife* and *career woman*. Some sentences were chosen to be polarized with respect to the two scales, whereas others were chosen to be neutral or irrelevant. The number of neutral or irrelevant sentences was varied to test between adding and averaging.

The active-passive scale evidently represents a continuous dimension. Numerous integration studies with such scales have supported averaging, whereas the once-popular summation rule has done poorly. Dull assumed that averaging would apply to judgments on this scale. Hence the addition of neutral statements should decrease response polarity.

The housewife-career woman scale, on the other hand, is more categorical than dimensional. Dull argued for a summation rule on the grounds that similarity between the description and each polar category of the scale should be judged only on the basis of number of common elements. Hence the number of neutral or irrelevant statements in the description should have no effect.

(It should be noted, incidentally, that this rating response involves a compromise between two similarity judgments, one for each polar category of the rating scale. The foregoing similarity averaging rule would imply that neutral statements would decrease similarity separately with each polar category. But this would tend to cancel in the rating compromise. A more appropriate test between averaging and summation would seem to require a unipolar rather than a bipolar rating scale.)

As claimed by Dull (1982) and reported by Brewer, the results supported the averaging rule for active-passive and a summation rule for housewife-career woman. But a rather different picture emerges from study of the original dissertation. The analyses of variance showed no significant differences between the two scales with respect to effect of number of neutral or irrelevant statements. There is thus no basis for the claim that different rules govern the two scales.

The claimed results were obtained from post hoc regression analyses. These analyses, unfortunately, severely confounded the nonorthogonal factors of number of relevant and number of irrelevant statements. They do not seem to allow any valid conclusion. The analyses of variance were appropriate, but they failed to support the claimed difference between the two scales.

Schematic Processing

In IIT, schematic processing is as important for known persons as for new or hypothetical persons, but the nature of these schemas may be different. The case of a new person may be illustrated with the application file of a likely prospect for graduate school. Some components of the processing may be in terms of categories, as when the term *overachiever* occurs in a letter of reference. Even a simple letter, however, may require a good deal of bottom-up processing to integrate the contents of the letter. This must be extended to integrate other letters and other information in the file.

Brewer's argument that perception of new persons rests on top-down categorical processing may hold for minimal social interactions, such as paying for gas at a self-service station, in which individual characteristics of the attendant are largely irrelevant. It would not seem to hold generally, however, as illustrated with the example of the graduate school applicant.

For known persons, the corresponding knowledge system is the basic schema. This may have a complex memory structure, as already indicated. But less integration may actually be involved for familiar than for new persons because the knowledge system representing the familiar person will include much from previous integrations.

Any particular instance of judgment or action about the known person will, of course, involve active assemblage, which is also a form of schematic processing. This assemblage is controlled jointly by the operative goal and the underlying knowledge structure. Nevertheless, categorical information may still be important, with the occupational stereotype of the family doctor, for example, or with sex stereotypes, which pervade interpersonal interaction.

THEORETICAL ISSUES AND IMPLICATIONS

The functional perspective leads in different directions from the more standard position adopted by Brewer. Categorical processing and person processing are both important, as Brewer emphasizes, but they need to be conceptualized within a larger framework of goal-oriented processing. Some issues associated with the functional perspective are discussed here, beginning with affect.

Affect

IIT postulates that affect and emotion are integral aspects of cognition. This cognitive view of affect arises naturally from the functional perspective, in which affect is considered signal information to guide judgment and action (Anderson, 1987, in press). One line of support for this postulate appears in findings of similar integration rules in affective and nonaffective judgments.

Fiske (1982) has also attempted to develop an approach to affect. With social stereotypes, for example, affective content of the stereotype may be transferred to group members, a view followed by Brewer and illustrated in Anderson and Lopes (1974). Stimulus cues activate the stereotype, considered as a knowledge structure in IIT. Selected aspects of this knowledge structure, including affect, are utilized in the valuation of the individual.

Brewer and Fiske both assert that integration models are piecemeal, data-driven, and disallow top-down or schematic processing. This is fundamentally incorrect. It fails to recognize the theoretical distinction between attitudes and attitudinal response, or between valuation and integration. Top-down processing is illustrated in the cited study of stereotypes. Schematic processing appears in the treatment of attitudes as knowledge systems (e.g., Anderson 1976a, 1976b, 1981a, 1981b). Schema-based processing is important in both valuation and integration. Top-down and bottom-up processing, however, generally occur together in IIT.

Affect and emotion surely must be included in social cognition. Except for IIT, however, current cognitive theories generally ignore or pay lip service to affect. Even Fiske (1982), despite her efforts to deal with affect, segregates it from cognition: "Cognitive analysis does not aim to address affect, by definition" (p. 55). This segregation illustrates that mainstream cognitive theories have been constructed on too narrow a conceptual foundation. Affect and emotion cannot be tacked on at the end; they need to be incorporated from the beginning (Anderson, 1983b, 1987, in press).

Functional Memory

Social psychology requires a functional conception of memory. The traditional conception of reproductive memory, which dominates mainstream information processing theories, is too narrow for social cognition. Unfortunately, reproductive memory seems also to dominate most current attempts to construe social cognition in an information processing framework. This preconception is reflected in the common reliance on recall measures of memory.

This preconception has a historical parallel. In attitude theory, as already indicated, it was once taken for granted that an attitude would be based on those stimuli that could be recalled. This was a primary assumption of the Yale school, which envisaged the attractive goal of basing attitude theory on the mass of results from verbal learning. This verbal memory hypothesis reappears in Hastie and Park's (1986) restriction of the term *memory-based* to verbal recall, as well as in the availability heuristic of Tversky and Kahneman (1973), which is a special case of the verbal memory hypothesis (Anderson, 1986). This same assumption is found in current attempts to base the study of cognitive organization on recall data.

This verbal memory hypothesis has generally been recognized to be inadequate, as already noted in the discussion of the two-memory hypothesis. As Crano (1977) later put it, "The simple isomorphism of retention and attitude, so long an article of faith of the classical attitude theorists, simply does not exist" (p. 94).

It follows that recall is inadequate to the needs of social cognition. On one hand, what is recalled may have little relation to judgment and action. On the other hand, major components of knowledge systems may not be recallable. This is a primary implication of the two-memory hypothesis, that attitudinal responses may be stored and retrieved even when their original stimulus base has been forgotten.

On commonsense grounds, moreover, it may be argued that important forms of social memory are not amenable to encoding in verbal or even visual form. Among these are affection and grief, admiration and envy, desire and pain. Such feelings may be hinted at in words, but the words are not the origin of the reality nor its memory.

A deeper reason for the inadequacy of recall measures derives from the functional perspective. Judgment and action typically involve inferences; the same given stimulus will have different implications relative to different goals. Whereas traditional memory theory has a natural concern with reproductive memory, functional theory is typically concerned with memory in relation to inferences and implications.

The functional measurement methodology of IIT is useful in functional theory, for it confers a capability for measuring an important class of inferences. This provides an approach to analysis of functional memory that can go beyond the limitations of recall data. Functional measurement is not routinely applicable, but it can provide information about processing that is not available from other methods.

Distributed Memory and Parallel Processing

IIT allows memory to be distributed as well as multiform (Anderson, 1983c). Memory for a trait adjective or a photograph need not be localized as a node in an associative network, but may be distributed arbitrarily. The possibility of distributed memory fits well with the foregoing multiformity assumption, which allows various nonverbal forms of memory. Person memory, for example, may be distributed across the two cerebral hemispheres, which are differentially specialized for language and affect (Anderson, in press). Because IIT has a central concern with integration of multiple stimuli in everyday goal-seeking, it has a natural affinity for distributed memory.

IIT also allows for parallel rather than serial processing. Serial processing is prominent in the flow diagrams that have characterized information processing theories. This seriality assumption, exhibited in Brewer's Fig. 1.1, may be the origin of her either-or assumption that processing must be either top-down or bottom-up.

Distributed memory and parallel processing have become popular in mainstream cognitive psychology, as in the microstructure approach considered in Rumelhart and McClelland (1986). IIT is less concerned with microstructure, however, more with cognitive units at a higher level, near that of everyday thought and action. The aggregated action of a distributed, multiform memory field may then be represented as a higher level unit that can, under certain conditions, be measured exactly with functional measurement. This can provide boundary conditions that any theory of microstructure must obey.

Meaning Constancy and Memory Bias

A basic issue in memory theory arose from studies of integration rules in IIT. These results imply that certain current claims of memory biases are dubious.

To illustrate the issue, consider stereotype studies, which have frequently shown that persons who act the same may yet be judged differently merely from membership in different social categories. The standard, almost unquestioned interpretation has been in terms of a general bias hypothesis: The stereotype biases or distorts the processing so that the same information takes on different meanings for different social categories.

This presumption of bias has been further interpreted in terms of memory. Here the main issue has concerned the locus of the bias: Is the encoding biased or is it the retrieval? But little of this work has taken cognizance of an alternative nonmemory interpretation, one that has substantial empirical support.

Meaning constancy revisited is an apt label for this issue of memory bias. Memory bias is related Asch's (1946) hypothesis that adjectives in a person description undergo dynamic interaction in which they change one another's meanings. This has been compared with a meaning-constancy hypothesis from IIT in numerous studies. The evidence overwhelmingly favors meaning constancy, not only in Asch's task, but in various other tasks as well (see Anderson, 1981a, Chapter 3 and Section 4.1.8). Stereotypes, in particular, may be integrated directly into the assemblage and into overt judgments of the person with no effect on the other information. This issue became clear, conceptually and empirically, through the cited studies. As noted in a later overview, "The main criticism of Asch's formulation is that it failed to clarify the conceptual issues . . . When the conceptual structure of the problem is made clear, Asch's evidence is seen largely to reach conclusions that are obvious and uninformative" (Anderson, 1981a, pp. 217–218).

The same issue arises in many memory studies in social cognition. The popular measure of recognition memory is subject to exactly the same noninteractive interpretation: stereotype, prototype, or other categorical information may act directly on the recognition response, unmediated by any effect on memory for other information. Assimilation to category expectation, as assumed by Brewer, may reflect halo processes affecting the response. In studies of illusory correlation, similarly, judgments of cooccurrence frequency may reflect not memory but judgment.

Because of this conceptual problem, many studies that are commonly taken to indicate memory bias, whether in storage or retrieval, are inconclusive (e.g., Cantor & Mischel, 1977; Cohen, 1981; Hamilton & Rose, 1980; Snyder & Uranowitz, 1978). Memory biases may be present in these studies, to be sure, but there is no way to tell. Although the tasks and procedures used in these studies were very like those in the tests of meaning constancy, the change-of-meaning interpretation was nevertheless taken for granted. As a consequence, the experimental designs failed to include any way to test and establish the basic conceptual assumption. This issue is discussed further in Anderson (1983a, 1983c).

Schema Theory

The foregoing functional perspective embodies a somewhat complex schema theory, for schemas appear in different forms at different loci in the information processing. One form is that of knowledge systems, exemplified by attitudes, which may subserve a diversity of particular attitudinal responses. This conception allows for cognitive structure in attitudes while retaining the usefulness of an algebraic theory of attitudinal responses (Anderson, 1976a, 1976b, 1981a, 1981b).

Schematic processing also occurs in attitudinal responses. Valuation, in particular, is a constructive process under control of the operative goal (Anderson, 1974, pp. 88–90). Even in simple personality impression studies, the assigned goal sets up a person schema that activates corresponding valuation and integration operators and guides stimulus processing.

A third form of schema, the assemblage, arises through the interaction of goal and knowledge systems. An assemblage rests on an operating goal plan and constitutes an organized system in its own right. Although assemblages typically have temporary active existence, they may themselves be stored for future use.

The distinction between attitudes as knowledge systems and particular attitudinal responses allows for cognitive organization while retaining the usefulness of the common definition of attitudes as evaluative responses. This common definition, although too narrow for social theory, does embody an important truth: attitudes are functional. Indeed, the evaluative character of attitudinal response exhibits the goal-directed character of attitudes.

Functional Perspective

A functional perspective is not new. It appears in Darwinian theory, in the pragmatic philosophers, in the functional school of attitude theory (see McGuire, 1969), and elsewhere. A functional perspective is also congenial to common sense, which sees everyday life in terms of motivations, goals, and actions.

To this functional tradition, the theory of information integration has made an effective contribution. The experimental work has elucidated the existence of a fairly general cognitive algebra in many areas of social psychology. Cognitive algebra has intrinsic interest as a mode of cognitive functioning. It also provides powerful new methods for further analysis of cognitive structure, in part through its capability for assessing processing flow and inferences (Anderson, 1983c, Sections C and D), in part through its capability for psychological measurement. This measurement is functional, for it assesses values as they operate in motivations and goals of the individual person.

Values constitute a fundamental biosocial capability, and they pervade the goal-directed character of everyday life. A theory of value is important for the study of social cognition. Mainstream cognitive psychology, however, has little to say about affect or value. Mainstream cognitive psychology is thus too narrow to deal with functional memory, for example, and it cannot get far in the study of judgment and action, for they depend on value. Social psychology needs to develop a new foundation for cognitive theory, a foundation with sufficient breadth to accommodate its central concerns.

ACKNOWLEDGMENT

This work was supported by Grant BNS82-12461 from the National Science Foundation to the Center for Human Information Processing, University of California, San Diego.

REFERENCES

Anderson, N. H. (1974). Cognitive algebra: Integration theory applied to social attribution. In L. Berkowitz (Ed.), *Advances in experimental social psychology* (Vol. 7, pp. 1–101). New York: Academic Press.

Anderson, N. H. (1976a). *Integration theory applied to cognitive responses and attitudes* (Tech. Rep. CHIP 68). La Jolla, CA: Center for Human Information Processing, University of California, San Diego.

Anderson, N. H. (1976b). *Social perception and cognition* (Tech. Rep. CHIP 62). La Jolla, CA: Center for Human Information Processing, University of California, San Diego.

Anderson, N. H. (1981a). *Foundations of information integration theory.* New York: Academic Press.

Anderson, N. H. (1981b). Integration theory applied to cognitive responses and attitudes. In R. E. Petty, T. M. Ostrom, & T. C. Brock (Eds.), *Cognitive responses in persuasion* (pp. 361–397). Hillsdale, NJ: Lawrence Erlbaum Associates.

Anderson, N. H. (1983a). *A theory of stereotypes* (Tech. Rep. CHIP 119). La Jolla, CA: Center for Human Information Processing, University of California, San Diego. In N. H. Anderson (Ed.), *Contributions to information integration theory* (in press).

Anderson, N. H. (1983b). *Psychodynamics of everyday life: Blaming and avoiding blame* (Tech. Rep. CHIP 120). La Jolla, CA: Center for Human Information Processing, University of California, San Diego. In N. H. Anderson (Ed.), *Contributions to information integration theory* (in press).

Anderson, N. H. (1983c). *Schemas in person cognition* (Tech. Rep. CHIP 118). La Jolla, CA: Center for Human Information Processing, University of California, San Diego. In N. H. Anderson (Ed.), *Contributions to information integration theory* (in press).

Anderson, N. H. (1986). A cognitive theory of judgment and decision. In B. Brehmer, H. Jungermann, P. Lourens, & G. Sevón (Eds.), *New directions in research on decision making* (pp. 63–108). Amsterdam: North-Holland.

Anderson, N. H. (in press). Information integration approach to emotions and their measurement. In R. Plutchik & H. Kellerman (Eds.), *Emotion: Theory, research, and experience* (vol. 4). New York: Academic Press.

Anderson, N. H. (1987). Review of *Political cognition*, R. L. Lau & D. O. Sears (Eds.). Hillsdale, NJ: Lawrence Erlbaum Associates. *American Journal of Psychology, 100,* 295–298.

Anderson, N. H., & Hubert, S. (1963). Effects of concomitant verbal recall on order effects in personality impression formation. *Journal of Verbal Learning and Verbal Behavior, 2,* 379–391.

Anderson, N. H., & Lopes, L. L. (1974). Some psycholinguistic aspects of person perception. *Memory & Cognition, 2,* 67–74.

Asch, S. E. (1946). Forming impressions of personality. *Journal of Abnormal and Social Psychology, 41,* 258–290.

Berscheid, E. (1982). Attraction and emotion in interpersonal relations. In M. S. Clark and S. T. Fiske (Eds.), *Affect and cognition* (pp. 37–54). Hillsdale, NJ: Lawrence Erlbaum Associates.

Cacioppo, J. T., Harkins, S. G., & Petty, R. E. (1981). The nature of attitudes and cognitive responses and their relationships to behavior. In R. E. Petty, T. M. Ostrom, & T. C. Brock(Eds.), *Cognitive responses in persuasion* (pp. 31–54). Hillsdale, NJ: Lawrence Erlbaum Associates.

Cantor, N., & Mischel, W. (1977). Traits as prototypes: Effects on recognition memory. *Journal of Personality and Social Psychology, 35,* 38–48.

Cohen, C. E. (1981). Person categories and social perception: Testing some boundaries of the processing effects of prior knowledge. *Journal of Personality and Social Psychology, 40,* 441–452.

Crano, W. D. (1977). Primacy versus recency in retention of information and opinion change. *Journal of Social Psychology, 101,* 87–96.

Dull, V. T. (1982). *Two strategies of social classification.* Unpublished doctoral dissertation. Santa Barbara, CA: University of California.

Fazio, R. H. (1986). How do attitudes guide behavior? In R. M. Sorrentino & E. T. Higgins (Eds.), *Handbook of motivation and cognition* (pp. 204–243). New York: Guilford.

Fiske, S. T. (1982). Schema-triggered affect: Applications to social perception. In M. S. Clark & S. T. Fiske (Eds.), *Affect and cognition* (pp. 55–78). Hillsdale, NJ: Lawrence Erlbaum Associates.

Hamilton, D. L., & Rose, T. (1980). Illusory correlation and the maintenance of stereotypic beliefs. *Journal of Personality and Social Psychology, 39,* 832–845.

Hastie, R. (1981). Schematic principles in human memory. In E. T. Higgins, C. P. Herman, & M. P. Zanna (Eds.), *Social cognition* (pp. 39–88). Hillsdale, NJ: Lawrence Erlbaum Associates.

Hastie, R., & Park, B. (1986). The relationship between memory and judgment depends on whether the judgment task is memory-based or on-line. *Psychological Review, 93,* 258–268.

McGuire, W. J. (1969). The nature of attitudes and attitude change. In G. Lindzey & E. Aronson (Eds.), *The handbook of social psychology* (Vol. 3, 2nd ed., pp. 136–314). Reading, MA: Addison-Wesley.

Rumelhart, D. E., & McClelland, J. L. (1986). *Parallel distributed processing* (vol. 1). Cambridge, MA: MIT Press.

Shanteau, J. (in press). Functional measurement analysis of reaction times in problem solving. In N. H. Anderson (Ed.), *Contributions to information integration theory.*

Snyder, M., & Uranowitz, S. W. (1978). Reconstructing the past: Some cognitive consequences of person perception. *Journal of Personality and Social Psychology, 36,* 941–950.

Tversky, A., & Kahneman, D. (1973). Availability: A heuristic for judging frequency and probability. *Cognitive Psychology, 5,* 207–232.

3 Objects in Categories and Objects as Categories

Jack Feldman
Georgia Institute of Technology

Brewer's chapter has provided an interesting and provocative integration of two streams of research: "person categorization," the focus of much recent activity in social cognition, and "person perception," the focus of much of the early research on impressions and judgments of people. The fundamental difference between these approaches, as Brewer presents them, is in the representation of people as members of categories *versus* the representation of people as unique individuals, capable of maintaining a separate identity in the perceiver's cognitive structure. Her description of "person perception" as concept formation is apt; the representation of persons *as individuals* has important theoretical implications, and bears on many applied issues as well. In any individualized treatment program (e.g., psychological or medical therapy), any educational setting (e.g., elementary or secondary classrooms, occupational counselling), or any employment situation (job interviews, performance appraisals, promotions, etc.), the impression that is formed by the decision maker influences the individual's life, sometimes profoundly (see, for instance, Feldman, 1986a; Jussim, 1986).

The following discussion does not question the importance of Brewer's distinction between top-down and bottom-up processing, nor her discussion of the factors promoting one or the other. Rather, the basic argument is that she did not go far enough in arguing that the cognition of social and nonsocial objects proceeds on identical principles—indeed, that the definition of an object as "social" depends as much on the perceiver as the object or person—and that only a single process is needed to encompass both.

ARE SOCIAL AND NONSOCIAL OBJECTS INHERENTLY DIFFERENT?

Brewer (p. 1) states that the majority of the time, the perception of nonsocial objects does not differ from that of social objects, and that when it does, it depends on the perceiver's processing goals and purpose. My argument is that the former statement is too weak, and that the degree to which any object is "personalized" depends on characteristics of the object in interaction with the cognitive structure, preexisting affect, and the purposes of the perceiver.

Much of the argument that "social things" are not processed as are "nonsocial things" depends on the analysis of Lingle, Altom, and Medin (1984) and Ostrom (1984). Persons are said to be dynamic rather than static, active rather than passive, and causal agents or sources rather than objects (Brewer, p. 1). I would argue that the perception of any object as dynamic, causal, and active depends on the degree of elaboration of that object in one's cognitive structure and the degree of affect associated with it, as well as on the nature of the object itself. Much of the argument is intuitive and anecdotal, because (to my knowledge) this has not been a topic of research.

Expertise implies a more elaborate cognitive structure, and the corresponding ability to attend to and encode aspects of a stimulus that a relative novice may overlook, or attend to only with greater relative effort (Alba & Hutchinson, 1987). The greater the degree of elaboration in a stimulus domain, then, the more differentiated any given set of objects is likely to be, whether they are people, postage stamps, automobiles, or rocks. A mountain range, for example, is likely to be dynamic to a geologist precisely because the details that connote change are more accessible to that person. Likewise, involvement with or strong affective response to a class of objects promotes and motivates cognitive elaboration and tends to give meaning to details that would otherwise be unnoticed. The person who has carefully restored an antique automobile is likely to be highly sensitive to symptoms of its mechanical welfare, perhaps noting that "she really wants to run today." Art enthusiasts talk about the "moods" of a painting changing, as do outdoorsmen when speaking of a mountain or a forest. It is hard to think of these as causal entities *unless* one shares, phenomenologically, the viewpoint of these highly involved experts. It is easy to think of animals as "people-like" social objects, and easier the closer they are to humans (does a clam have moods?), but how often have we been upset at discovering a person who thinks of our beloved pet as we might think of a chair or toaster, or been amused at a person who treats a plant as we might a pet, or someone who lavishes affection on an automobile, boat, stereo system, etc.?

While it is true that some objects (e.g., cabbages) are harder to treat as "social" than some others (e.g., kings), the point here is that people differ on this tendency with respect to any given object, as a function of their learning history and motivational/affective state. Any child who has had to memorize a dreary list of the monarchs of England since the Romans probably regards them much like cabbages, while the avid historian (or the good historical novelist) sees them as living characters. In short, "personhood" or "objecthood" is as much in the eye of the beholder as in the beheld, a point to which I will return.

Lingle et al. (1984) do not point out any *necessary* differences in the cognitive representations of social and nonsocial "things." Their examples can be matched by counterexamples depending only on knowledge, affect, or both. For instance:

1. Social categories are not necessarily more (or less) heterogeneous than natural object categories (p. 77). Consider "things to take on a camping trip" (Barsalou, 1983) or "edible things."

2. Social categories' representational attributes do not necessarily require more inference (p. 85). For example, the nutritional value of foods, or the performance potential of automobiles, may require a great deal of inferential work.

3. Membership and inference attributes (p. 86) are not necessarily any more complementary for natural than social categories. Lingle et al.'s "fat person" example is misleading. One can infer "photosynthesis" from "fruit," but not the reverse, and one does not need to reference photosynthesis to identify a fruit.

4. The use of probabilistic and exemplar information does not necessarily differentiate social and nonsocial categories (p. 97). Their example (mammal *verus* hostile person) is somewhat misleading. For example, compare the ease of generating examples of "unreliable vehicle" versus "psychologist" or "boxer."

5. Natural object categories (p. 99) may overlap as much or more than social categories. For instance, consider "grass" and the categories "animal fodder," "decorative plants," "means of erosion control."

Not to belabor the point further, it seems reasonable to conclude that Lingle et al. (1984) have provided a thoughtful and useful outline of issues to be considered in studying *any* categorization process, but that these issues are not any more relevant to social categories than to any other. Since their discussion is central to Brewer's conceptualization, the earlier arguments may be taken as questioning the degree to which a purely social theory of person perception and personalization is warranted.

ARE TWO PROCESSES NEEDED TO EXPLAIN PERSONALIZATION?

Brewer's conceptualization of complementary bottom-up and top-down processes of person representation fits very well with a model of categorization that assumes a relatively fixed cognitive structure. One implication is that a person must be seen either as a category member or an individual—that is, a member of a unique, single-object category. Recent views of category structure (Barsalou, 1986) paint a different picture—one in which categorization is a highly flexible response based on patterns of association; these associations presumably can be influenced by affect as well as frequency and recency of use, and can be more or less articulated—that is, linked into a complex pattern. In this view, categories are constructed as necessary (though some are more readily constructed than others); their structure can be influenced by goals, features of context, and other states of the perceiver and the environment.

Barsalou (1986) cites evidence showing that:

1. There are substantial individual differences in the graded structure of categories (the degree to which a given exemplar is "typical") (p. 13). There is also substantial variability over time (p. 17).

2. Graded structure may be influenced by context and point of view (pp. 9–13), including whether or not subjects must give reasons for their response. Some categories become relatively context-independent with frequency of use; expertise would naturally be associated with context-independence.

3. Categories may be represented by prototypes (central tendency), ideals, or exemplars, in the sense that graded structure may be determined by any of these for different categories or for the *same* category at different times and in different contexts (pp. 4–9).

Gara and Rosenberg (1979; see also Lingle et al., 1984) have shown that individuals may come to represent categories—in their terms, function as "supersets." This corresponds to the common observation that many individuals come to "know" others, at least initially, by explicitly comparing them to some well-known (and affectively relevant) person. It is said that in the entertainment industry, well-known stars become "types," as in "Get me a Clint Eastwood type to play the sheriff."

The foregoing suggests a unitary process of representation, in which people acquire the capacity to represent others in a variety of ways; *which* way will be chosen depends on the relative degree of elaboration of person information (i.e., "expertise" about that individual), affect attached to that person, processing goals and context, and recent experience. Needless to say, these factors are likely to be correlated.

The following points suggest the possible nature of the representation process.

1. A given person, to be perceived at all, must be categorized (identified, in Brewer's terms) in some way. Initial categorization probably takes place into broad, culture—common categories and/or categories with strong affective connotations (e.g., sex, race, social class). Temporary and chronic category ac-

cessibility are both important in the automaticity of this process (see Bargh, 1984, and Bargh, Bond, Lombardi, & Tota, 1986).

2. Affect, outcome dependence, goals or other factors (e.g., unexpected behaviors) elicit conscious attention/attribution processes; attention to behaviors cues trait schemata, which may be conceptualized as categories like any other, perhaps represented by "ideals." (This is discussed more fully later.)

3. Over time, the person becomes highly elaborated in memory—associated with a great many other persons, social categories, and trait concepts. As a function of frequency of interaction, the person representation becomes highly accessible and context-independent—and now serves as a standard or norm (Kahneman & Miller, 1986) against which to assess others. However, a change in processing goals may also allow the person representation to act as a category exemplar. Expertise in some area of knowledge would facilitate such flexibility—so that, for example, Jackie Stewart and A. J. Foyt are both auto racers, and one may think of "Jackie Stewart" types and "A. J. Foyt" types of racers meaningfully. The same can be said of nonsocial objects, such as the cars each is likely to have driven. Johnson and Raye (1981) and Alba and Hasher (1983) both argue against a purely schematic memory. Individuating information is *available* in memory, but is not always *accessible,* unless an effortful search is undertaken. The degree of existing elaboration, the affect associated with the person or events in memory, and the perceiver's goals would all be likely to influence recall, and thus the "personalization" of the individual in memory. The central point is that no *shift in process* is necessary to reach a personalized state; top-down and bottom-up processing occur simultaneously, and only a simple process like the one hypothesized above, or some functional equivalent, is necessary to determine the representation at a given moment.

ARE VISUAL AND VERBAL MODES OF REPRESENTATION MIRROR IMAGES?

Brewer's discussion of the visual representation of at least some categories, and the general importance of visual representations, is well stated and informative. The idea of visual representation seems applicable to both ideal and exemplar-based categories as well as those whose prototypes are determined by central tendency. Klatzky's (1984) chapter makes it clear that visual memory, whatever the underlying process, stores information not easily represented semantically.

Interestingly, the chapter also contains suggestions that visual memory operates similarly to memory for verbal stimuli. For example, reduction of memory for pictures with homogeneous stimulus sets, and the corresponding effect in visual paired-associate learning, recalls the confusion of memory when verbal stimuli belonging to the same category are presented (p. 239). The possibility that knowledge, strategies, and goals influence visual representations suggests that knowledge structures are as important in the construction of mental imagery as in the construction of verbal categories. The existence of reliable individual differences in visual information processing (p. 205) suggests that skill in the manipulation of visual concepts can be developed like any other skill, and that visual elaboration, like verbal elaboration, can take place as a function of experience and affective involvement with an object or category.

Studies of priming effects (pp. 249–250) and visual aftereffects produced by imagined stimulation (pp. 249–251) seem analogous to studies of category priming in person perception; so do studies of facial recognition as influenced by category accessibility, and research on the effects of schemata on the segmentation of behavior sequences (pp. 257–258).

Again, without belaboring the point we may hypothesize that visual and verbal representation processes are not fundamentally different once any innate differences in processing capacity are taken into account. Klatzky (1984, pp. 261–265) discusses how concepts may drive pictoliteral processing, and pictoliteral processing may drive conceptualization. Some people may be particularly good at translating from one representation to another—illustrators, for example, or cinematographers, or architects—while others may emphasize one of the two realms.[1]

Brewer's discussion of coherent visual categories that do not easily elicit verbal labels is paralleled by Barsalou's (1983) discussion of ad hoc or goal relevent categories, which are coherent but do not easily elicit prototypical images. Perhaps the key to both phenomena is the relative degree of elaboration of visual and verbal information, in addition to the nature (e.g., heterogeneity) of the objects themselves. A two-way classification, as presented in Table 3.1, may help clarify the issue. In Table 3.1, ease of visual representation and ease of verbal representation are orthogonal (though they may be correlated in nature). The ''Easy-Easy'' cell includes basic taxonomic categories, such as animals (birds, mammals), person categories (age, sex), and so forth. Easy verbal but difficult visual representation (ad hoc categories) is matched by the difficult verbal/easy visual representation, while difficulty on both is represented by ''ignorance.'' Movement from one cell to the other is a function of increasing knowledge, though the mode of category representation also varies with the nature of the objects. For example, ''items in a basic emergency tool kit'' is probably exemplar—defined, with category members becoming more easily

---

[1]Indeed, it is entirely possible that people may form categories based on other sensory modalities, given experience and motivation. Tactile, proprioceptive and kinestetic cues are important in many skilled performances (e.g., acrobatics; acting; sculpture; flying; motor racing; metalworking) which may require information processing under extremes of time pressure and distraction. It would be surprising if highly developed skills did not involve categories of behavior defined by various kinds of ''feeling'' referenced to internal standards. At the highest levels, these would also be susceptible to conceptual analysis and cognitive penetration.

TABLE 3.1
A Classification System for Category Representation

		Visual Representation	
		Easy	Difficult
Verbal Represen- tation	Easy	Taxonomic categories	Ad hoc/goal relevant categories
	Difficult	Pictoliteral categories	Domain-specific ignorance

named and visualized with experience. Finally, as context-independence is achieved, a prototypical or ideal exemplar may represent the abstract category attributes—for instance, a small adjustable pliers combining the characteristics of size, cost and versatility that determine graded "tool kit" structure may represent that category. A person category—say, "dramatic heroine," may be built up the same way, from exemplars, via visual and verbal elaboration until a single individual or joint representation is found to typify the category. Alternatively, one salient individual can, with sufficient experience, define the category—as John Wayne became the archetypical cowboy for an entire generation.

ARE DIMENSIONAL AND CATEGORICAL REPRESENTATIONS DIFFERENT?

Brewer's model assumes that person categories are nested within ". . . partitions along a few primary dimensions" (p. 10). Age and sex are two such automatically processed dimensions. This seems to reflect an assumption that dimensional and categorical representations are somehow different, in that trait perceptions represent a judgment of "amount" along an inherently continuous scale, while category perceptions represent placement in discrete and discontinuous classes. Fiske & Pavelchak (1986, p. 186) make the same sort of distinction. While one may argue about the "dimension-like" or "category-like" nature of any particular distinction (sex has always seemed categorical to me, while "femininity," subjectively, seems dimensional), this is at best an argument based on individual differences in the construction of "reality." More importantly, it is most parsimonious to use a single idea of representation until forced by the data to do otherwise. A categorical theory, assuming "ideal" representations, can serve. Barsalou (1986) reviews evidence that graded structure in such a category is determined by similarity to an ideal that may, in fact, not exist (e.g., "foods to eat on a diet" may be compared to a hypothetical calorie-free treat to determine their goodness as category members). It is not a long inferential leap to imagine that traits operate similarly, or may do so in certain contexts—that a hypothetical "perfect extrovert" may be constructed for use as an ideal category representation under some circumstances, or a close-to-ideal exemplar selected. The ability to differentiate more or less finely within such a category would be based on experience, which would develop attention to stimulus features in experts (and their presence in the ideal) that would be unknown to novices. Either linear or configural judgments would be possible.

The important difference is that a dimensional judgment reflects some quantity—a person has some *degree* of extraversion, masculinity, etc., or on a bipolar dimension, has some *balance* of quantities (*amounts* of masculinity-femininity). A categorical judgment represents a *qualitative* impression. The difference is that "middle" scores on a dimension have meaning, as do low scores. The midpoint of "masculinity-femininity" is thus "androgyny." In a categorical judgment (whether expressed as a check on a bipolar scale or not) a middle score means *neither category applies*—the person is not "equally masculine and feminine," the concepts are *irrelevant*. Essentially, either the perceiver, the perceived, or both are "aschematic" for that dimension (Markus, 1977).

This viewpoint helps make some anomolous data sensible. For example, the Behaviorally Anchored Rating Scale (BARS) attempts to define dimensions of job performance by anchoring a rating scale with examples of behavior scaled according to the method of equal-appearing intervals. The rater marks that point on the scale defined by the type of behavior expected of the ratee. Researchers in this area have found that, while behaviors indicative of good or poor performance are easy to elicit, "middle" behaviors are rare and difficult to scale (L. James, personal communication). This suggests a two-category representation, defined by ideal "good" and "poor" workers; the "middle" range is simply undefined. Fiedler's contingency model of leadership (Fiedler, 1978) depends on an individual difference measure, "esteem for the Least Preferred Coworker" (LPC), to define leadership style (which interacts with situational factors to determine effectiveness). Comparisons are typically made between high and low scorers on the LPC measure, which requires a rating of one's least preferred coworker on a series of evaluative scales. "Middle" LPC scores are not much discussed, and do not seem meaningful in terms of reliable behavioral tendencies. The "high LPC" and "low LPC" individuals may be rating against different ideal representations in a coworker category, while "middle" scorers may simply *not think* in those terms.

Klatzky (1984) notes that the perceptual system allows only a certain minimum size of difference to be encoded; Barsalou (1986) shows that ideals may represent a category in certain contexts as well as from the category's inception, and that central tendency, ideals, and frequency of exemplar instantiation may contribute simultaneously to graded structure. These points suggest strongly that it may be useful to ask how our understanding of judgment and impression processes generally may be improved by taking a category membership point of view rather than a dimensional point of view—for instance, inquiring as to the nature, occurrence, and development of ideals, the similarity judgment process comparing ideals to exemplars, and functions relating the decision threshold for category membership to contextual and individual difference variables.

CONCLUSION: PEOPLE AS OBJECTS AND OBJECTS AS "PEOPLE"

The issues raised here, and stimulated by Brewer's thoughtful paper, are intended to be somewhat heretical and controversy-provoking. They do not depart much, if at all, from conclusions reached by others, but I have tried to push their implications for social cognition somewhat further than a more typical format would allow.

Basically, I am arguing for a much more flexible and dynamic view of cognitive structure and process—one that has as its central premises that:

(a) Cognitive structure is constantly changing as experience accumulates and learning occurs (while realizing that learning depends on existing structure; e.g., Feldman, 1986b; Siegler, 1983).

(b) Cognitive structure is flexible in use, in that new structures (like categories) can be built to order, and new relationships between structures constructed (see Barsalou, 1983)—and that, the more material and skill there is available, the easier this becomes (see Alba & Hutchinson, 1987).

(c) Not only structures but processes can be called out as needed, and part of our task is to determine the nature of these "subroutines' and the circumstances under which they operate. This is not made easier by the fact that one process (e.g., conceptual operations on verbal material) may influence another (e.g., the generation of visual images).

(d) Affect matters, both as a consequence of and a motive driving social cognition.

One of the interesting consequences of the above view, based more on intuition than any logically defensible derivation at this point, has been referred to earlier: that objects may be invested with affect, and cognitively elaborated, to the point that they are perceived to be as "social" as any individual. Also, individual objects or people can be sufficiently invested with affect, and so frequently encountered or elicited (perhaps voluntarily) in a variety of contexts that they come to represent a category or to exemplify and entirely new category. Such a process, taken to extremes, may be labeled pathological; the individual whose affect is invested in some class of objects, and whose cognitive structure is highly elaborated in that domain, but who is relatively detached from and ignorant of interpersonal relations, is regarded as eccentric at best[2] and perhaps psychopathic at worst. The person whose representational skills in the domain of persons are highly elaborated, but who is relatively ignorant otherwise, is similarly unusual. Depending on the degree and direction of affect, such a person may be regarded very highly, or maybe seen as manipulative and self-seeking.

There are likely to be substantial cultural differences in the degree to which given objects are "social." The Japanese, for example, do not regard racing vehicles as anything more than tools; last season's machinery is routinely shredded. The British, in contrast, revere old machinery to the point of restoring vintage examples for special competition and museum display. The Japanese, though, have entire museums devoted to swords, and regard sword makers and polishers (which are separate crafts) as "living national treasures."

In short, what is social and what or who is an "individual" depends very much on who you ask and the circumstances of the inquiry.

REFERENCES

Alba, J. W., & Hasher, L. (1983). Is memory schematic? *Psychological Bulletin, 93,* 203–231.

Alba, J. W., & Hutchinson, J. W. (1987). Dimensions of consumer expertise. *Journal of Consumer Research, 13,* 411–454.

Bargh, J. A. (1984). Automatic and conscious processing of social information. In R. Wyer & T. Srull (Eds.), *Handbook of social cognition* (Vol. 3, pp. 1–43). Hillsdale, NJ: Lawrence Erlbaum Associates.

Bargh, J. A., Bond, R. N., Lombardi, N. J., & Tota, M. E. (1986). The additive nature of chronic and temporary sources of construct accessibility, *Journal of Personality and Social Psychology, 59,* 869–898.

Barsalou, L. W. (1983). Ad hoc categories. *Memory and Cognition, 10,* 82–93.

Barsalou, L. W. (1986). The instability of graded structure: Implications for the nature of concepts. In U. Neisser (Ed.) *Concepts reconsidered: The ecological and intellectual bases of categories.* Cambridge, England: Cambridge University Press.

Feldman, J. M. (1986a). A note on the statistical correction of halo error. *Journal of Applied Psychology, 71,* 173–176.

Feldman, J. M. (1986b). On the difficulty of learning from experience. In H. Sims, Jr. & D. Gioia (Eds.) *The thinking organization* (pp. 263–292). San Francisco: Jossey-Bass.

Fiedler, F. E. (1978). The contingency model and the dynamics of the leadership process. In L. Berkowitz (Ed.), Advances in experimental social psychology (Vol. 11, pp. 60–112). New York: Academic Press.

Fiske, S. T., & Pavelchak, M. A. (1986). Category-based *vs.* piecemeal-based affective responses: Developments in schema-triggered affect. In R. M. Sorrentino & E. T. Higgins (Eds.) *The*

---

[2]Like the lady with dozens of cats, each with a name and distinct personality; the hot-rodder who names his car and spends countless hours perfecting its appearance and performance; or the more familiar computer "hacker."

handbook of motivation and cognition: Foundations for social behavior (pp. 167–203). New York: Guilford Press.

Gara, M. A., & Rosenberg, S. (1979). The identification of persons as supersets and subsets in free-response personality descriptions. *Journal of Personality and Social Psychology, 37,* 2161–2170.

Johnson, M. K., & Raye, C. L. (1981). Reality monitoring. *Psychological Review, 88,* 67–85.

Jussim, L. (1986). Self-fulfilling prophecies: A theoretical and integrative review. *Psychological Review, 93,* 429–445.

Kahneman, D., & Miller, D. T. (1986). Norm theory: Comparing reality to its alternatives. *Psychological Review, 93,* 119–138.

Klatzky, R. L. (1984). Visual memory: Definitions and functions. In R. Wyer & T. Srull (Eds.), *Handbook of social cognition* (Vol. 2, pp. 233–270). Hillsdale, NJ: Lawrence Erlbaum Associates.

Lingle, J. H., Altom, M. W., & Medin, D. L. (1984). Of cabbages and kings: Assessing the extendability of natural concept models to social things. In R. Wyer & T. Srull (Eds.), *Handbook of social cognition* (Vol. 1, pp. 71–117). Hillsdale, NJ: Lawrence Erlbaum Associates.

Markus, H. (1977). Self-schemata and processing information about the self. *Journal of Personality and Social Psychology, 35,* 63–78.

Ostrom, T. M. (1984). The sovereignity of social cognition. In R. Wyer & T. Srull (Eds.), *Handbook of social cognition* (Vol. 1, pp. 1–38). Hillsdale, NJ: Lawrence Erlbaum Associates.

Siegler, R. S. (1983). Five generalizations about cognitive development. *American Psychologist, 38,* 263–277.

Compare and Contrast: Brewer's Dual Process Model and Fiske et al.'s Continuum Model

Susan T. Fiske
University of Massachusetts at Amherst

The distinction between category-based and attribute-based impression formation seems to be an idea whose time has come. With the last decade's emphasis on theory-driven social cognition, more data-driven social cognition has been neglected. The most recent *Annual Review* chapter on social cognition (Higgins & Bargh, 1987) illustrates the resurgence of data-driven processes in the field generally. Within research on impression formation more specifically, two recent models attempt to deal with the lopsided reliance on either data-driven or theory-driven processes by synthesizing the two. The target article is one of these attempts, and the other is a model developed by my collaborators and myself. While each model proposes that perceivers can form impressions both in stereotypic, category-oriented ways and in more individuated, attribute-oriented ways, the resemblance does not go much farther.

Our model proposes a continuum of impression formation processes, from category-based at one end to piecemeal, attribute-based at the other end. The model addresses the basic question posed by Asch 40 years ago (1946): Do people form impressions based on the overall Gestalt of the person or based on the attributes as isolated elements? We propose that people do both. The model also integrates social schema theories (see Fiske & Taylor, 1984; Markus & Zajonc, 1985) with algebraic models of impression formation (i.e., weighted averaging, N. Anderson, 1974; expectancy-value, Fishbein & Ajzen, 1975). Our model proposes that people engage in both holistic and elemental processing, proposing a continuum between them. Each type of processing is mostly likely to occur under specific informational and motivational conditions (Fiske, 1982; Fiske & Neuberg, in press; Fiske & Pavelchak, 1986).

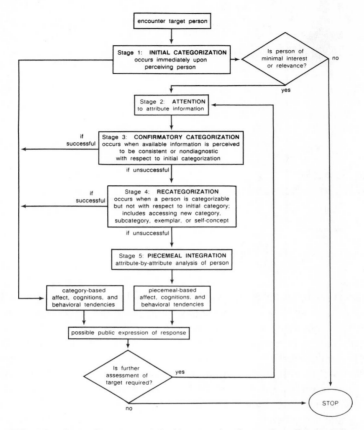

FIG. 4.1.   A continuum model of impression formation: From category-based to individuating responses, as a function of information, motivation, and attention. From Fiske & Neuberg, in press. Figure Copyright Susan T. Fiske, 1986.

MAJOR FEATURES OF THE CONTINUUM MODEL

The category-based/piecemeal continuum model makes several assumptions about impression formation processes (see Fig. 4.1). First, the model posits a rapid *initial categorization* that occurs regardless of the perceiver's intent. The initial category is likely to be based on obvious physical cues, overt labels, or other information immediately available upon encountering the target, and it is unaffected by additional attribute information (Neuberg & Fiske, 1987). If the target is uninteresting and irrelevant to the perceiver, that may be all the impression formation that occurs.

Second, however, if the target is indeed interesting or relevant, the model posits that *attention* to available attribute information mediates the possibility of responses along the remainder of the continuum. Without attention and effort, additional attribute information (whether confirming, neutral, ambiguous, or inconsistent) cannot be combined with the initial categorization (Fiske, Neuberg, Pratto, & Allman, 1986).

Third, the model posits that more category-based processes have *priority* over more attribute-based processes along the continuum. This premise stems from: the basic demands of cognitive economy; the considerable literature documenting the effects of social categories on perception, inference, and memory; the observation that subtle and not-so-subtle forms of stereotyping continue despite societal norms against it; and our own think-aloud data showing people's preference for categorizing (Fiske, Neuberg, Beattie, & Milberg, 1987).

INFORMATION CONFIGURATIONS

The available information configuration determines ease of categorization and, consequently, affects where on the continuum a perceiver's processes are located. Targets with stereotypic attributes elicit category-based responses, through *confirmatory categorization*. Targets who partially fit an initial category, but whose remaining attributes are ambiguous, may also be fit to the initial category by confirmatory categorization. Targets who partially fit an initial category, but whose remaining attributes are also partially inconsistent, are subtyped or newly categorized through *recategorization* processes. Finally, other targets, whose attributes simply do not fit any available category, elicit fully individuated, attribute-by-attribute *piecemeal* processes (see Fiske & Neuberg, in press, for a review of our own and other supportive work).

MOTIVATIONAL EFFECTS

Motivational conditions also importantly affect whether people make more category-oriented or more attribute-oriented responses. Outcome dependency, accountability, necessity to communicate, fear of invalidity, self-esteem threats, and other motivations can encourage relatively category-based or relatively attribute-based processes, under different circumstances (again, see Fiske & Neuberg, in press, for references). To integrate the budding literature on motivation and impression formation, we propose that motivations combine with circumstances to create specifiable goals that favor one or the other end of the continuum. Motivation is posited to operate via goal-directed attention to attributes (Erber & Fiske, 1984; Neuberg & Fiske, 1987). That is, if a perceiver is motivated to form an accurate impression of the target—for example, due to short-term, task-oriented outcome dependency—the perceiver will attend to different information than if motivated to maintain a negative category for the target—for example, due to self-esteem threats. Because motivation affects the amount and kind of attention paid to the target's attributes, it potentially influences processes at each successive stage: category confirmation, recategorization, and piecemeal integration.

COMPARISON TO BREWER'S MODEL

Superficially, Brewer's proposed model is strikingly similar to ours. In its current form, her model proposes a branching sequence of processes, which resembles our similarly explicit statement of processing stages. And both models suppose that the more category-oriented processes dominate the more attribute-oriented processes. The first stage in both models comprises immediate, basic categorization, followed by a relevance judgment that determines whether additional processing occurs. The models diverge from this point on, however, in several crucial respects that make the superficial resemblance superfluous.

In Brewer's model, different stages are proposed to have distinct types of *cognitive representations*. In our opinion, this premise is not logically well-founded. In effect, Brewer confounds one logical type with another (Ryle, 1949): the methods used by researchers and the cognitions in the heads of perceivers. Just because researchers studying certain types of cognitions have used certain methods (e.g., multidimensional scaling) or certain stimuli (e.g., pictures or verbal labels) does not mean that subjects predominately represent the particular cognitions in that particular way. For example, Brewer specifically hypothesizes that automatic identification judgments are represented as categories located in multidimensional space. We adhere to a network model, regardless of processing type, believing that multidimensional space is a descriptive tool for scientists to describe people's knowledge, rather than an actual type of cognitive representation.

Similarly, Brewer proposes that her second stage, category-based typing, depends on pictoliteral prototypes, using holistic, nonverbal pattern-matching. We do not propose a separate type of representation at different levels, believing that a variety of visual and verbal information types all can be represented within a network model. Nor would we suggest that visual information predominates at this particular stage or any other.

And again, Brewer's third stage, individuation, depends on category sub-types, using a feature differentiation process. That is, the person is represented as a category member with some distinctive features. We certainly agree with Brewer that subtypes are a frequent reference point for impression formation, and her research indeed has been instrumental in making this point. Nevertheless, category subtypes and exemplars are not logically limited to certain types of individuated representation that differ in kind from category-based or personalized impressions.

Finally, Brewer's fourth stage, personalization, is hypothesized to depend on individual schemata within a propositional network representation, using integration and elaboration processes. The individual is represented as a unique instance with certain features including category membership. Brewer argues that the representation is wholly verbal at this level. Our view is that verbal representations have been part of a network model all along, with greater elaboration in moving from category-based to individuated representations. Moreover, our most individuated type of processing allows both visual and verbal types of information, as do all our earlier stages.

There is another reason to avoid positing different forms of representation in different types of processing, in addition to the apparent logical error. It simply is not testable. This is because representation and process cannot be separated; one cannot meaningfully posit a representation without describing the processes that operate on it. That is, our access to cognitive representations depends on their role in some cognitive process (e.g., memory retrieval). One cannot empirically examine a representation in isolation from all processes. Hence, one has to make simultaneous assumptions about both representation and process. Because of this, there will always be too many degrees of freedom to competitively test specific representations within one representation-processing model against those within another representation-processing model; it is impossible to hold representation constant while varying process, or vice versa (J. Anderson, 1978). Therefore, any class of representation can produce empirical effects that mimic any other class of representation, given a few adjustments in one's processing assumptions. This means that efforts to choose between images and propositions, for example, will be doomed to indeterminancy. Given the empirical indeterminancy of such debates within cognitive psychology, it does not seem fruitful to propose one type of representation to the relative exclusion of another.

Finally, it does not make intuitive sense to argue specific types of representation for specific modes of impression formation: It seems unlikely that highly personalized portraits do not include visual information or that stereotypic portraits do not include verbal information. Perceivers easily image the appearances of their near and dear, as well as knowing verbal information about stereotyped outgroups.

Another critical feature differentiates Brewer's model and ours. Her model posits different *rules of inference* following each stage of processing. For example, Brewer's decision rule for moving on from automatic identification is whether the target is relevant enough to the perceiver to warrant further processing; the decision rule for moving to categorization versus personalization is self-involvement; the decision rule for moving to individuation is degree of category fit. Out model similarly includes an initial interest/relevance judgment (to distinguish between people one passes in the street and people who meaningfully enter into one's life).

But, unlike Brewer, we posit that both motivational involvement and information fit are decision rules that apply at each subsequent stage. For example, a target can be a good or poor fit to an initial category, a good or poor fit to a subtype, a good or poor fit to an exemplar. Similarly, motivations influence the likelihood and type of categorization, as well as the likelihood and type of recategorization and piecemeal processing. Because of the importance of these decision rules in each type of processing, we specify informational and motivational influences in considerably more detail, based on our own and others' research. For example, the range of motivations we consider is broader, and we also describe some ways that motivation can influence each stage after initial categorization.

Our model also differs from Brewer's in the centrality of *attentional processes*. Although the Brewer model notes attentional processes that distinguish features of individuals from other category members, our model portrays attentional processes as important in category selection at the initial categorization stage and as mediating each of the following stages of confirmatory categorization, recategorization, and piecemeal integration. Perceivers cannot process what they do not notice, so the direction of attention determines what may enter into impressions. Moreover, perceivers cannot integrate information without the attentional capacity and effort available to do so; hence, attentional resources determine whether people move beyond the more category-oriented processes to the more attribute-oriented processes. Finally, the goal of attention determines its nature (e.g., unbiased search vs. selective search), which then determines what is admitted for further cognitive elaboration at each stage.

The distinction between *a branching versus a continuum model* constitutes another important difference between Brewer's formulation and ours. In Brewer's view, self-involvement creates a dichotomous choice between personalization, on the one hand, and categorization or individuation (subtyping), on the other. In our view, involvement can affect each process along the continuum from confirmatory categorization, through recategorization, to piecemeal integration. Brewer's model assumes that impression formation proceeds in two wholly different manners, depending on involvement. The dichotomy implies, first, that when perceivers are involved they never stereotype, which seems unrealistic. Competitive involvement, for example, can enhance stereotyping. And even otherwise involved people (e.g., spouses who happen to be from different social categories or families who label one child "the athletic one" and another "the smart one") may use category information to explain each other's behavior. Brewer's dichotomy also implies that one never forms a fully personalized account of another unless one is fairly involved, which also seems unrealistic. For example, mere proximity can cause repeated contact with an outgroup member at the next desk, with the result that one develops a highly personalized impression. The advantage of our continuum model, on the other hand, is that it allows most impressions to incorporate both the category and other attributes, but to different degrees at different points along the continuum.

Finally, Brewer's entire paper is explicitly motivated as an effort to show how social cognition resembles nonsocial cognition, minimizing any differences due to *social and nonsocial stimulus qualities*. Instead, her model assumes that any differences in social versus nonsocial cognition are due to the perceiver's purposes and processing goals. These points are insufficiently developed in several respects. First, although social cognition researchers have long noted differences between social and nonsocial cognition (Fiske & Taylor, 1984; Heider, 1958; Ostrom, 1984; Tagiuri & Petrullo, 1958), the differences have merely supported the claim that *social* cognition research is inherently interesting, important, and complicated. Social cognition researchers have not exactly used the differences as an excuse for neglecting insights from nonsocial cognitive research. Brewer does not present any evidence to suggest that her model draws on nonsocial cognition research to a greater extent than do any other current models of social cognition, as a result of claiming equivalence between social and nonsocial stimuli.

Second, although the Brewer framework specifically aims to emphasize goals, little is said about goals after the introduction. Goals are mentioned twice: as influencing category accessibility (Bruner, 1958; Higgins & King, 1981; Wyer & Srull, 1981) and as instigating personalism through outcome dependency (Erber & Fiske, 1984). These scattered references do not constitute a novel emphasis on goals.

Third, Brewer's distinction between goals and stimulus qualities may be unnecessary in the first place. Any difference between social and nonsocial cognition that can be interpreted as due to a perceiver goal can equally well be interpreted as due to a stimulus quality. It is often the specific features of social stimuli that give rise to the specific goals of impression formation. For example, social stimuli are independent causal agents, in a way that nonsocial objects rarely are. Consequently, the social perceiver's goal frequently emphasizes the quest for prediction and control, which is not as inherently likely to arise in nonsocial cognition. Social stimulus qualities themselves instigate the processing goal. As another example, social stimuli are uniquely similar to the perceiving self. Hence, the perceiver's goal may include social comparison: searching for things in common or seeking to differentiate oneself. Again, stimulus qualities are inextricably linked to goals. One cannot easily separate impression formation differences as mainly due to either stimulus qualities or perceiver goals that are unique to social or nonsocial domains. For this and the previous reasons, then, a compelling case is not yet made that the Brewer model uniquely goes beyond social/nonsocial stimulus differences to emphasize processing goals.

There are other *specific points* of distinction between Brewer's model and ours. For example, we separate confirmatory categorization from recategorization, while Brewer lumps both into a categorization/typing stage, with a simple outcome of fit/no fit. We believe it is useful to separate confirmatory categorization from recategorization for several reasons: Recategorization requires more attention to the individual's attributes, elicits the process of generating a new knowledge structure rather than mere agreement, occurs under specifiably different information conditions, and is potentially more accurate. In short, people go through different processes to decide either, yes, this person fits my initial impression of being a typical X (confirmatory categorization) or, no, this person is not really an X, but perhaps an different kind of X or even a Y (recategorization).

As another specific point, Brewer's model and ours each mean different processes by "individuation." By fully individuated processing, we suggest a detailed attribute-by-attribute integration of available information, piecemeal processing, which can occur when categorization and recategorization processes break down. This can be faciliated both by informational and motivational exigencies. For example, if categories and subcategories do not fit, the perceiver forms a more or less detailed impression of the target on the basis of combining the individual attributes. The combinatorial process may occur in various ways, ranging from a quasi-algebraic combination to links that take meaning more into account. But fully individuated piecemeal processing focuses entirely on the target person's attributes, as given, with a minimum of category-based inference and organization. In contrast, Brewer provides an individuating process that includes category plus exceptions, if the perceiver is uninvolved and the initial category does not fit. Her "individuation" is apparently equivalent to our "recategorization," although the proposed eliciting conditions and ultimate consequences differ.

In sum, our model differs most significantly from Brewer's in that we propose a common type of representation that simply becomes more elaborated in more individuated processing, rather than proposing completely distinct types of representations in different types of processing. Also in contrast to Brewer's, our model proposes that the decision rules at each stage are quite similar: Information can fit to varying degrees and motivations can encourage accuracy to varying degrees, either factor resulting in processes along a continuum from categorization to individuation. Moreover, we have specified how processes along the continuum are influenced by informational conditions (fit between label and attributes) and motivational conditions (motivations combined with circumstances to produce specific goals), neither point much developed by Brewer. Attention is the central mediator of both informational and motivational influences that place processes along the continuum. Our model is explicitly continuous, rather than dichotomous, because relatively less reliance on the category and greater reliance on attributes is best characterized not as discrete but as gradual. Finally, as in previous social cognition work, the model draws on general principles of cognition, while not minimizing the interesting and complicated features of specifically social cognition.

Thus, our effort and Brewer's are concerned with many overlapping issues, but the models differ dramatically in their proposed representations and processes, in the amount of emphasis on informational and motivational conditions influencing these processes, as well as in the theme of attention that emerges throughout our model. In broadest outline, certainly, both models concur that information and motivation influence how impression formation proceeds, as more category-oriented or more attribute-oriented.

ADVANTAGES AND DISADVANTAGES OF EACH

One way to evaluate a model is to apply some standard criteria for a good theory (Deutsch & Krauss, 1965; Quine & Ullian, 1970). Perhaps not surprisingly, we believe our model has some distinct advantages according to such criteria. Most important, it is definitively *testable*. That is, by positing a continuum of processes from the more category-based to the more attribute-based, the model explicitly predicts which independent variables will move the perceiver farther along the dependent variable continuum. Decreases in category-attribute fit move the perceiver toward more attribute-based processes. Increases in motivations to be accurate move the perceiver toward more attribute-based processes. Increases in motivations to arrive at particular answers freeze the perceiver toward the category-oriented end. Attribute-oriented attention mediates the effects of both information fit and motivational factors on the extent of category-oriented or attribute-oriented processes. These predictions can be and are being tested (in addition to our work, see Mackie & Worth, 1986; Sujan, 1985, on informational effects within our model; and see Omoto & Borgida, in press; Kruglanski, 1986; Tetlock, 1985, on relevant motivational effects).

Brewer's model, on the other hand, presents some difficulties for comprehensive testing. As indicated by the research cited in support, the dichotomous branching model lends itself mainly to isolated tests of individual stages and processes hypothesized for each. This creates the danger of empirical myopia. For example, if one studies visual information relevant to social categories and verbal information relevant to personalization, this does not allow one to discover visual information's relevance to personalization and verbal information's relevance to categorization. A theory that posits discrete steps leading to dichotomous choices lends itself to such limitations.

Our model is also more explicitly *integrative* of previous results. We have demonstrated that a considerable range of literature can be organized and understood within our framework (Fiske & Neuberg, 1986; Fiske & Pavelchak, 1986). Studies that manipulate both information configurations and motivational circumstances all fit within the overall framework. Brewer's model uses research to illustrate key points, but it does not explicitly organize existing knowledge to the same extent.

The continuum model is also more *parsimonious* than Brewer's dual mode model. Our model posits a single representation (networks) and a single set of decision rules (information fit and motivational goals) and a single mediator (attribute-oriented attention). Brewer's model posits a variety of representations and decision rules and possible mediators. We believe there is no compelling case for totally separate representations and processes at multiple discrete stages of impression formation. It is neither cognitively economical for perceivers nor theoretically economical for psychologists.

Finally, Brewer's model is not completely *internally consistent*. For example, if involvement is seen as a continuous variable, how can impression processes be dichotomized? In positing a dichotomy between impression formation that involves and does not involve the self, the model fails to allow for impressions that occur at intermediate levels of involvement or that develop with developing involvement. That is, how would a perceiver move from one branch (i.e., individuation) to the other (personalization)? As another example, the model is sometimes described as a unidirectional stage model, but at other times as bidirectional, incorporating both top-down and bottom-up processes. Hence, the model's sequential assumption is either inconsistent or unclear. As a final example, although pictoliteral prototypes are posited for categorization processes, research using verbal stimuli is cited, and although propositional networks are posited for personalization, research using visual stimuli is cited.

Brewer's model does have some distinct advantages over ours. It reminds verbally oriented impression formation researchers that visual information is important. It presents a fairly developed theory of subtypes. It discusses the merits of dimensional and categorical representations in some detail. Nevertheless, in its current form, my collaborators and I feel it needs further development.

CONCLUSION

The beginning of this comment suggested that the distinction between category-based and attribute-based impressions is an idea whose time has come. In our effort and in Brewer's, there is an attempt to synthesize previously competing or apparently incompatible perspectives. In the tradition of (1) thesis (Asch's Gestalt approach), (2) antithesis (Anderson's algebraic approach), (3) second thesis (the schema approach), our work represents a synthesis. As such, it may be viewed as a constructivist effort (McGuire, 1983): Rather than pitting theories against each other to see which is right, one attempts to specify circumstances under which each is useful. This is the spirit in which both models are offered.

In the course of our research agenda over the last several years, we first encountered Brewer's model, in preliminary form, as a convention paper (Brewer, 1985), apparently prepared simultaneously with our ongoing work (e.g., Fiske, 1982, 1983, 1985; Fiske & Neuberg, in press; Fiske & Pavelchak, 1986). It has been a privilege to observe the convergence of Brewer's ideas and ours over time, as we each have benefited from each other's and our colleagues' suggestions. This comment is intended to continue that iterative process. Professor Brewer brings to her work a strong combination of concern with the real-world psychology of desegregation and with the fine-grained task of cognitive explanation. This blend shows in the quality of her considerable contributions.

ACKNOWLEDGMENT

The preparation of this comment was supported by NSF Grant BNS 85-96028 and by NIMH Grant 1 RO1 MH41801. The author would like to thank Edward Emery and Steven Neuberg for their helpful suggestions on an initial draft.

REFERENCES

Anderson, J. R. (1978). Arguments concerning representations for mental imagery. *Psychological Review, 85,* 249–277.

Anderson, N. H. (1974). Information integration: A brief survey. In D. H. Krantz, R. C. Atkinson, R. D. Luce, & P. Suppes (Eds.), *Contemporary developments in mathematical psychology* (pp. 236–305). San Francisco, CA: Freeman.

Asch, S. E. (1946). Forming impressions of personality. *Journal of Abnormal and Social Psychology, 41,* 258–290.

Brewer, M. B. (1985, April). *Forming impressions of others: From social object to person.* Presidential address presented at the meeting of the Western Psychological Association.

Bruner, J. S. (1958). Social psychology and perception. In E. E. Maccoby, T. M. Newcomb, & E. L. Hartley (Eds.), *Readings in social psychology* (3rd. ed., pp. 85–94). New York: Holt, Rinehart & Winston.

Deutsch, M., & Krauss, R. M. (1965). *Theories in social psychology.* New York: Basic Books.

Erber, R., & Fiske, S. T. (1984). Outcome dependency and attention to inconsistent information. *Journal of Personality and Social Psychology, 47,* 709–726.

Fishbein, M., & Ajzen, I. (1975). *Belief, attitude, intention, and behavior: An introduction to theory and research.* Reading, MA: Addison-Wesley.

Fiske, S. T. (1982). Schema-triggered affect: Applications to social perception. In M. S. Clark & S. T. Fiske (Eds.), *Affect and cognition: The 17th Annual Carnegie Symposium on Cognition* (pp. 55–78). Hillsdale, NJ: Lawrence Erlbaum Associates.

Fiske, S. T. (1983). Affective responses to social stereotypes. Grant from the National Science Foundation.

Fiske, S. T. (1985). Intent and category-based responses to mental patients. Grant from the National Institutes of Mental Health.

Fiske, S. T., & Neuberg, S. L. (in press). A continuum model of impression formation from category-based to individuating responses: Influences of information and motivation on attention and interpretation. In M. P. Zanna (Ed.), *Advances in experimental social psychology* (Vol. 23). New York: Academic Press.

Fiske, S. T., Neuberg, S. L., Beattie, A. E., & Milberg, S. J. (1987). Category-based and attribute-based reactions to others: Some informational conditions and stereotyping and individuating processes. *Journal of Experimental Social Psychology 23*, 399–427.

Fiske, S. T., Neuberg, S. L., Pratto, F., & Allman, C. (1986). *Stereotyping and individuating: The effects of information inconsistency and set size on attribute-oriented processing.* Unpublished manuscript, University of Massachusetts at Amherst.

Fiske, S. T., & Pavelchak, M. A. (1986). Category-based versus piecemeal-based affective responses: Developments in schema-triggered affect. In R. M. Sorrentino & E. T. Higgins (Eds.), *The handbook of motivation and cognition: Foundations of social behavior* (pp. 167–203). New York: Guilford Press.

Fiske, S. T., & Taylor, S. E. (1984). *Social cognition.* New York: Random House.

Heider, F. (1958). *The psychology of interpersonal relations.* New York: Wiley.

Higgins, E. T., & Bargh, J. A. (1987). Social cognition and social perception. *Annual Review of Psychology, 38,* pp. 369–425.

Higgins, E. T., & King, G. (1981). Accessibility of social constructs: Information-processing consequences of individual and contextual variability. In N. Cantor & J. F. Kihlstrom (Eds)., *Personality, cognition, and social interaction* (pp. 69–122). Hillsdale, NJ: Lawrence Erlbaum Associates.

Kruglanski, A. W. (1986, May). Motivational bases of attributions. Paper presented at the symposium on *New Directions in Social Cognition,* New England Social Psychological Association.

Mackie, D. M., & Worth, L. T. (1986, August). Processing implications of schema-based and piecemeal evaluation of consumer products. Paper presented at the American Psychological Association, Washington, DC.

Markus, H., & Zajonc, R. B. (1985). The cognitive perspective in social psychology. In G. Lindzey & E. Aronson (Eds.), *The Handbook of Social Psychology* (Vol. 1, 3rd. ed., pp. 137–230). New York: Random House.

McGuire, W. J. (1983). A contextualist theory of knowledge: Its implications for innovation and reform in psychological research. In L. Berkowitz (Ed.), *Advances in Experimental Social Psychology,* Vol. 16 (pp. 1–47). New York: Academic Press.

Neuberg, S. L., & Fiske, S. T. (1987). Motivational influences on impression formation: Outcome dependency, accuracy-driven attention, and individuating processes. *Journal of Personality and Social Psychology, 53,* 431–444.

Omoto, A. M., & Borgida, E. (in press). Guess who might be coming to dinner: Personal involvement and racial stereotypes. *Journal of Experimental Psychology.*

Ostrom, T. M. (1984). The sovereignty of social cognition. In R. S. Wyer, Jr., & T. K. Srull (Eds.), *Handbook of social cognition* (Vol. 1, pp. 1–38). Hillsdale, NJ: Lawrence Erlbaum Associates.

Quine, W. V., & Ullian, J. S. (1970). *The web of belief.* New York: Random House.

Ryle, G. (1949). *The concept of mind.* New York: Barnes & Noble.

Sujan, M. (1985). Consumer knowledge: Effects on evaluation strategies mediating consumer judgments. *Journal of Consumer Research, 12,* 1–16.

Tagiuri, R., & Petrullo, L. (Eds.). (1958). *Person perception and interpersonal behavior.* Stanford, CA: Stanford University Press.

Tetlock, P. E. (1985). Accountability: The neglected social context of judgment and choice. In L. Cummings & B. M. Staw (Eds.), *Research in organizational behavior.* Greenwich, CT: JAI.

Wyer, R. S., Jr., & Srull, T. K. (1981). Category accessibility: Some theoretical and empirical issues concerning the processing of social stimulus information. In E. T. Higgins, C. P. Herman, & M. P. Zanna (Eds.), *Social cognition: The Ontario Symposium* (Vol. 1, pp. 161–198). Hillsdale, NJ: Lawrence Erlbaum Associates.

5 The Dynamics of Categorization and Impression Formation

Sarah E. Hampson
Oregon Research Institute
Eugene, Oregon

The most novel aspect of Brewer's model of impression formation is her proposal that there are two modes by which social information is processed—category-based, top-down processing versus person-based, data-driven processing. Which of these modes will be used is primarily determined by the perceiver's goals. According to Brewer's model, category-based and person-based processing are alternative routes leading to different forms of representation of the target person. One consequence of postulating two different modes of impression formation is that it suggests a fresh appraisal of a long-standing issue—the differences between social and nonsocial cognition. Brewer argues that category-based processing is very similar in social and nonsocial cognition, whereas person-based (personalized) processing is rare in nonsocial cognition.

WHAT IS THE UNIT IN SOCIAL COGNITION?

This has always been a controversial question in personality research (e.g., Fiske, 1974), and in social psychology the debate often pivots around whether it is the group or the individual that is the focus of interest (e.g., Hewstone & Jaspers, 1984). In social cognition, there is a similar difference of opinion—whether the person or the behavior performed by the person is the preferred unit (e.g., Cantor & Mischel, 1979; Hampson, 1982). The choice of unit is critical because it determines the shape of the subsequent model of social cognition.

Brewer takes the target person as the unit of impression formation. Herein lies one of our concerns about her model. We (Hampson, John, & Goldberg, 1986) believe it is this emphasis on a physically bounded entity (the person) that has led to the protracted debate about the similarities and differences between object and person perception. We propose that instead of taking the person as the unit in impression formation, a genuine appreciation of the dynamic nature of social stimuli leads to *behavior* as being the unit of analysis. The ultimate purpose of the social perceiver is to understand what people are *doing*, not what they are *are*, although understanding what they are (i.e., category-based perception) may provide valuable clues as to what they are doing.

We use the term "behavior" in its broadest sense, and perhaps "event" is a better word. Events involve motor behaviors, but these are often the least important part of the action. Impression formation involves the interpretation of behavioral events in order that the target person's underlying *intentions* may be inferred. It is the inferred intentionality (or lack of) that gives meaning to behavior, and it is through the observer's constructive perception of the target's behavior that the event is understood.

STATIC VERSUS DYNAMIC SOCIAL PROCESSING

The most crucially important distinction is between the target person and the behavioral event in which the target person is engaged. We believe that focusing on the target person encourages a static view of social stimuli and therefore overestimates the similarities between social and nonsocial cognition. Brewer particularly emphasizes the physical aspects of the target person in the typing process involved in category-based processing. For example, she proposes that person categories may be represented pictoliterally, and she used some of her own studies, in which subjects sorted photographs of people's faces, to exemplify the kind of research generated by an emphasis on visual aspects of social stimuli.

However, by taking behavioral events as the starting point, the dynamic and goal-oriented nature of social cognition becomes central. These events can be presented in visual or verbal forms, since more useful models of social cognition are unlikely to appear as the result of favoring one mode of stimulus information over another. In everyday life, we have to process a variety of direct and indirect kinds of social information. The challenge is to generate models of social cognition that account for the ways that people use, with such ingenuity, whatever information is available to derive hypotheses about what is going on around them.

Perhaps an everyday example will help to clarify this point. If, as I am returning to my parked car, I see a person writing on a piece of paper and placing it on my windscreen, my understanding of that event will be substantially influenced by whether or not the target person is wearing the uniform of a traffic warden. The psychological processes involved in recognizing her uniform are not interesting to social psychologists. Presumably, they are identical to those associated with any form of everyday object perception. What is of interest is my radically different understanding of the event depending on the social category in which I place the target (e.g., traffic warden, distributor of advertising information, my best friend). The social category allows me to make inferences about what the target is trying to do (fine me, sell me something, tell me to give him a lift). The categorization process is important primarily for what it buys the social perceiver in terms of explanatory power.

Although much of social cognition is concerned with the processes of person perception, the phrase "impression formation" is a holdover from an earlier era of social psychology and tends to be misleading. Again, it emphasizes the static view, both of the target person and the perceiver. Previous information is used to assist in understanding a target's current actions, but most of the time social perception is not concerned with character sketches. Just think for a moment how difficult and unsatisfying it is to write letters of recommendation. Impression formation is the study of how people make sense of the available target information in the light of their current goals.

THE ROLE OF TRAITS

Brewer sidesteps the controversy over whether trait encoding occurs spontaneously at an early stage in social information processing or whether it occurs at a relatively late stage (e.g., Smith, 1983; Smith & Miller, 1983; Winter & Uleman, 1984; Winter, Uleman, & Cunniff, 1985; Uleman, Winborne, Winter, & Shechter, 1986; Wyer & Srull, 1986) by proposing that some traits (e.g., friendly, hostile) are used at the initial identification stage, whereas the remainder are used in person-based processing. The issue is not central to her discussion because she does not regard traits as the unit of person representation. Instead of slotting people into multidimensional trait-space, Brewer prefers to match people to pictoliteral categories (category-based processing) or to insert them into a propositional network (person-based processing). However, in neither of these modes of processing is the role of traits given a thorough airing, which is surprising since so much of the research on impression formation has used trait descriptions, and traits form such a substantial part of the everyday language of lay social cognition (Goldberg, 1981).

Although traits are dimensional, in the sense that people may be described as characterized by a trait to varying degrees, this does not necessarily mean that traits form a mental multidimensional space in which target persons may be (rather laboriously) located, as Brewer claims (pp. 9–10). She favors persontypes as social categories (e.g., occupational roles), although she does not provide a comprehensive list of potential social categories.

We have argued else where that traits are semantic categories used for identifying behavioral events (Hampson, 1982; Hampson et al., 1986). According to our model of traits, a behavior can be identified as being more or less prototypical of a trait category on the basis of a feature-matching process. Thus, when behavior is taken as the unit of social cognition, traits provide additional categories to those suggested by Brewer for category-based processing. Brewer is not explicit about the role of traits in category-based processing, but she notes that traits may be inferred from the visual images that constitute the mode of representation in this type of processing (p. 15).

Our research on traits as cognitive categories suggests that traits share many similarities with object categories although there also appear to be some interesting differences. Contrary to the assumptions of Brewer (p. 1), we have found evidence of at least some hierarchical organization of trait categories comparable to the hierarchies found in the object domain (Hampson et al., 1986). We suspect that social categories may differ from nonsocial categories primarily in terms of the attributes of social categories. Instead of a hierarchical organization of attributes, one in which subordinate categories possess all the attributes of categories above them, plus their own, we suspect that trait categories constituting a hierarchy may be distinguished by their particular profile of values on the *same* set of attributes (John, 1986).

We consider that traits are also used in person-based processing, but the procedures for deciding which trait is applicable differ when traits are applied to people, as opposed to behaviors. Whereas traits label behaviors via a feature-matching process, traits are applied to people via a set of ascription rules, which may vary from trait to trait (Rorer & Widiger, 1983). These ascription rules will include many of the principles identified by Kelley (1967) for making dispositional versus situational attributions.

DUAL PROCESSING VERSUS SEQUENTIAL PROCESSING

There is no compelling reason to separate the two modes of social processing into diverging routes. Instead, we assume that category-based processing occurs prior to person-based processing. The information gained in categorization will be relevant to the person-based representation. As a result of findings from recent investigations of the role of traits, it becomes clear that both modes of processing rely extensively on top-down processes, but perhaps of only partially overlapping forms (e.g., traits as behavioral labels versus traits as person-descriptors).

Brewer (p. 20) proposes that when a particular person is characterized by category-discrepant features, then the category-based representation will be individuated. However, the distinction between an individuated category-based representation and a personalized person-based representation seems difficult to maintain empirically. It would be more parsimonious to draw the distinction between nonindividuated category-based processing, and individuated processing. If the explanation achieved by categorizing the target fails to yield an adequate understanding of the event for the perceiver's current purposes, then further individuated processing will be instigated. For example, if categorizing the person in the earlier example as a traffic warden fails to explain her behavior (perhaps she removes the parking ticket as I approach), I may be compelled to make some inferences about her as a person (e.g., she is ''kind'') in order to understand what she is doing.

SUMMARY AND CONCLUSIONS

Brewer has proposed two modes of social information processing (category-based versus person-based) in which the unit of social cognition is the target person. Contrary to Brewer, we argue that the appropriate unit for social cognition is the behavioral event. The goal of social cognition is social understanding, and this is achieved by explaining events. We believe that traits play a crucial role in social understanding. They serve as categories both for behaviors and for people, although the attribute-matching rules for applying a trait to a behavior will not be the same as the ascription rules for applying that same trait to a person. We suggest serial rather than dual processing in which nonindividuated social processing takes place prior to individuated processing.

ACKNOWLEDGMENT

The author's work is partially supported by Grant MH-39077 from the National Institute of Mental Health, U. S. Public Health Service. Lewis R. Goldberg provided his usual assistance in translating from British to American. Correspondence concerning this commentary should be addressed to Sarah E. Hampson, Oregon Research Institute, 1899 Willamette Street, Eugene, OR 97401.

REFERENCES

Cantor, N., & Mischel, W. (1979). Prototypes in person perception. In L. Berkowitz (Ed.), *Advances in experimental social psychology (Vol. 12)*. New York: Academic Press.

Fiske, D. W. (1974). The limits for the conventional science of personality. *Journal of Personality, 42*, 1–11.

Goldberg, L. R. (1981). language and individual differences: The search for universals in personality lexicons. In L. Wheeler (Ed.), *Review of personality and social psychology* (Vol. 2, pp. 141–165). Beverly Hills, CA: Sage Publications.

Hampson, S. E. (1982). Person memory: A semantic category model of personality traits. *British Journal of Psychology, 73*, 1–11.

Hampson, S. E., John, O. P., & Goldberg, L. R. (1986). Category breadth and hierarchical structure in personality: Studies of asymmetries in judgments of trait implications. *Journal of Personality and Social Psychology, 51,* 37–54.

Hewstone, M., & Jaspers, J. M. F. (1984). Social dimensions of attribution. In H. Tajfel (Ed.), *The social dimension: European developments in social psychology* (Vol. 2, pp. 379–404). Cambridge, England: Cambridge University Press.

John, O. P. (1986). How shall a trait be called? A feature analysis of altruism. In A. Angleitner, G. Van Heck, & A. Furnham (Eds.), *Personality psychology in Europe* (Vol. 2). Lisse, The Netherlands: Swets & Zeitlinger.

Kelley, H. H. (1967). Attribution theory in social psychology. In D. D. LeVine (Ed.), *Nebraska Symposium on Motivation (Vol. 15).* Lincoln: University of Nebraska Press.

Rorer, L. G., & Widiger, T. A. (1983). Personality structure and assessment. In M. R. Rosenzweig & W. W. Porter (Eds.), *Annual review of psychology* (Vol. 34, pp. 431–463). Palo Alto, CA: Annual Reviews.

Smith, E. R. (1983). Attributions and other inferences: Processing information about the self versus others. *Journal of Experimental Social Psychology, 20,* 97–115.

Smith, E. R., & Miller, F. D. (1983). Mediation among attributional inferences and comprehension processes: Initial findings and a general method. *Journal of Personality and Social Psychology, 44,* 492–505.

Uleman, J. S., Winborne, W. C., Winter, L., & Shechter, D. (1986). Personality differences in spontaneous personality inferences at encoding. *Journal of Personality and Social Psychology, 51,* 396–403.

Winter, L., & Uleman, J. S. (1984). When are social judgments made? Evidence for the spontaneousness of trait inferences. *Journal of Personality and Social Psychology, 47,* 237–252.

Winter, L., Uleman, J. S., & Cunniff, C. (1985). How automatic are social judgments? *Journal of Personality and Social Psychology, 49,* 904–917.

Wyer, R. S., & Srull, T. K. (1986). Human cognition in its social context. *Psychological Review, 93,* 322–359.

6 Impression Formation: What Do People Think About?

Edward E. Jones
Princeton University

Brewer's theoretical essay is undoubtedly an important contribution to the field of social cognition, and in particular to our more focused attempts to understand how impressions are formed. The dual process model she presents is provocative, both because it is an ambitious attempt to synthesize a large body of literature and because it is boldly stated and avoids wimpish caveats. Therefore, it is an ideal exemplar of a target article for this fledgling publication—ideal because ambitious reviews inevitably leave out references that any given critic believes to be important, and because clearly stated models provide ample opportunities for dissent and qualification.

The main themes I stress in elaborating, if not criticizing, Brewer's model are the paradoxical claims that she ignores a central portion of the history of impression formation research on the one hand, and that her model is somewhat dated on the other hand. Let me deal with each of these themes in order.

WHAT HAPPENED TO BEHAVIOR?

Brewer is apparently critical of the relative concentration of impression formation research on the integration of information conveyed by trait lists or verbal descriptions. As a corrective, she wants to call our attention to the role of physical (especially facial) characteristics and related visual imagery. This is all well and good, but is it not amazing that there is no mention of *behavioral information* which, after all, is the most crucial source of person perception information in our daily lives? There are literally hundreds of experimental studies involving the impression formation of actors in realistic settings, where verbal descriptions are not involved, where physical characteristics are held constant, and where the varied information is the behavior of the actor. I am sure that those who label themselves social cognition students would hardly argue that behavior is uninformative, but can a valid theory of impression formation truly be erected by models that attempt to explain what happens to information that is a mixture of traits, category labels, and physical cues? The field of "impression formation" or "person perception" was not born with Asch to leap through Anderson to the current generation of information processing researchers. There was a modestly important development associated with attribution approaches, responsible for many of the "hundreds" of experiments referred to above. And one of the most exciting and appealing features of the attributional approach (at least for me) was that it broke away from the semantics of trait list integration to focus on how people perceive and interpret social behavior. And yet a brief visitor from the planet Cognit might look at Brewer's essay and conclude that no one has ever worried about how naive persons conceptualize the behavior of their fellow humans or has ever conducted research built around interpretations of systematically varied, complex behavioral stimuli.

THE PERCEIVER AS PART OF THE SITUATION

Such a historical oversight is not unrelated to the second theme that fulfills the paradox: Brewer's person perceiver is basically a passive information processor. Oh, of course, the perceiver is active in that he or she has goals, construes the information at hand in line with expectancies, and frames the construed information in goal-relevant schemas. But the perceiver is not active in eliciting information or in creating the conditions under which information about the target person is generated. In real life, the perceiver is a "player." He or she is either actively eliciting information or at least forms part of the situation to which the target person is behaving. Brewer's model totally ignores the problems and research opportunities that this more active, imbedded view of the perceiver presents.

More generally, the model pays occasional lip service to such variables as "contextual cues," but is essentially mute concerning the enormous importance of situational factors in the person perception process. This stems in part from the failure to recognize that the central problem in person perception is the interpretation of a target person's behavior, for this of course requires an understanding of the situation to which the behavior is addressed.

Brewer's model focusses on modes of information processing and contrasts the top down processing of category-based impression formations with the data driven processing of person-based impression formations. In view of the voluminous literature on stereotypes and prototypes, I would quarrel with her characterization of the "prevailing view" as that of a bottom-up process. Nevertheless, the distinction is probably useful, and Brewer nicely articulates some of its intriguing theoretical and practical consequences. But the present dual process model leaves out too much at the point of entry. So many of the really fascinating things that go on in the process of forming an impression happen as information is generated and initially encoded. The present model treats this as somewhat incidental, as "primitive categorization" that is carried by automatic processing, and then goes on to tell us what happens to this already coded (and therefore at least partially interpreted) information once it arrives in the flow chart.

By comparison, Trope's (1986) dual process model tells us more about the identification process itself and does so in a way that captures the interaction between situations, behaviors, and "priors." Thus our expectancies (priors) not only influence how we perceive situations, but situations influence how we perceive behaviors and behaviors influence how we construe situations. An integrated theory that combined these features of Trope's model with the more explicitly categorical features of Brewer's model in the subsequent information processing stages would be very powerful.

ARE THERE REALLY TWO PROCESSES, ONE, OR "N"?

In her provocative parsimony, Brewer suggests that "self involvement" determines whether the top-down (categorization) or the bottom-up (personalization) process occurs. When we personalize, social categories are relevant but subordinate and a "different type of cognitive structure" is involved since person-based knowledge is represented in memory as a "propositional network." A major distinguishing feature is where the processing stops—at the highest useful level of abstraction (category-based mode) or at the lowest useful level of abstraction (person-based mode). What is "useful" depends on task demands imposed by the environment when category-based encoding is involved, and the needs and goals of the perceiver in the case of personalized information processing.

This separation of environmental "task demands" and perceiver goals may not survive analytic scrutiny. The ease with which a goal can become a situational requirement, and vice versa, makes me question whether this distinction is useful. Task settings are often selected to accommodate perceiver goals, and goals often are defined by the task settings in which we find ourselves. If there is a distinction, it may involve degrees of environmental constraint—how much choice does the perceiver have in selecting tasks and in implementing self-defined purposes? It is not apparent whether or how the degree of situational constraint affects information processing. Do I process information differently if I have the freedom to choose among many available goals (which is how I interpret the condition in which personal needs are operative) than if the environment somehow restricts the things I can do (i.e., makes task demands)? Is there a further implication that we have more freedom of action when we are "personally involved?" Once again, the dual process model appears to omit explicit reference to the role of variations in situational constraint.

In addition, the problem of identifying which of the two processing modes is operative seems to be a serious one. Let us say that Joe is personally involved with Jane and Sam is not, but both are asked to describe their impression of her. If Joe's impression is more differentiated and has more data-proximate categories, is this because Joe goes from the data up or because Joe went further down from the more abstract categories that failed to fulfill his purposes? Is Joe simply more persistent in working over the information at hand, or is he actually proceeding in an inductive rather than a deductive manner? There is a suggestion that order of recall will help us to maintain the dual process distinction, but I find it hard to believe that this is going to be anything like a truly reliable discriminator since perceivers inevitably go back and forth between the data and its conceptualization. The well-established finding that our impressions of acquaintances and fellow in-group members are more differentiated and complex than our impressions of strangers and out-group members, for example, does not require different information processing modes.

THE QUESTION OF PERCEIVER GOALS

Brewer's model attaches great importance to the purposes and goals of the perceiver. "Perceiver motives and objectives . . ." are "the primary determinant of processing mode." How do they enter the model? Well, needs affect dimensional salience and influence category selection. We are not treated to any concrete examples of perceiver motives, but there appear to be crucial occasions when our motives can be collected under a label called "self-involvement"—crucial because self-involvement leads to person-based information processing. But if motives and goals and purposes and needs are so important, they deserve more than lip service. Again, there is a long history of theorizing and experimenting about interaction goals—going back at least to my paper with Thibaut in 1958 (Jones & Thibaut, 1958), and recently reviewed by Showers and Cantor (1985)—that permits us to go beyond hand-waving. Swann's (1984) very thoughtful essay is useful in clarifying the relation between interaction goals and the actors' information requirements.

Because of the main contention that there are indeed two distinct information processing modes, and the further contention that the choice of mode is determined by the presence or absence of self-involvement, must we assume that interactions either are or are not self-involving? One suspects that not only are there many gradations of self-involvement, but there are many kinds. I may be extremely self-involved when I am negotiating with a trooper over yet another speeding ticket, but does this self-involvement induce person-based information processing? Is it the same kind of self-involvement produced by a stormy argument with my wife? By an attempt to put a troubled student at ease? By interacting with classmates at a 25th reunion? Since Brewer assigns such a terribly important role to ''self-involvement,'' it is incumbent on her eventually to tell us with as much precision as possible, just what she means by this term and why it does all the things she says it does.

HANDLING INCONSISTENT INFORMATION

Most of the interesting and important things about impression formation happen when expectancies are disconfirmed. In some objective sense they almost always are, though we know that disconfirming evidence can be, and often is, ignored. Brewer's essay is particularly stimulating when it discusses the use of social categories in the impression formation process. When information is inconsistent with the social category in which we have already classified the target person, and it is too salient or consistently present to be ignored, Brewer notes that we can preserve the general category by forming a category subtype, or by ''particularizing''—attaching distinguishing features to the individual but not the category as a whole.

There are, of course, a number of additional possibilities that do not require category change. Brewer's analysis could be enriched by starting from the realization that a given individual can be categorized in a number of ways, some of which are more informative or salient than others. One might expect that when information is inconsistent with the most salient category, other more compatible categories will become salient. Perhaps, to reflect on Brewer's example of ''the U.S. President who was an alcoholic, we might readily shift to ''hard drinking ex-General.'' Presidents aren't alcoholic, then, but in the rare instance in which they are also Generals they might drink a lot. One suspects that multiple category systems play an important role in the preservation of individual category based expectancies.

In addition, to return to a now familiar refrain, expectancies can be retained in the face of disconfirming behavioral data if the behavior can be attributed to the situation in which it was observed. Brewer does not distinguish between category-based and target-based expectancies (Jones & McGillis, 1976), though the distinction may be particularly important in describing how inconsistencies are handled. Category-based expectancies are probabilistic; they come with a built-in acknowledgment that there will be exceptions. Some women are assertive, some blacks are distinguished scientists, some white sprinters are very fast, and some Harvard graduates are not very bright. Such exceptions can be easily handled without any change in the category. Intuition suggests that we might even contrast such exceptions with the category prototype, as in ''boy, that Harvard man is *really* stupid,'' though there is little solid evidence for such effects in the experimental literature. Target-based expectancies are those that derive from prior information about the particular person being perceived. The information may be based on observed behavior (Gilbert & Jones, 1986), self-descriptive claims, or reputational gossip (Jones, Schwartz, & Gilbert, 1985). To the extent that the target-based expectancy is based on credible or authoritative information, it is less likely to be probabilistic and more likely to be anchored in an implicit personality schema (or, in Brewer's terms, a propositional network). When the person behaves in an unexpected way, a perceiver's first task is to find a reason that is compatible with the personality schema in which the expectancy is embedded. A most convenient way to accomplish this is to attribute the unexpected behavior to some feature of the situation that would have elicited much the same kind of response in almost anyone, regardless of their personality (cf. Kulik, 1983; Kulik, Sledge, & Mahler, 1986). This same kind of situational escape valve can also operate when category-based expectancies are violated, but there are many more alternative modes of resolution in the latter case.

CONCLUDING REMARKS

Much of this critique points to features of Brewer's model that need further elaboration or conceptual analysis. It objects less to what is said than to what has been omitted. Nevertheless, the omission of the vast attributional literature in a paper on impression formation does seem to reflect at least an unfortunate "sealing off" of the attributional and social cognition literatures. In addition, I have argued that the model is incomplete, and therefore retrogressive, in leaving social interaction out of social cognition. To treat the perceiver as nothing but an information processor is to ignore his role as an information producer and elicitor. I submit that we shall never really understand the relationship of person perception to interpersonal relations until we incorporate the perceiver as an information producer who may or may not be aware of his informational contributions.

REFERENCES

Gilbert, D. T., & Jones, E. E. (1986). Exemplification: The self-presentation of moral character. *Journal of Personality, 54,* 101–123.

Jones, E. E., Schwartz, J., & Gilbert, D. T. (1983–1984). Perceptions of moral expectancy violation: The role of expectancy source. *Social Cognition, 2,* 273–293.

Jones, E. E., & McGillis, D. (1976). Correspondent inferences and the attribution cube: A comparative reappraisal. In J. Harvey, W. Ickes, & R. Kidd (Eds.), *New directions in attributional research* (Vol. 1). Hillsdale, NJ: Lawrence Erlbaum Associates.

Jones, E. E., & Thibaut, J. W. (1958). Interaction goals as bases of inference in interpersonal perception. In L. Tagiuri & L. Petrullo (Eds.), *Person perception and interpersonal behavior.* Stanford: Stanford University Press.

Kulik, J. A. (1983). Confirmation attribution and the perpetuation of social beliefs. *Journal of Personality and Social Psychology, 44,* 1171–1181.

Kulik, J. A., Sledge, P., & Mahler, H. I. M. (1986). Self-confirmation, attribution, egocentrism and the perpetuation of self-beliefs. *Journal of Personality and Social Psychology, 50,* 587–594.

Showers, C., & Cantor, N. (1985). Social cognition: A look at motivated strategies. In M. R. Rosenzweig & L. W. Porter (Eds.), *Annual review of psychology* (Vol. 36). Palo Alto, CA: Annual Reviews Inc.

Swann, W. B. (1984). Quest for accuracy in person perception: A matter of pragmatics. *Psychological Review, 91,* 457–477.

Trope, Y. (1986). Identification and inference processes in dispositional attribution. *Psychological Review, 93,* 239–257.

7 Category-Specificity Effects in Social Typing and Personalization

Roberta L. Klatzky
Susan M. Andersen
University of California, Santa Barbara

Brewer's dual-process model of impression formation distinguishes between categorization, or "typing," and what she terms "personalization." The first process identifies someone as a particular "type" of person, a member of a larger group, and the second identifies the person as an individual. In our opinion, Brewer's model organizes many of the phenomena of social cognition in a provocative way. We nonetheless take issue with her particular view of social categorization.

Brewer assumes that social categories are mediated by a single type of representation, i.e., by a "pictoliteral" image (Klatzky, 1984). Such representations have certain essential characteristics: They are verbally unmediated, highly specific, and (at least weakly) analogous to physical images. Although Brewer assumes that social categories may exist at various levels of abstraction, she does not emphasize this fact, nor does she indicate that the pictoliteral assumption is violated in some cases. Thus, Brewer's pictoliteral claim carries with it the implication that all functional social representations, at any level of abstraction, directly convey *only* physical features. Even if one adds some internal, interpretive process that can extract further information (e.g., likely affective or behavioral responses), the representation is still limited to features conveyed by physical appearance.

We argue that distinct types of social categories exist. These types differ not only in their predictiveness, but in the degree to which they contain concrete and visualizable attributes. Hence, we challenge the basic assumption that all social categories with which we "type" people are "pictoliteral." We further argue that social-category structures differ in their processing efficiency and in the degree to which people apply them in various person perception tasks.

LEVELS OF CATEGORIZATION IN SOCIAL TYPING

In our work, we have found evidence that two particular types of representations function in social categorization, representations that differ profoundly in visualizability and distinctiveness. Specifically, we have examined the role of trait-based categories and social stereotypes in social categorization. In trait categorization, an individual is assigned to a category representing everyone who possesses a trait attribute, for example, "tough," "emotional," "bright," or "boring." In stereotyping, people categorize others by thinking of them as members of a larger group, with whom they share *many* features. Groups of this sort often bear a specific, socially shared label, such as "redneck" or "do-gooder."

Our view of trait-defined categories and social stereotypes can be understood within the context of "network" approaches to knowledge representation (Anderson & Bower, 1972; Collins & Quillian, 1969; Higgins, Rholes, & Jones, 1977; Srull & Wyer, 1980; Wyer & Carlston, 1979). In a network model, conceptual representations or "nodes" are connected to one another by means of associative "links," including connections between attributes and objects (e.g., soft-bed). In this terminology, we suggest that traits are linked by attribute-object links to one or more—usually more—distinct social stereotypes (and to a number of distinct individuals). By contrast, stereotypes have object-attribute links, not only to traits and not only, as Brewer argues, to physical features, but to many other types of attributes as well, such as typical overt behaviors, probable inner states, values, attitudes, and so on.

Our work has focused on the relative predictive power of traits and social stereotypes. In our model, retrieval of a stereotype should provide access to all of its features (including many trait concepts), whereas retrieval of a trait term should provide only indirect access to such attributes, through mediating links to social stereotypes. Hence, retrieving a trait should be less predictive than retrieving a stereotype, leading to far fewer associated attributes and inferences, because its connections to associated attributes are indirect.

The proposition that trait categories have low predictive power is at odds, in some respects, with the literature on "trait prototypes" (Buss & Craik, 1980; Cantor & Mischel, 1977: Ebbesen & Allen, 1980; Hampson, John, & Goldberg, 1986; Schneider & Blankmeyer, 1983; Tsujimoto, 1978). This work has indicated that trait-defined categories (such as *extravert* and *introvert*) are very predictive, in that they are associated with large numbers of prototypical attributes, that they can be effectively defined in terms of behaviors, and that they can lead to biases and overgeneralizations about individuals who are categorized in these terms. To account for this, we argue that trait terms are associated with a number of different attributes because they are linked in memory to a variety of social stereotypes.

We've conducted a number of studies to explore these assumptions. Our first set of studies has verified a number of critical predictions (Andersen & Klatzky,

1987). First, we predicted that trait-based categories would be strongly associated in memory with a set of distinct social stereotypes. Second, we predicted that these social stereotypes would be associatively "richer" and thus more predictive than the related trait-defined categories. Third, we predicted that stereotypes would be linked to more concrete, visible attributes than would the trait-defined categories. Finally, our most critical prediction was that traits would share virtually all of their "core" associates with related stereotypes, while the stereotypes would maintain unique associates. That is, although the stereotypes associated with a common trait may overlap substantially, they will also be quite distinctive, because each has unique associates as well as the common associate of the trait. By contrast, the trait categories should represent features that are common to related stereotypes, and their associates should therefore be sparse relative to those of the stereotypes themselves.

Our first study was designed to verify the existence of social stereotypes related to the trait domains of extroversion and introversion. Subjects were asked to sort, according to similarity, a set of featural adjectives, including a subset of those used by Cantor and Mischel (1977) and some related others. These adjectives consisted of the terms *extraverted* and *introverted* and five other sets of six adjectives, each of which seemed, based on face validity, to be associated with one of five social stereotypes. We constructed a measure of interitem similarity by counting the total number of times each pair of items was placed in a common stack, and submitted the resulting similarities to a complete-link cluster analysis (Hartigan, 1979).

Three different rules for determining the cluster solution all yielded the same 6-node solution, from which we identified the following clusters: the clown /comedian, the politician/diplomat, the bully/gang member, the brain/genius, the wallflower/neurotic, and the guru/wiseman. The labels that subjects provided for the type of person represented by each stack clearly verified the 6-node solution and our cluster labels. The most frequently provided labels in each category were Comedian/Clown, Politician, Bully, Depressed/Suicidal, Brain/Genius, Guru/Wiseman. Of course, numerous related labels were also given, such as "Woody Allen" for the comedian, "a senator" or "Ronald Reagan" for the politician, "a mafioso" for the bully, "a computer science major" for the brain, "an anorexic" for the neurotic, and "Ghandi" for the guru.

In sum, people can categorize trait adjectives with considerable intersubject agreement and can identify distinct social stereotypes summarizing diverse sets of attributes within each of two trait domains. These data provided an empirical basis for exploring the relative predictiveness of these traits and social stereotypes. Our next study was designed for this purpose.

In this study, we assessed the richness of traits and social stereotypes by asking subjects to list all of the attributes that a person in each category would possess. Consistent with previous work, we used the number of listed features as a measure of category predictiveness, and analyzed both the raw number of items retrieved and the number of nonredundant attributes retrieved. Controlling for redundancy is important because a conceptual feature of a social category might be expressed by several closely related terms (strong/powerful; conceited/thinks he's hot stuff), and subjects were not instructed to self-edit in any way (see also Cantor & Mischel, 1979; Rosch et al., 1976).

We hypothesized that the social stereotypes would be associated with more attributes than would the trait-defined categories, at least when redundancy among attributes is controlled (see also Cantor & Mischel, 1979), and that they would be richer in concrete, observable attributes. The results showed that subjects listed no more redundant features in response to the social stereotypes than in response to the trait-defined categories, but they did list more nonredundant attributes for the social stereotypes than for the trait-defined categories. Using this measure, all three social stereotypes in each domain were associated with more features than were the related trait-defined categories.

The specific types of features subjects listed in response to each category label were also examined so as to identify any differences in the content of traits and stereotypes. To do this, the listed features were categorized as one of 8 content types: (a) a demographic fact; (b) a physical feature; (c) an overt behavior or behavioral characteristic; (d) a relatively "invisible" trait characteristic; (e) a feeling about a behavior; (f) a general thought or feeling; (g) an evaluation by another person(s); (h) a miscellaneous description (see also Fiske & Cox, 1979; Ostrom, 1975). The results showed that the subjects generated fewer physical features, overt behaviors and behavioral characteristics, and demographic facts in response to traits than in response to stereotypes.

These findings support the suggestion that social stereotypes are *richer* than traits in terms of the number of associates they possess, and more *vivid* as well (cf. Nisbett & Ross, 1980), in terms of the number of visualizable features. The members of social-stereotype categories appear to be easier to visualize than the members of trait-defined categories. Both traits and stereotypes, in fact, are associated with nonvisible features (e.g., is cunning) as well as with visible ones (e.g., wears pin-striped suits). Hence, it is likely to be an overgeneralization to suggest that all social categorization that results in "typing" in "pictoliteral."

In our next study, the pattern of shared association between trait-defined categories and social stereotypes was assessed. Subjects were given the most commonly offered attributes generated for each category in our previous study. They were also presented with the set of trait categories and social stereotypes and were asked to assess the degree of association between each attribute and each category. We hypothesized that virtually all items highly associated with a trait-defined category would also be strong associates of related social stereotypes, but that the reverse would not hold. Stereotypes, to put it more simply, were expected to be associated with more idiosyncratic, distinctive features than were the trait-based categories. As an example, politicians may have all the

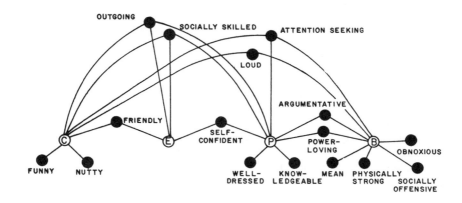

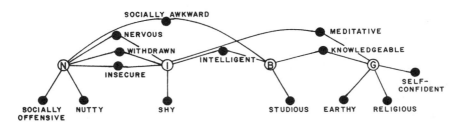

FIG. 7.1.   Hypothetical network relations connecting the trait-defined category *extravert* with related social stereotypes (top) and connecting the trait-defined category *introvert* with related social stereotypes (bottom). From Andersen and Klatzky, 1987, copyright American Psychological Association.

characteristics of extraverts but extraverts do not tend to have all the characteristics of politicians.

The data confirmed our predictions, as shown in Fig. 7.1. We used the rating data to construct a representation of the patterns of association in two hypothetical networks connecting traits and related social stereotypes. The networks, shown in the figure, link two categories if they share (i.e., are high associates of) a common attribute. Virtually all of the core attributes of traits were shared with related stereotypes, whereas far fewer of the core attributes of stereotypes were shared with related traits.

Figure 7.1 further indicates that the attributes most associated with a trait category were also highly associated with multiple related stereotypes, while the attributes most associated with stereotypes were not necessarily highly associated with the relevant trait category or with other stereotypes. These findings suggest the possibility that the reason traits are used in social description—even though they are relatively impoverished—is that their association with social stereotypes mediates social prediction. That is, social stereotypes may be activated (or partially activated) when a trait is retrieved, making available at least a subset of the rich set of associates of these stereotypes. This precise hypothesis, of course, merits further research, but it is supported by our data.

Together, these studies indicate that trait-defined person categories are highly abstract and are associated in memory with a variety of more specific social stereotypes. Our theoretical analysis suggested initially that trait-defined categories, in comparison to social stereotypes, should have two characteristics: (a) they should be only weakly associated with other properties (except for virtual synonyms); and (b) virtually all of their associates should be shared by related stereotypes, which tend to be highly visible. Our trait categories acted just this way.

The trait/stereotype distinction suggests, then, that singular trait descriptions, such as, "unsophisticated," "daring," or "sensual," are quite abstract and uninformative, whereas related social stereotypes in the same domain, like "country bumpkin," "showoff," or "gourmet," respectively, should always be more predictive and robust. As to the generality of this proposition, it should be noted the trait categories *extravert* and *introvert* actually differ from one another quite markedly and nevertheless show similar associative structures in relation to related social stereotypes.

In short, these studies confirm two major tenets that we hold in disagreement with Brewer's model. First, they show that there are qualitatively different ways of categorizing or "typing" others. In our view, the difference between trait categories and stereotypes is not simply one of level of specificity, which Brewer's model allows. Indeed, stereotypes are far more specific and robust than are traits, just as Brewer's work has suggested that social stereotypes like "the grandmotherly type" are more robust than are age-based categories such as "the elderly." But our work also indicates that traits are considerably less visualizable than are stereotypes, suggesting that social categorization is not exclusively "pictoliteral." In fact, both traits and stereotypes were found to be associated with a number of relatively "invisible" features, such as preferences, feelings, and beliefs. These features suggest that neither traits nor stereotypes are entirely analogous to visual images.

It may be, in fact, that Brewer has made an error in not distinguishing between what Smith and Medin (1981) called the "core" features of a concept and those that, by contrast, permit the "identification procedure" to take place. The core features of a category are those that truly define it; a core feature of the category "boy," for example, is "young." Such a feature, however, may not play a direct role in categorization. The features used in categorization are those that provide perceptually available cues to age, such as shape of head, elasticity of skin, stature, and so on. In the critical task Brewer employed in her own work, subjects were given pictured exemplars (photographs) and asked to sort (i.e., categorize) them. Not surprisingly, subjects sorted the photographs by perceptually available features. However, the fact that they were able to do this task does not mean that these physical and visible features are the only attributes associated with the category in question. A number of less direct, inferred features may, in fact, be at the core of the category, including, for example, inferred beliefs, feelings, relatively *invisible* traits, and behaviors. This variety of attributes—which is not directly part of a "pictoliteral" representation (Klatzky, 1984)—appears to be included among the core features of both traits and stereotypes, when the task begins with category labels (cf. pictured exemplars) and asks subjects to generate the attributes (as in our second study).

Nonetheless, in this first body of research, we examined only the mental representation of traits and stereotypes. One could argue that the structural differences between traits and stereotypes are uninteresting unless they have information-processing consequences. We would respond that the differential specificity of traits and social stereotypes should importantly influence person perception processes. That is, if social stereotypes are more specific and vivid than are trait-defined categories, they ought to operate more efficiently in social information processing (cf. Higgins & King, 1981; Nisbett & Ross, 1980; Tversky & Kahneman, 1973; see also Taylor & Fiske, 1978). Most network models assume that associative retrieval is slowed by intervening links (Anderson, 1983), and so the indirect links between trait terms and other properties should slow attribute retrieval for traits. Furthermore, lack of distinctiveness and visualizability ought to reduce both the vividness (Nisbett & Ross, 1980; although see Taylor & Thompson, 1982) and the salience (Taylor & Fiske, 1978) of traits relative to social stereotypes. In terms of a network model, these factors would be expected to affect category activation and the strength of the linkages to other concepts in memory, again to the disadvantage of the traits. All of these assumptions imply that more time should be required to comprehend sentences connecting a social category with an associate when the category is a represented as a trait than when it is represented as a social stereotype.

Together with John Murray, we have begun to assess the relative efficiency of trait categories and social stereotypes in social information processing. In these studies, subjects were exposed to a number of sentences that contained either a trait category (e.g., daring person) or stereotype (e.g., showoff or hero), paired with an act that such a person might perform. Subjects were asked to rate the sensibility of the sentence, and their reaction times were recorded.

In one study, we paired each trait or stereotype with a relevant prototypic act (e.g., for hero, "saved a damsel in distress"), and in the second study, we paired each trait or stereotype with a very general act (e.g., "sat down"). In both cases, consistent with our prediction, subjects judged the sensibility of stereotype-based sentences far more quickly than that of the trait-based sentences. Thus, social stereotypes appear to operate considerably more efficiently than do trait-defined categories in social prediction.

Assuming that comprehension requires finding associations that link a category label with an act, these data further support the argument that traits are associated with fewer features and that they provide fewer constraints on incoming information than do stereotypes. Because these studies made use of a variety of traits and stereotypes, the results generalize well beyond the domains of extraversion and introversion, used in our first body of work (Andersen & Klatzky, 1987).

To summarize, we suggest that there are at least two types of social categorization or "typing"—assignment to a trait category and assignment to a stereotype. We argue that these two types of categorization lead to different predictions about individuals, neither of which makes exclusive use of visible attributes. We also suggest, however, that differences in the visibility of the features associated with social categories may affect their structure and efficiency in social information processing.

CATEGORIZATION IN SOCIAL TYPING VS. PERSONALIZATION

On a different note, the assumption in social cognition is that people tend to use information processing strategies that require the least amount of effort, i.e., those that operate most efficiently and are thus the most cognitively economical (Fiske & Taylor, 1984; Taylor, 1981). Our earlier arguments suggest that making use of these most-efficient strategies will lead to stereotyping, not to trait-typing. This makes sense, of course, when there is little reason to exert energy in the processing of social information. Brewer argues, however, that under certain circumstances, people will exert substantial effort to "personalize" others rather than simply "typing" them. In this process, the category constructed represents a specific person rather than a stereotype, and trait associations are extensively used.

We agree with Brewer's argument that personalization is likely to be different from typing in a number of important respects, but we would argue that a form of typing is always present even in the domain of personalized categories. Even individualized person concepts have associated attributes, and in our approach (see also Smith & Medin, 1981), these attributes are themselves social categories. Hence, there is likely to be an essential similarity between social categorization in the form of typing and person-based categorization; general attribute concepts are always a part of our descriptions of specific individuals, whether typed or personalized.

On the other hand, there may be important differences between typing and personalization in the nature of the general concepts with which individuals are linked in the two cases. In another series of studies, we examined the direct application of traits and stereotypes to individuals that were likely to be typed or personalized. Consistent with points made by Brewer, the general idea behind this work was that traits and stereotypes are likely to differ in the manner in which they are applied. We predicted a specific and complex pattern of usage as follows. Traits may sometimes be useful in social categorization precisely because of their weakness as predictors. That is, they may tend to be used more readily than stereotypes to describe others about whom very little is known. Considerably more behavioral observation may be required to justify a stereotype-based categorization than to justify a trait-based categorization. Paradoxically, it is also possible that traits may tend to be used more readily than stereotypes in describing one's intimates (Hampson, 1983), because as attributes they are more amenable for use in the idiosyncratic combinations necessary to capture our most familiar and well-articulated impressions. In this case, stereotypes are too constraining to be applied directly. The implication is that social categorization by means of stereotypes should take place most readily in the middle range of familiarity, when there is enough opportunity for observation to make robust categorical judgments feasible, but not so much as to invalidate the stereotype.

Two studies were conducted in which participants assessed the similarity between a given target (e.g., self, mother, Ronald Reagan, Barbara Walters) and a series of trait and stereotype labels. In the first study, we tested the notion that traits would be used with increasing frequency, and that stereotypes would be used with decreasing frequency, as a function of intimacy. The data confirmed this prediction by showing that people directly applied social stereotypes in social perception tasks involving public figures—their favorite TV character, Ronald Reagan, Barbara Walters—but not in those involving intimates—the self, their best friend. These results were exactly reversed for the trait terms, which were applied most in cases of considerable intimacy (self, best friend; see also Hampson, 1983).

In the second study, we tested the prediction that traits might be used more frequently not only in describing intimates but also when describing individuals about whom very little is known. In the latter case, the nonconstraining nature of traits may again be an advantage. Hence, we expected to observe a curvilinear relationship between intimacy and the use of traits, such that they would be used more heavily in cases of high and low intimacy than in cases of moderate intimacy. A complementary curvilinear pattern was expected for stereotypes, such that they would be used most to describe moderately known, highly visible others. The data clearly supported this prediction: People used traits more than stereotypes to describe themselves and their intimates, and they also used traits more for total strangers, whereas stereotypes were used most to describe public figures who are readily observed but not intimate.

In our view, traits are essentially attributes—of various persons and of various other social categories, such as stereotypes. They may serve alone, in which case they designate weakly predictive categories, or collectively with other attributes. Using Brewer's terms, trait categories are likely to play a role both in "typing" and "personalization." Similarly, stereotype concepts might sometimes be used in personalization, if the person in question appears to fit most of the stereotype's associated attributes. This means that the separation between social categorization and specific person categorization may be a rather fuzzy one.

In general, our work is consistent with the dual-process model of social categorization proposed by Brewer. However, it challenges Brewer's assumption that social categorization is "pictoliteral," by emphasizing differences in the nature and function of the social categories used in "typing" others. It also suggests possible differences between efficiency and diagnosticity in social categorization, and in doing so suggests that research on the interrelation between typing and personalization in impression formation is a fruitful direction for future inquiry.

REFERENCES

Andersen, S. M., & Klatzky, R. L. (1987). Traits and social stereotypes: Levels of categorization in person perception. *Journal of Personality and Social Psychology, 53,* 235–246.

Anderson, J. R. (1983). *The architecture of cognition.* Cambridge, MA: Harvard University Press.

Anderson, J. R., & Bower, G. H. (1972). *Human associative memory.* Washington, D.C.: V. H. Winston & Sons.

Buss, D. M., & Craik, K. H. (1980). The frequency concept of disposition: Dominance and prototypically dominant acts. *Journal of Personality, 48,* 379–392.

Cantor, N., & Mischel, W. (1977). Traits and prototypes: Effects on recognition memory. *Journal of Personality and Social Psychology, 35,* 38–48.

Cantor, N., & Mischel, W. (1979). Prototypes in person perception. In L. Berkowitz (Ed.), *Advances in experimental social psychology* (Vol. 12, pp. 3–52). New York: Academic Press.

Collins, A. M., & Quillian, M. R. (1969). Retrieval time from semantic memory. *Journal of Verbal Learning and Verbal Behavior, 8,* 240–247.

Ebbesen, E., & Allen, R. B. (1979). Cognitive processes in implicit personality trait inferences. *Journal of Personality and Social Psychology, 37,* 471–488.

Fiske, S. T., & Cox, M. G. (1970). Person concepts: The effect of target familiarity and descriptive purpose on the process of describing others. *Journal of Personality, 47,* 136–161.

Fiske, S. T., & Taylor, S. E. (1984). *Social cognition.* New York: Random House.

Hampson, S. E. (1983). Trait ascription and depth of acquaintance: The preference for traits in personality descriptions and its relation to target familiarity. *Journal of Research in Personality, 17,* 398–411.

Hampson, S. E., John, O. P., & Goldberg, L. R. (1986). Category breadth and hierarchical structure in personality: Studies of asymmetries in judgments of trait implications. *Journal of Personality and Social Psychology, 51,* 37–54.

Hartigan, J. (1979). Cluster analysis of variables. In W. J. Dixon & M. B. Brown (Eds.), *Biomedical computer programs: P Series* (pp. 623–632). Berkeley: University of California Press.

Higgins, E. T., & King, G. (1981). Accessibility of social constructs: Information processing consequences of individual and contextual variability. In N. Cantor & J. F. Kihlstrom (eds.), *Personality, cognition, and social interaction* (pp. 69–121). Hillsdale, NJ: Lawrence Erlbaum Associates.

Higgins, E. T., Rholes, C. R., & Jones, C. R. (1977). Category accessibility and impression formation. *Journal of experimental social psychology, 13,* 141–154.

Klatzky, R. L. (1984). Visual memory: Definitions and functions. In R. Wyer & T. Srull (Eds.), *Handbook of social cognition* (Vol. 2). Hillsdale, NJ: Lawrence Erlbaum Associates.

Nisbett, R. E., & Ross, L. (1980). *Human inference: Strategies and shortcomings of social judgment.* Englewood Cliffs, NJ: Prentice-Hall.

Ostrom, T. M. (1975, August). *Cognitive representation of impressions.* Paper presented at the American Psychological Association convention, Chicago.

Rosch, E., Mervis, C. B., Gray, W. D., Johnson, D. M., & Boyes-Braem, P. (1976). Basic objects in natural categorization. *Cognitive Psychology, 8,* 382–439.

Schneider, D. J., & Blankmeyer, B. L. (1983). Prototype salience and implicit personality theories. *Journal of Personality and Social Psychology, 44,* 712–722.

Smith, E. E., & Medin, D. L. (1981). *Categories and concepts.* Cambridge, MA: Harvard University Press.

Srull, T. K., & Wyer, R. S., Jr. (1980). Category accessibility and social perception: Some implications for the study of person memory and interpersonal judgments. *Journal of Personality and Social Psychology, 38,* 841–856.

Taylor, S. E. (1981). Categorization approach to stereotyping. In D. L. Hamilton (Ed.), *Cognitive processes in stereotyping and intergroup behavior* (pp. 83–114). Hillsdale, NJ: Lawrence Erlbaum Associates.

Taylor, S. E., & Fiske, S. T. (1978). Salience, attention, and attribution: Top of the head phenomena. In L. Berkowitz (Ed.), *Advances in experimental social psychology* (Vol. 11, pp. 249–288). New York: Academic Press.

Taylor, S. E., & Thompson, S. C. (1982). Stalking the elusive "vividness" effect. *Psychological Review, 89,* 155–181.

Tsujimoto, R. N. (1978). Memory bias toward normative and novel trait prototypes. *Journal of Personality and Social Psychology, 36,* 1391–1401.

Tversky, A., & Kahneman, D. (1973). Availability: A heuristic for judging frequency and probability. *Cognitive Psychology, 5,* 207–232.

Wyer, R. S., Jr., & Carlston, D. E. (1979). *Social cognition, inference, and attribution.* Hillsdale, NJ: Lawrence Erlbaum Associates.

8 Where is the Stimulus Person in Impression Formation?

Leslie Zebrowitz-McArthur
Brandeis University

Despite considerable evidence indicating that our perceptions of people's psychological attributes are strongly tied to their facial appearance (See McArthur, 1982, and Berry & McArthur, 1986, for reviews of this research), there has been almost no systematic and theoretically guided research on this topic. Brewer's model, with its emphasis on pictoliteral representations of people is a refreshing exception. However, it does not quench my thirst for a clear elucidation of this issue. The reason is that Brewer's model, like its predecessors, is concerned primarily with the *processes* of impression formation, and little attention is paid to the *contents* of these impressions, to their *origins,* or to the *stimulus information* on which they are based. The purpose of the present commentary is to pose some questions which are raised by a concern with these latter three issues.

INITIAL CLASSIFICATION DIMENSIONS

Brewer's model holds that people are initially and automatically identified "on a limited number of stimulus dimensions that are processed simultaneously" (p. 8). The proposed contents of these initial classification dimensions include a stimulus person's gender, age, skin color, degree of relevance to the perceiver's immediate goals, hostility, and strength. While some data are offered to support the first of these classification dimensions, none are offered regarding the automaticity of the others. In addition, it is not clear why the model assumes that people are automatically identified along *dimensions*, while in the more controlled processing which follows, people are evaluated in terms of *categories*. Why isn't the automatic identification also in terms of categories?

103

In addition to desiring more elaboration of the contents of the initial classifications, I am interested in the origins of the tendency to automatically identify
people along the dimensions that Brewer specifies—why these dimensions?
Brewer suggests that the dimensions of gender, age, and skin color ''are used so
frequently and consistently as to be become automatic, processed unconsciously,
and without intention'' (p. 6). But this begs the question. Why are they used so
frequently and consistently? Do perceivers learn to identify people along these
dimensions? If so, what controls this learning process?

Not only does the model leave unanswered the question of what determines
what the initial classification dimensions are, but also it does not address the
question of what stimulus information elicits classification along these dimensions. What aspects of stimulus persons determine where they will be classified
along dimensions such as age, hostility, strength? The answer to this question is
not self-evident even for a dimension like age, where one may ask what factors
contribute to variations in the perceived age of a stimulus person. And, the
answer to this question is crucial in any effort to predict what impressions will be
formed of a given stimulus person.

CATEGORIZATION

According to Brewer's model, after a person has been classified along some
basic stimulus dimension, the perceiver may engage in further information processing about the individual. This processing may be person-based or category-
based. Brewer devotes most of her attention to category-based processing, which
involves determining the social category to which the stimulus person belongs,
after which impressions and evaluations of the person are transferred from that
category. She argues that the requisites for category-based processing—high
information load and input from multiple stimulus persons—are characteristic of
many real life social settings, and she consequently assumes that category-based
processing is a common basis for impression formation in everyday life. I do not
find this assumption very compelling.

First, the experimental evidence for category-based processing has been provided in measures of *recall* for social information, which may not yield the same
effects as *impression* measures would. Second, the memory overload which has
been shown to yield category-based processing in experimental settings may be
rare in real life encounters, where information about various stimulus persons is
revealed in behaviors that are dynamic, multimodal, and extended in time.
Finally, those situations which are most conducive to category-based processing
may often result in a termination of processing immediately after the initial
classification, with the result that, according to the model, no impression is even
formed. To the extent that category-based processing is in fact less frequent than
Brewer assumes, it is unfortunate that her model devotes so little attention to

questions concerning person-based processing. There are also some important questions regarding category-based processing that the model does not thoroughly address. In particular, what is the content of the person categories that perceivers employ? What is the origin of these categories? And, what is the stimulus information on which categorization is based?

Person Category Contents

Brewer gives us a taste of the contents of person categories, but her model does not fully specify them. For example, she reports that subjects' verbal descriptions of "person types" incorporate roles, traits, and behaviors, but she does not articulate what contents distinguish one person type from another. Our understanding of person categories would be greatly enhanced if the specific roles, traits, and behaviors associated with various person types could be described in a conceptually integrated fashion.

Brewer also tells us that person types are nested within superordinate sets defined by partitionings along the dimensions used in the initial identification of persons. Thus, person categories are not expected to cross-cut the initial classification boundaries. In support of this proposal, Brewer cites the results of a cluster analysis to determine what photos subjects associated in a sorting task. Although she claims that relatively few of the clusters cross age-sex boundaries, her Fig. 1.3 reveals that 5 clusters do cross these boundaries, while 7 do not. It thus appears that person categories are not necessarily nested within partitions defined by the initial identification of the person. The implication is that, contrary to Brewer's suggestion, different representations of the same social role will not necessarily be developed when the role occupant is male vs. female, old vs. young.

Finally, Brewer describes person categories as pictoliteral representations, which are (1) more specific and configural than nonvisual concepts; (2) unmediated by verbal descriptions; and (3) point-by-point mappings of the stimulus that can be operated on in a manner analogous to the processing of external stimuli. Although it may be difficult to provide specific verbal descriptions of such nonverbal pictoliteral contents, I believe that this will be necessary if the construct of person types is to be maximally useful in predicting and understanding impressions.

Stimulus Determinants of Categorization

Although some stimulus determinants of categorization are suggested by Brewer, these are not fully developed. More specifically, she reports that subjects show high agreement on which facial photographs go together as a category, which suggests that there are systematic facial determinants of categorization. However, she does not specify what is the effective facial information for a person's categorization nor does she speculate as to what other stimulus information may affect categorization. I am very curious to know more about the 12 subclusters of photos that her research has identified. What is needed is a systematic analysis of subjects' category descriptions as well as a systematic analysis of the physical characteristics of the faces so that the defining characteristics of the various person types can be determined.

One stumbling block to such an analysis is the lack of any guidance from Brewer's model as to what facial characteristics will be associated with what impressions. Recent work by McArthur and her colleagues illustrates the value of the ecological theory of social perception (McArthur & Baron, 1983) in addressing this question.

The ecological theory holds that social perceptions will be influenced by facial characteristics that typically reveal attributes whose detection is adaptive either for the survival of the species or for the goal attainment of individuals. Among these characteristics are those that distinguish infants from more mature organisms, and considerable research has established that the facial characteristics that identify infants do in fact reveal their dependency and approachability. (See Berry & McArthur, 1986, for a review of pertinent research.) The ecological theory further predicts that a strong attunement to adaptively significant facial characteristics may be overgeneralized. In particular, it has been hypothesized that adults with immature facial qualities are perceived to have childlike psychological attributes.

Considerable research has provided strong support for the overgeneralization hypothesis. More specifically, adults with the infantile features of large, round eyes, a short nose, a small and rounded chin, or low vertical placement of features—which yields a large forehead and a small chin—are perceived as physically weaker, more submissive, more naive, warmer, and more honest than those with more mature versions of these facial characteristics (Berry & McArthur, 1986). Although babyfacedness may not be a factor that distinguishes the person types in Brewer's cluster analyses, the ecological theory may nevertheless prove fruitful in generating predictions regarding the facial and psychological characteristics that do distinguish the person categories that her work has identified.

It must be noted that an analysis of the facial characteristics of the various person types is not really encouraged by Brewer's emphasis on knowledge structures. Indeed, Brewer rejects the possibility that subjects' sorted the photographs on the basis of specific physical features and then inferred personality traits from those features. She claims, rather, that sorting was guided by preexisting mental images. In support of this position, Brewer notes that when subjects were explicitly instructed to sort according to shared physical features they produced a set of subclusters somewhat different from that which emerged when they sorted according to character.

These divergent results need not imply that subjects do not use physical features when they sort according to character. Indeed, how can existing mental images possibly serve as a basis for consensual sorting? There has to be something in the physical appearance of the faces that leads subjects to agree as to which ones go together. Perhaps when subjects sort according to character they rely on facial *gestalts* (e.g., babyfacedness, attractiveness, healthiness, friendliness), whereas they rely on individual feature comparisons when asked to sort according to shared physical features. This would account for the different clusters that emerge under different instructions.

The impact of facial characteristics on impressions is underscored by Brewer's observation that "visual information generates trait inferences" even when categories for those images cannot be articulated with a verbal label (p. 15). However, this direct link between visual information and trait perceptions seems to contradict the assumption that "impressions are based on an active categorization process in which available 'person types' are matched to the information given about the new person" (p. 17). Why is it necessary to posit the mediating construct of person types in the perceiver's head to account for impressions? An unmediated link between visual information and impressions would be more parsimonious.

Another significant problem with the proposed pattern-matching process is that the model does not specify what is being matched or how it is determined when an adequate fit has been achieved. Although Brewer allows that the categorization of a particular stimulus person depends upon the initial classification along primary dimensions (e.g., gender, age), the other determinants of categorization that are considered (category accessibility, contextual cues, and processing goals of the perceiver) have little to do with the stimulus person per se. Are we to assume that a perceiver will form identical impressions of two 25-year-old women who are encountered at the same time in the same situation? Brewer's cluster analysis suggests that this would not occur, and the question remains as to what person categories perceivers will employ and what is the informational basis for categorization.

Social Category Origins

The origin of the person categories that people employ is an issue that information processing theories, like Brewer's, rarely address. Indeed, I have dubbed person schemas "immaculate conceptions," because they are discovered, full grown, in the head of the perceiver, and no one ever asks how they got there. Brewer is to be commended for broaching this question. Unfortunately, however, I do not find the answer very satisfactory. She argues that "from personal and shared social experience, the individual perceiver derives a set of person 'types' that are represented in the form of abstract images or interrelated features" (p. 12). But, what is the nature of this experience? Should we expect a great deal of commonality across perceivers in the categories of person perception or do person types vary from perceiver to perceiver?

As noted above, person types are defined as *pictoliteral* representations, which depict the stimulus with a point-by-point mapping of the stimulus. This suggests that there are person types out in the world that people learn to detect. If so, then to answer my question about the origins of person categories, one must specify the nature of these external stimulus persons. However, Brewer suggests (pp. 29-30) that the sensitivity to natural combinations of features which characterizes category prototypes in the world of objects does not characterize category formation in the social domain. The question thus remains as to where various social categories come from.

CONCLUSIONS

Brewer argues that classical theories of impression formation are bottom up, focusing on stimulus determinants. My own view is that classical theories have *not* focused sufficiently on stimulus determinants. Asch's Gestalt model, Anderson's weighted averaging model, as well as more recent schema theories have all been concerned with the cognitive processes through which perceivers infer psychological characteristics from behavioral or other information. While attending to the question of *how* impressions are formed, these theories are not particularly concerned with *what* specific physical, psychological, or behavioral characteristics give rise to the impressions or with what the impressions are. As a result, existing research on person perception is marked by an inadequate taxonomy for representing the content of our impressions of other people; an inadequate specification of the stimulus information that gives rise to these impressions; and an apparent disinterest in developing general theories which can explain the origins of these impressions. It is against this background that I respond to Brewer's model. She describes it as incorporating top-down processing as well as data-driven constructions, which is true. Nevertheless, I would place Brewer's model in the same category as the classical theories in its emphasis on the *processes* of impression formation. To be sure, it is necessary to elucidate the pertinent cognitive processes if we are to achieve an adequate understanding of impression formation, and Brewer's model makes some significant contributions to this endeavor. But, it is equally important to elucidate the contents of impressions, their origins, and the stimulus information on which they are based. Here there remains much work to be done.

REFERENCES

Berry, D. S., & McArthur, L. Z. (1986). Perceiving character in faces: The impact of age-related craniofacial changes on social perception. *Psychological Bulletin, 100,* 3–18.

McArthur, L. Z. (1982). Judging a book by its cover: A cognitive analysis of the relationship between physical appearance and stereotyping. In A. Hastorf & A. Isen (Eds.), *Cognitive Social Psychology* (pp. 149–211). New York: Elsevier North Holland.

McArthur, L. Z., & Baron, R. M. (1983). Toward an ecological theory of social perception. *Psychological Review, 90,* 215–238.

9 The Content of Awareness and Top-Down versus Bottom-Up Processing

Clark McCauley
Bryn Mawr College

The dual process model presented in this volume is important as a serious attempt to advance our understanding of how social cognition fits into the larger business of human cognition. Certainly many of those studying social cognition lean to the view that social cognition, especially perceptions of other persons, is more than simply the application of the research of those calling themselves cognitive psychologists. Brewer's model is thus likely to be of considerable interest to both cognitive and social-cognitive psychologists, and the broad-ranging scholarship evident in the order she brings to a diverse literature will likewise recommend her presentation of the model even to those who might disagree with her direction.

AWARENESS AS MODEL

In trying to grasp and evaluate the dual process model, I found it useful to begin from a view of cognition recently offered by Yates (1985) in his paper "The content of awareness is a model of the world." Although this view is not new, it has recently been receiving more explicit attention (see also Murphy & Medin, 1985, concerning the importance of theories about the world in determining the categories with which we perceive that world). The major assertion of this view is that perceptions are constructs mistaken for the stimuli that they exist to account for. Additional assertions include the following: These constructs are categories of experience, they are created to account for patterns of the environment relevant to action in the environment, they are created so as to maximize the stimulus information accounted for or predicted and to minimize the number of categories required, they must be internally consistent although they may be inconsistent with stimulus information, and they are amodal insofar as a given construct can account for correlated stimulus information from multiple sensory modalities. With the additional assumption that a category is represented by its most typical member or prototype (Rosch, 1977), this view leads Yates to the conclusion that objects and events can only enter awareness in terms of one or more prototypes instantiated with whatever important details or unique characteristics are not accounted for by the prototypes. Although no claims are made about the nature of mechanisms that mediate between stimulus information and awareness, this view does deny that such mechanisms are accessible to awareness.

This awareness model (short for "awareness as model") should be congenial to many cognitively oriented psychologists, as it makes explicit ideas that can be traced to Wundt, Berkeley, and Mill and that appear in more recent work by Piaget, Neisser, and Rock (see Yates, 1985, for more about the origins of the model). The model is interesting in the present context because it compares closely with the dual process model in some respects and contrasts sharply in others. The awareness model is largely congruent with the description of top-down processing in the dual process model (see below), though it goes beyond that description in claiming that stimulus information is only accounted for rather than incorporated in categorical perception. But the awareness model is most useful in concentrating our attention on bottom-up processing, since this kind of processing should not be possible if only instantiated prototypes are admitted to awareness.

IS BOTTOM-UP PROCESSING ALWAYS PERSON-BASED?

From the perspective of the awareness model, consider now what the dual process model says about the nature of and evidence for a phenomenon of bottom-up processing. The first reference in this regard is to Asch (1946), who noted our capacity to understand another person in terms of a distinct and unique individuality. Brewer suggests that Asch assumes thereby that a perceiver opens a kind of "mental slot" to receive and process data toward formation of an integrated impression of an unfamiliar person. But does Asch assume anything inconsistent with perception of an instantiated prototype, that is, anything inconsistent with top-down processing? It does not seem so, especially given Asch's insistence on the integrated and gestalt quality of the impression that results from even the first few tidbits of information about the stimulus person. As Yates (1985) notes, "Defining objects as instantiated prototypes also naturally makes objects (but not stimuli) gestalts . . . ." (p. 251). The gestalt is understandable as the prototype or prototypes that can best account for the whole pattern of stimulus information. In other words, the metaphor of a "mental slot" is too unstructured and undynamic to represent Asch's view of impression formation. Information may indeed be integrated on-line to form or modify a unified impression, but there is nothing in Asch to suggest that the unity depends on seeing the unfamiliar person *sui generis* or disconnected from familiar types and categories of persons. It is just this disconnection that I take to be the meaning of bottom-up or "piecemeal" processing.

Moving from Asch to more recent research on social cognition, Brewer notes evidence that information about persons observed in a group context is often organized in terms of the group rather than in terms of individual members of the group. Individual organization is more likely to the extent that characteristics such as race and sex make an individual stand out as different. These are not controversial contentions, but the derivation from them is, namely, the distinction between category-based top-down cognition and bottom-up person-based cognition. The problematic aspect of this distinction is the joining of a division based on the numerosity of the object of person perception—one person or a group—with a division based on the nature of the cognitive activity. Both individuals and groups can be perceived either categorically—prototypically—or "piecemeal," as Brewer recognizes in proposing that it is the perceiver's goals and not the target characteristics that determine whether perception is top-down or bottom-up. Similarly there is no obvious impediment to replacing "Individual #1" and "Individual #2" in Brewer's Fig. 1.4 schematic of top-down versus bottom-up processing with, respectively, "Group #1" and "Group #2." Thus top-down processing may usefully mean categorical processing and bottom-up processing may usefully mean piecemeal processing, but there is no real opposition between category-based processing and person-based processing. In what follows I will examine top-down versus bottom-up processing with the understanding that bottom-up or piecemeal processing can be applied to either individual or group targets of perception.

HOW "PRIMITIVE" ARE CATEGORIZATIONS OF AGE, SEX, AND RACE?

In the description of the dual process model, the first step is said to be a "primitive categorization" in terms of such categories as age, sex, and skin color. The awareness model, as noted earlier, denies that perceivers have access to processing short of the instantiated prototype, and denies that perceivers can choose to stop processing at some level of abstraction short of the categorical. The models agree to the extent of asserting that the units of person perception are categorical rather than scalar and in asserting a Roschian view of categories represented by prototypes. It is true that the dual process treatment of prototypes as visual images seems to conflict with the assertion of the awareness model that prototypes are amodal, but this difference may be more apparent than real (see for instance Brewer's linking of pictoliteral representations with schemas) and will not be pursued here. A more important conflict concerns the status of categorizations of race, sex, and age as "primitive." The awareness model leads us to expect economy of prototypes so as to maximize the information accounted for while minimizing the prototypes in awareness. Thus we are led to suspect that age, race, and skin-color, though susceptible to awareness as independent but relatively vague prototypes, are likely to be available in awareness as instantiation of some more specified prototype. Here the awareness model anticipates Brewer's suggestion that a woman doctor is more than simply the intersection of woman and doctor. But is the "woman" perceived as a primitive or subordinate to "woman doctor"? The awareness model raises doubt about whether age, sex, and race are primitive categorizations; indeed the awareness model suggests that these are derived from top-down processing.

With this doubt as instigation, let us examine the evidence offered in support of the contention that processing of gender is automatic. Faces judged for honesty and likeableness are later recognized more accurately than faces judged for gender (Bower & Karlin, 1974). Though consistent with automatic processing as asserted by the dual process model, this result is equally consistent with the awareness model. "Because sensations are assimilated to prototypes in order to be perceived, the information that people become aware of when confronted with stimuli is predicted to depend on the vagueness of a prototype (the degree to which information in sensations is deemed irrelevant) . . . information deemed irrelevant in constructing the prototype may not be automatically perceived or remembered at all" (Yates, 1985, p. 261). According to the awareness model, then, facial features are relevant and recalled only in relation to prototypes, but fewer features are relevant to judging gender than to judging honesty or likeableness. Thus the recognition results may be obtained because the gender prototype is less specified or more vague than the prototype of honesty or likeableness, rather than because gender is automatically and independently perceived while honesty and likeableness require more top-down processing.

Similarly the "Stroop effect" with social judgments, if replicated beyond the preliminary research reported by Brewer in this volume, can be attributed to the greater vagueness of sex prototypes than occupational prototypes. That is, sex may be specified by an occupational prototype and so interfere with judgments of occupation whereas occupation is not specified by sex prototypes and so does not interfere with judgments of sex. In general, the awareness model suggests that perceptual experiments will reflect the nature of the objects in awareness rather than the processes by which these objects come to awareness (Yates, 1985).

Brewer suggests that the empirical clusterings derived from free sortings of photographs are further evidence of primitive categorization by age and sex. This evidence again needs examination. At a purely descriptive level, subjects' verbal descriptions of their categories (e.g., "white collar workers who are uptight about their jobs'') seldom mention age or sex. However, Brewer emphasizes the fact that relatively few of the clusters cross age-sex boundaries as an indication of the fundamental or primitive nature of these categories. Recourse to her Fig. 1.3 indicates that six of thirteen clusters do cross age or sex boundaries, so it is not clear how strong this indication is. What is clear is that the verbal descriptions sound like prototype descriptions, suggesting support for the awareness model in its assertion that the content of awareness will tend to be a relatively small number of well-specified prototypes rather than more and vaguer prototypes such as age and sex.

TOP-DOWN PROCESSING

After the first step of primitive categorization, the dual process model asserts a choice between top-down and bottom-up processing. The needs and objectives of the perceiver are said to determine the mode of processing, much as these are said to determine the creation of prototypes in the awareness model. Indeed, as already noted, top-down processing in the dual process model is largely congruent with the assertions of the awareness model. Both understand perception as categorical, both understand categories as represented by prototypes, both understand these prototypes in analog terms, and, more particularly, both understand impression formation as category matching. Both can comprehend the literature Brewer ably reviews to indicate the consequences of category activation for attention to, memory for, and organization of information about persons.

Before moving on to bottom-up processing, there is a question to be raised about the study by Darley and Gross (1983) that Brewer cites as indicating the effects of categorization on information processing. The study showed that judgments of a child's academic level were unaffected by information about her social class unless the class information was joined with ambiguous performance data. Another way of putting this result is that judges ignored social-class stereotypes (McCauley, Stitt, & Segal, 1980) except when ambiguous individuating information was available. As Brown (1985) points out about studies by Locksley (Locksley, Borgida, Brekke, & Hepburn, 1980; Locksley, Hepburn, & Ortiz, 1981) that seemed to show no stereotype effects when diagnostic individuating information was available, this is too good to be true. Instead, as Brown suggests, there is probably some sensitivity among college students to avoid displaying the ''prejudice'' of category based judgments and to depend rather on individuating behavior. In the study by Darley and Gross such sensitivity might permit the stereotype linking academic ability with social class to be expressed under cover of the ambiguous individuating behavior but not without this cover. This would be a case of rationalizing a category-based judgment with pseudo-individuating information, rather than a case of judgment based on category-biased interpretation of individuating information.

BOTTOM-UP PROCESSING

The dual-process model makes bottom-up processing the converse of top-down processing in that all information is directly associated with the individual (or group, as argued above), and any organized structure of perception is arrived at only second and subordinate to the elements of information. The awareness model denies the possibility of awareness of elements except in subordination to and instantiation of one or more prototypes. But there may be less to this difference than at first appears. What stands in the way of understanding bottom-up processing as the creation of a new category of experience for which the perceived group or individual is the prototype? Certainly the subordination of features to the individual or group would be thus maintained, as for instance when ''Janet is a nurse'' is understood in terms of ''only those aspects of nursing that are characteristic of Janet in that role'' (Brewer, this volume). If this subordination is the essence of bottom-up processing, then the essence is preserved. Let us examine instance and evidence for bottom-up processing with this possibility in mind.

Bottom-up processing is said to differ from top-down in that information inconsistent with a category will be ignored or differentiated from the prototype in top-down processing, whereas behavior contrary to expectation will be processed extensively and incorporated into the representation of the individual in bottom-up processing. If we take the results of Asch's studies of impression formation as examples of bottom-up processing, this contention will not stand. Asch (1952, p. 220) clearly reports his subjects using denial to cope with contradictory information. For instance a *worker* described as *intelligent* created problems of impression formation that Asch's subjects often solved by denying either that the stimulus person was *really* intelligent or that he was a worker (some made him a foreman). More abstractly, the whole idea of bottom-up processing of information inconsistent with expectations leads to a question about the source of those expectations. Unless the inconsistent information is directly contradictory of previous information, the experience of inconsistency suggests that the ''representation'' that is the outcome of bottom-up processing has some quality of going beyond the given. Once this much is admitted, it is difficult to see how the representation is to be distinguished from a prototype, that is, how bottom-up processing is to be distinguished from top-down.

Bottom-up processing is also said to be distinguishable from top-down in free recall. Recall from top-down processing is predicted to begin with individuating features and progress to categorical identification, whereas recall from bottom-up processing should progress in the reverse order. Wyer and Srull (1986) are cited for the assumption of a recency effect in recall that provides the rationale for this prediction, but it is not clear that individuating features and category identifications would show up in the same "bin" for Wyer & Srull, so the recency prediction is not certain. With or without a recency effect, it is not at all obvious why top-down processing, with its emphasis on the prototype, should be credited with the prediction of recall for features first, while bottom-up processing, with its subordination of the built representation to the building features, should be credited with prediction of recall for features last. Evidence consistent with the recall predictions is cited from Hampson (1983), who found that frequency of trait terms in free description increased with familiarity with the person described. This evidence is equally consistent with the view that more familiarity leads to more information and more specified prototypes to account for this information, that is, with a top-down or awareness model of impression formation.

Another prediction about bottom-up processing is that it permits recall of both person category and the behavior from which the category was inferred (the former presumably subordinate to and less easily recalled than the latter), whereas top-down processing permits recall of the category but not behavior that was consistent with it. The first part of this assertion receives only squinting support from the research cited. Lingle (1983) did indeed find that subjects could remember both traits and behaviors about stimulus persons (though it is not clear why bottom-up processing should be expected in his study), but he found a dependency such that behaviors were better remembered that were consistent with the trait category recalled. This kind of dependency is consistent with top-down rather than bottom-up processing.

The last prediction about bottom-up processing to be dealt with here is that this mode of processing is more likely for impressions of persons or groups who are more similar to the perceiver. The evidence cited is that more complex and differentiated impressions are formed for members of the ingroup than for members of the outgroup. The difficulty here is that more complex and more differentiated impressions are not necessarily associated with bottom-up processing. Indeed Brewer's Fig. 1.4, a schematic of the difference between bottom-up and top-down processing, does not convey any obvious difference in complexity of structure. There are not, for instance, more levels in the schematic of bottom-up processing. Indeed the essence of the processing difference, as noted above, appears to be what is subordinate to what, not the degree or levels of subordination. From the perspective of the awareness model, the greater complexity of ingroup impressions in comparison with outgroup impressions can be understood in terms of having or attending to more information about members of the ingroup. More specified prototypes are created to account for the greater information, as was suggested in understanding the relation of familiarity to trait attribution (Hampson, 1983).

CONCLUSION

In these comments, I have attempted to accomplish two related purposes. One is to advance a view of perception as model of the world that I believe should be congenial to many cognitively oriented psychologists. Application of this awareness model to examples and issues of research in social cognition has some heuristic value in its own right. In addition, I have tried to use the awareness model as a perspective for understanding and evaluating the dual process model. The upshot of that application is that I believe the strongest part of the dual process model is an account of top-down processing that is largely congruent with the awareness model. I am not persuaded that there is a phenomenon of bottom-up processing to be opposed to top-down processing, though some of what is offered in the dual process model in relation to bottom-up processing might usefully be considered in terms of our tendency to create new categories or prototypes for persons or groups close to us.

REFERENCES

Asch, S. E. (1946). Forming impressions of personality. *Journal of Abnormal and Social Psychology, 41,* 258–290.

Asch, S. E. (1952). *Social psychology.* Englewood Cliffs, NJ: Prentice-Hall.

Bower, G. H., & Karlin, M. B. (1974). Depth of processing pictures of faces and recognition memory. *Journal of Experimental Psychology, 103,* 751–757.

Brown, R. (1985). *Social psychology, the second edition.* New York: Free Press.

Darley, J. M., & Gross, P. H. (1983). A hypothesis-confirming bias in labeling effects. *Journal of Personality and Social Psychology, 44,* 20–33.

Hampson, S. E. (1983). Trait ascription and depth of acquaintance: the preference for traits in personality descriptions and its relation to targert familiarity. *Journal of Research in Personality, 17,* 398–411,

Lingle, J. H. (1983). Tracing memory-structure activation during person judgments. *Journal of Experimental Social Psychology, 19,* 480–496.

Locksley, A., Borgida, E., Brekke, N., & Hepburn, C. (1980). Sex stereotypes and social judgment. *Journal of Personality and Social Psychology, 39,* 821–831.

Locksley, A., Hepburn, C., & Ortiz, V. (1982). Social stereotypes and judgments of individuals: an instance of the base-rate fallacy. *Journal of Experimental Social Psychology, 18,* 23–42.

McCauley, C., Stitt, C. L., & Segal, M. (1980). Stereotyping: from prejudice to prediction. *Psychological Bulletin, 87,* 195–208.

Murphy, G. L., & Medin, D. L. (1985). The role of theories in conceptual coherence. *Psychological Review, 92,* 289–316.

Rosch, E. (1977). Human categorization. In N. Warren (Ed.), *Studies in cross-cultural psychology* (Vol. 1, pp. 3–50). New York: Academic Press.

Wyer, R. S., & Srull, T. K. (1986). Human cognition in its social context. *Psychological Review, 93,* 322–359.

Yates, J. (1985). The content of awareness is a model of the world. *Psychological Review, 92,* 249–284.

10 Social Categorization: Structures, Processes, and Purposes

Douglas L. Medin
University of Illinois

INTRODUCTION

Being more of a consumer than a contributor to research on social cognition, I assume my comments on Brewer's paper can be simply a listing of likes and dislikes. And, indeed, there is a great deal to like about Dr. Brewer's contribution. Because preferences are often idiosyncratic and since readers of *Advances in Social Cognition* include contributors and not just consumers, I will say why I like what I like. My comments are organized as follows. The first section briefly reviews a few facets of the dual process model that are particularly useful and attractive. Because I do not have a corresponding set of dislikes or criticisms, the main section of this comment discusses some general issues in social categorization. The final section summarizes recommendations for future social cognition research in light of the preceding sections.

STRONG POINTS

One favorite question I often pose to researchers in social cognition is as follows: Suppose that my best friend whom I see almost every day is Chinese. I may have some impression of what Chinese people in general are like. The question is how much will my impression of Chinese people be influenced by my relationship with my Chinese friend. One answer is: quite a bit. Based on the Kahneman and Tversky work on cognitive heuristics (e.g., Kahneman & Tversky, 1973; Tversky & Kahneman, 1973, 1974, 1980), one might expect that experiences with my friend would be highly available and would receive a great deal of weight in my overall judgment. The alternative possibility is that I am barely cognizant of the fact that my best friend is Chinese and that consequently my overall impression of Chinese people is scarcely affected at all by my friendship.

A second question I have often wondered about concerns *when* category level information becomes available. Consider the situation of knowing a man for a number of years before finding out that he is gay versus knowing from the onset that he is gay. Will the former situation have more impact on your impression of gay people (because it is unbiased by preconceptions) or will the latter (because it may directly confront preconceptions about gay people)?

Both of these questions are somewhat naive because they oversimplify the social situation in so many ways. For example, if our friendship is more than superficial, my Chinese friend and I will discuss reactions and issues associated with race and because of our relationship I will be likely to learn about and have experiences with other Chinese people which will also influence my impressions. Despite these oversimplifications, these questions concerning social categorization seem worth asking.

One of the strong points of Brewer's dual process model of impression formation is that it provides a framework in which the above questions become focused and meaningful. Her distinction between the individuation of social categories and the cognition of persons (personalization) corresponds to the scenario involving a best friend who is Chinese. The second scenario, which may involve both decategorization and recategorization, also revolves around personalization versus individuation of categories (see Fig. 1.1 from Brewer's article). I hasten to add that the answers to the two questions are not entirely obvious in Brewer's framework, because one needs to couple representational assumption with a corresponding set of processing assumptions. One might be tempted to read Brewer's Fig. 1.1 as implying that one's representation of their Chinese friend would be personalized and, therefore, would not influence one's overall impression of Chinese people. That reading, however, entails a particular processing model operating on the knowledge representations implied by the Figure. One could readily formulate alternative processing models for the same representation that would lead to a strong influence of personalized knowledge on category-level judgments. The key point is that Brewer has proposed some intriguing distinctions concerning the representation of social information that can be used to ask theoretical and applied questions concerning social categorization. Although a variety of processing assumptions is possible, each is associated with a set of empirically testable constraints.

Another strong point of Brewer's model is that she entertains the idea that there are multiple types of representation at different stages of processing and at different levels of abstraction. It may not matter so much whether or not her conjectures are correct as it does that they serve to help free one from the normal default assumption that there is basically a single type of processing yielding a single form of representation. The idea of multiple representation and processing types appears to be gaining currency in the area of social cognition, and I do not mean to imply that Brewer should be given exclusive credit for the general idea. The idea of multiple representation and processing types does stand in contrast to most of the research on the categorization of natural objects which assumes (incorrectly, I think) that people are relentlessly doing the same thing (e.g., abstracting prototypes) more or less all the time (see Medin & Smith, 1984, for a recent review). People in social cognition, such as Brewer, not only seem to be posing the right sorts of questions concerning multiple representation forms but also making progress in answering them.

The final strong point of Brewer's dual process model that I wish to emphasize is the role of salient distinctions (e.g., male versus female, old versus young) in organizing social categories. Even more than natural object categories, social categories are severely underconstrained, and a fundamental question is why we have the social categories that we have rather than others. In particular, social categories are often overlapping and not hierarchically organized, and Brewer's ideas concerning salient initial distinctions may provide some useful constraints on category construction and between-category relationships. Again, these ideas are less precisely worked out than they are agenda-setting, but the agenda is full of intriguing possibilities.

Overall then, Brewer has written a very provocative paper. The dual process model may be more of a research framework than an explicit theory, but I think it may prove to be an extremely useful framework. Her paper also raises some more general issues concerning (social) categorization to which attention will now turn.

GENERAL ISSUES

Perhaps one of the benefits of outside commentators is that they may raise issues that normally form part of the background or context in an area of research but which nonetheless are worthy of attention. Although my questions may be off the mark they are intended in that spirit.

Goals and Purposes of Social Categorization

Figure 1.1 and Table 1.1 in Brewer's target chapter lay out some fairly complex processes and structures, and one might well ask what the cognitive system is trying to do. Why should there be categorization, individuation, and personalization? One common answer to why people might categorize is that it is in the interest of cognitive economy. That is, categorization is a way of coping with information overload. I confess to being very skeptical about this answer. To my knowledge, no one has identified a memory disorder attributable to a person's having so many items of information stored away that there is no room for any new facts. (Of course, access to this information is a different question.)

I think that categorization, including social categorization, is primarily to cope with the problem of too little rather than too much information. We may be at a loss as to how to interact with a new person we meet if we have no way of generating any expectations at all concerning how the person will think and act. Indeed, people seem to attend to many sources of information that may improve the accuracy of their predictions. For example, if males act differently from females, then one can draw inferences and make predictions more accurately if they have separate representations for males and females than if they have only an undifferentiated person representation. Adding information about age and occupation may allow more fine-grained predictions and expectations. Any one person falls into a very large number of potential categories. Presumably it is the case that the more categories used to refine our expectations, the less likely we are to be misled (assuming bias-free processing). In any event, if every person were treated as absolutely unique, then there would be no basis at all for generating expectations. This would be analogous to the situation of a physician's being confronted with a totally new disease unlike any other. Again, the problem is ignorance, not an overabundance of information.

If social categories are developed to deal with the problem of having too little information, then there ought to be a corresponding set of implications for appropriate knowledge structures. For example, prototype representations in terms of modal or characteristic properties allow one to generate expectations that will be on the average true, but there are several sources of information to which prototype representations are insensitive. For example, representations in terms of averages give no indication of range or variability and contain no knowledge concerning patterns of within-category correlated properties that might be used to set up category subtypes. This insensitivity to subtypes is a serious problem for prototype models that employ top-down abstraction processes that treat categories as homogeneous (for detailed critique, see Medin, 1983; McClelland & Rumelhart, 1985).

Taking advantage of information in particular contexts also can improve predictions. For example, a mushroom found in the wild can be expected to have a much higher probability of being poisonous than one found in a grocery store. Similarly, people may behave differently at work than they do at home or at a party.

If the foregoing analysis is at all accurate, then the representations associated with Fig.1. (p. 5) will prove to be inadequate because they are too static and context-independent. There may be no general answer to the question of whether representations are organized around persons, groups, or situations. The response should depend on what information is needed and how well that information can be predicted from knowledge about who the person is, what groups they can be classified into, or what situation is instantiated. Although I would agree that self-involvement is associated with needing or wanting ever finer predictions, dynamic, context-dependent representations may prove to be the rule rather than the exception (Barsalou & Medin, 1986). In general, I think greater attention to the purposes of social categorization could be used to motivate and refine our theories concerning knowledge representation.

Structure and Process

It is trite but true that we never evaluate theories of representation by themselves but always representation-process pairs. Still, it is easy to be distracted by issues concerning representations and let the associated processing principles fade into the background so much that we may have the illusory belief that some task gives us a pure look at representation. For example, the early work on ill-defined concepts by Rosch and Mervis (1975) involved asking people to list attributes of concepts. The procedure served Rosch and Mervis quite well. It is important to realize, however, that in the process of listing attributes people are almost surely doing something other than directly reading and reporting their knowledge representations. Keil (1981) has noted that there is a rich set of properties and predicates associated with ontological knowledge that provides conceptual structure. In attribute listing paradigms almost all of these properties are never mentioned. Similarly, the descriptions associated with Fig. 2.2 in Brewer's paper may be constrained by the social context, and ought not to be thought of as a direct index of explicit knowledge (Grice, 1975).

Another minor quibble. Some of the categorization processes discussed by Brewer may indeed involve abstraction during the initial storage process. But one should also keep in mind the possibility that initial encoding may be more individuated or personalized and that categorization-like behavior emerges at the time of retrieval because the person is unable to obtain unique access to the relevant individual information. Although, in general, direct abstraction at storage and indirect abstraction at retrieval may operate in similar ways, it may be important for some purposes (particularly in thinking about top-down versus bottom-up processes) to keep the potential distinction in mind. Overall, I think work on social categorization should aim to be one level more precise in describing and evaluating experiments on representation and processing of social information.

Structure

Much of the work on categorization, including social categorization, has relied on either features or dimensions in describing similarity. As a consequence, similarity of conceptual structures has often been defined in terms of matching and mismatching attributes or distance in some appropriate multidimensional space. Brewer argues for "pictoliteral" representations because they preserve temporal, spatial, and configural relations among category features. Although this is a step in the right direction, I think it is a small step where a larger one is needed. First of all, pictoliteral representations need processing machinery to operate on them so that the relational information is preserved. More importantly, however, more radical departures from the traditional similarity-based approach may be in order. Elsewhere, Murphy and I argue that the relationship between a concept and an example is like that of theory and data (Murphy & Medin, 1985). In this sense, categorization is less attribute matching than it is an inference process. For example, jumping into a swimming pool with one's clothes on is, in all probability, not associated with the concept *intoxicated*, yet that information might well be used to decide that a person is drunk. A concept may be invoked when it has sufficient explanatory relation to an object, rather than when it matches an object's attributes.

One structural consequence of viewing concepts as like theories or embedded with theories is that some properties may not be simply more salient than others, but also more *central*. For example, I believe that almost all bananas and almost all boomerangs are curved, but the property, curved, seems more central to boomerang than to banana. An interesting parallel to this observation is provided in a recent study by Asch and Zukier (1984). Participants were given trait descriptions of people that, on the surface at least, seemed to be contradictory. For example, they might be told that a person is both *kind* and *vindictive*. The participants reported no difficulty in integrating these conflicting descriptions into a unitary impression and, indeed, they often commented that they knew a person who fit the description in question. Asch and Zukier identified a number of integration strategies, and one of the more common ones was to make one property more central than the other. For example, a typical resolution for a person who is both kind and vindictive is to assume that the person is fundamentally vindictive and that kindness is only in the service of furthering his or her nefarious ends. I believe we need to know much more about representational structures and that the notion of centrality is going to play an important role in these accounts.

Theories are only indirectly constrained by data because there are typically mediating assumptions and operationalizations that lie between the core assumptions and the data actually collected. These factors allow the theory to be somewhat of an idealization, and it is not always clear which assumptions, if any, should be questioned when (apparently) contradictory data arise. This is true for theories in general, as well as for the theories we use to describe other people in particular. If people are constantly developing and evaluating theories and explanations of others, then another aspect of conceptual structure is the mediating factors that determine when and how our theories become modified. Some parts of our theories are likely to be more flexible or mutable than others. If one's introverted friend acts very sociable, do we decide that the friend is not introverted after all, that he or she is compensating, or that the particular circumstances are special? (See Weber & Crocker, 1983, for related questions.) We need a theory of mutability if we are going to make much progress in understanding conceptual change. (A very interesting start along these lines is the recent work of Kahneman and Miller [1986] on norm theory.)

Overall, a serious limitation on our current accounts of conceptual structure is that we have been working with overly limited notions of structure. We have a ways to go if our aim is to get at the character of knowledge structures rather than to simply provide a caricature of them.

CONCLUSIONS

Almost all of the issues I have listed (and, therefore, almost all the criticisms) apply not only to social categorization in particular but to categorization research in general. Still, work in the area of social cognition provides some unique opportunities because questions such as how explanatory structures interact with conceptual structures are highlighted in the social domain. Brewer's dual process model provides a heuristic framework that allows us to go a step deeper in addressing some difficult but important theoretical questions. It also affords us a new view of other difficult questions concerning how we process information about others. In some respects this new view is disturbing because it suggests that we have further to go than we might have thought. In particular, I have suggested that we need to scrutinize more closely the purposes of categorization, aim for more precision in evaluating combinations of structural and processing assumptions, and enrich our impoverished views of conceptual structures. Brewer's work suggests that, if our journey is going to be a little longer, at least there will be fascinating questions to puzzle us along the way.

ACKNOWLEDGMENTS

Preparation of this paper was supported by NSF Grant BNS 84-19756. Marie Banich and Brian Ross provided valuable comments on an earlier version of this paper.

REFERENCES

Asch, S. E., & Zukier, H. (1984). Thinking about persons. *Journal of Personality and Social Psychology, 46*, 1230–1240.

Barsalou, L. W., & Medin, D. L. (1986). Concepts: Static definitions or context-dependent representations? *Cahiers de Psychologie Cognitive, 6*(2), 187–202.

Grice, H. P. (1975). Logic and conversation. In P. Cole & J. L. Morgan (Eds.), *Syntax and semantics, Vol. 3: Speech Acts* (pp. 41–58). New York: Academic Press.

Kahneman, D., & Miller, D. T. (1986). Norm theory: Comparing reality to its alternatives. *Psychological Review, 93*(2), 136–154.

Kahneman, D., & Tversky, A. (1973). On the psychology of prediction. *Psychological Review, 80,* 237–251.

Keil, F. C. (1981). Constraints on knowledge and cognitive development. *Psychological Review, 88,* 197–227.

McClelland, J. L., & Rumelhart, D. E. (1985). Distributed memory and the representation of general and specific information. *Journal of Experimental Psychology: General, 114,* 159–188.

Medin, D. L. (1983). Structural principles in categorization. In T. J. Tighe & B. E. Shepp (Eds.), *Perception, cognition, and development: Interactional analyses* (pp. 203–230). Hillsdale, NJ: Lawrence Erlbaum Associates.

Medin, D. L., & Smith, E. E. (1984). Concepts and concept formation. In M. R. Rosenzweig (Ed.), *Annual Review of Psychology, 35,* 113–138.

Murphy, G. L., & Medin, D. L. (1985). The role of theories in conceptual coherence. *Psychological Review, 92*(3), 289–316.

Rosch, E., & Mervis, C. B. (1975). Family resemblances: Studies in the internal structure of categories. *Cognitive Psychology, 7,* 573–605.

Tversky, A., & Kahneman, D. (1973). Availability: A heuristic for judging frequency and probability. *Cognitive Psychology, 5,* 207–232.

Tversky, A., & Kahneman, D. (1974). Judgment under uncertainty: Heuristics and biases. *Science, 185,* 1124–1131.

Tversky, A., & Kahneman, D. (1980). Causal schemas in judgments under uncertainty. In M. Fishbein (Ed.), *Progress in social psychology.* Hillsdale, NJ: Lawrence Erlbaum Associates.

Weber, R., & Crocker, J. (1983). Cognitive processes in the revision of stereotypic beliefs. *Journal of Personality and Social Psychology, 45,* 961–977.

11 Conditional Responses in Person Perception: The Categories of our Discontent

Chris S. O'Sullivan
University of Kentucky

The main focus of my comments are processes that appear to be contradictory to Brewer's model, but are actually compatible with it. In that way, I hope they suggest expansions of the model, to account for apparent exceptions. The exceptions that I am thinking of are cases in which we adopt or switch to the person-based mode of processing when our goals are impersonal, and others in which we adopt a category-based mode despite self-involving goals. I think such mode switching is affect-driven: Negative affect tends to drive us into category-based processing, and positive affect tends to drive us into person-based processing. I propose that, because the source of the affect that motivates the mode switching is the *other's* behavior, a context-sensitive and interactional component be added to the model. It can easily accommodate such an addition.

There are a few other points I raise later, dealing with the effect of context on the identification of ingroup members and with problems involved in categorizing atypical people.

Although there are sufficient findings in the literature to support many aspects of Brewer's proposal, I have found myself referring not to the literature but to anecdotes and common experiences. It was through consideration of everyday events that I came to appreciate the model. Also, reference to experience rather than experiments was often necessary because of the dirth of an experimental literature (and difficulties in building such a literature) on evolving and emotionally imbued interactions and relationships.

MODE-SWITCHING DUE TO OTHERS' BEHAVIOR:
COPING WITH AFFECT

Person-Based Processing with Impersonal Goals:
Reciprocity, Ingratiation, and Flirting

An axiom of the model is that person-based processing is more effortful than category-based processing. Thus, it is only when the perceiver's interactive goal is self-involving (and sufficient capacity is available) that the perceiver is motivated to engage in data-based, rather than category-based, processing. Two types of interactions that do not fit this prediction come to mind.

First, suppose that, fairly early in the semester, an undergraduate actually visits during your office hours. The student has come simply to express enthusiasm for your class; she or he is stimulated by your lecture, and wants to learn more and discuss his or her own ideas. I propose that your response will be to start processing the student, whom you may have previously categorized on the basis of appearance, in a person-based way. Perhaps you would resort to person-based processing only if the student's expressed appreciation was clearly person-based: If the enthusiasm were primarily for the material, it is possible that you would merely individuate; but if the student's perception were that it was not so much the material, but your perspective (on any issue) that was provocative and compelling, would you not be induced to reciprocate?

Such an event is not incompatible with the model. Brewer suggests that perceived similarity promotes personalized processing, and an hypothesis of similarity may be implicit in the student's approaching you, and in your acceptance of the terms of interaction. The proposal also implies that positive affect tends to promote person-based processing, in that similarity produces both affective involvement and person-based processing. The point here is that positive affect directed toward oneself and person-based treatment of oneself may elicit a person-based response.

Contrast this scene with one that begins exactly the same way, but in which it becomes clear that the student is merely a brown-noser, attempting ingratiation for a better grade. One's attention will immediately lapse, and her comments, even if interesting, may get perfunctory attention.

A similar sort of interaction may also occur with a colleague or staff-member. Suppose you are delivering something to a colleague mindlessly, on your way to a more involving task. Without really attending to the person, you identify him, and hand over the item. If someone asked you later whether he still had a cold, or whether you noticed he had cut off his beard, you would be at a loss. Suppose, then (some of you may have to imagine a sex-change to participate in this exercise), that he complimented you on your outfit. You might still be able to remain blissfully mindless. But if he then went on to inquire whether you had worn it for his benefit, you would be forced to attend to the person and the interaction in order to generate an *ad hoc* response (even if you decided that the best response was to ignore the comment).

The nature of your processing response, beyond greater attention and effort, would depend on your perception of the other's behavior. As with the student, your reading of his processing mode would influence your affective response. If you interpret the comment as category-based, you will be irritated (instead of or in addition to being pleased). This interpretation would probably derive from previous observations of the colleague as a chronic and pervasive flirt (a categorization). In fact, the ratio of resentment to flattery would be determined by the level at which you felt you had been categorized to merit such treatment: The more inclusive (higher in the hierarchy) the categorization necessary for this person to flirt with someone, the greater the resentment. If, on the basis of past observation, you felt that he had gone no further than a primary identification (female) in his treatment of you, you would be least pleased and most annoyed. The ratio would be more equal if you believed that the comment was motivated by subtyping. It could become predominantly positive if the subtype were very exclusive or if you managed to perceive the comment as person-based.

In both cases above (the interested student and the complimentary colleague), I suggest that there is reciprocity. Apparent person-based processing will elicit person-based processing in return (via positive affect), and apparent category-based processing will elicit category-based processing in return (via negative affect).

One reservation should be added to this principle: Reciprocity is not automatic in such cases. A prerequisite is that the other is not found deeply unattractive or unworthy of respect. In other words, a repulsive other will have a harder time eliciting person-based reciprocity. The underlying reason may be that one will reject any implication of similarity with some others, and will cognitively insist on categorical difference. If the student's thoughts and questions were insipid, you would experience irritation and would cut short any incipient person-based processing effort. If you found your flirtatious colleague attractive, you would be more inclined to interpret his behavior as person-based and to respond in kind, but if you found him categorically unacceptable, the interaction designated flirting might be redesignated as sexual harrassment.

Category-Based Processing with Self-Involving Goals

Complementary to the processes outlined above, I propose that person-based processing will switch to category-based processing if negative affect is aroused, and if one feels one is being treated in a category-based way. There is a complication here, however, because there are three (or even four, including that above), routes to person-based processing. Brewer lists personal relationships, outcome dependency, and social identity as reasons to engage in person-based processing. In this section, I shall be dealing only with the first two bases of self-involvement because I think they interact with negative affect and reciprocity in different ways.

Two routes to person-based processing. In Brewer's Fig. 1.1, a diamond representing the decision point to utilize person-based or category-based processing contains the question "Self-involving?" One reason that question is answered affirmatively is outcome dependency: Thus, if one's own welfare is dependent on the other's behavior, one will process the other very carefully, to avoid such error-prone heuristics as category-based inferences. This sort of affective involvement in the other is very different, I contend, from affective involvement due to a close relationship. When one's own well-being depends on the other, one may have no further interest in and may not personally care about the other. In contrast, with affection-based involvement, one cares about many aspects of the other, including the other's well-being in matters that have no bearing on oneself.

Whatever the reason for self-involvement, processing will be bottom-up, and the consequences for impression formation and recall will be the same. Brewer suggests that person-based processing bears a similarity to processing of information about the self. The similarity is that information about the self and about person-based others is best represented in propositional networks, rather than pictoliterally and prototypically. This common characteristic follows naturally from the complexity of such representations (which prohibits necessarily simplistic pictoliteral representation), and their uniqueness (which renders prototypes irrelevant).

I suggest, furthermore, that affection-motivated person-based processing resembles processing of information about the self in another way that is not shared by outcome dependent person-based processing. Specifically, we include others to whom we are affectively bound in some of our ego-defensive attributions. Perhaps through empathy and identification, we take the actor's, rather than the observer's, perspective on events in their lives. In particular, our self-serving biases extend to them, and no others (Aristotle described a true friend as "another self").

Relatives, friends, and lovers: Dealing with negative affect through category-based processing. These affection-linked groups of people we process in a person-based way, and in some sense they are an extension of ourselves. As noted before, the basis of inclusion of others in a self-like perspective may be perceived similarity. In fact, the degree of perceived similarity is often exaggerated with others who are emotionally close and included under the umbrella of the actor's perspective. Thus parents often exaggerate the similarity between themselves and their children (and children often recoil from the similarities they perceive). Most of us have experienced the delusion of similarity that marks incipient romantic relationships. With close friends, as well, one expects consensus in opinions on important matters, and expects them to adopt one's own sympathetic perspective on one's behavior. Such delusions of similarity extend to personality traits (Feinberg, Miller, & Ross, 1981). While perception of similarity usually produces positive affect, it also happens that positive affect produces perception of similarity.

What happens, then, when this loved other behaves offensively? When the similarity bond breaks down? Purely on the basis of intuition, I suggest that one resorts to categorical attribution. When the offspring behaves reprehensibly, the parent characterizes the behavior not as springing from the child's self but from the child's category (e.g., "teen-ager," or "terrible two's"). This parental attribution allows distancing of the other from the other's behavior, by providing an excuse for the behavior. Although it does not provide the same cognitive relief of assigning the cause to a temporary influence, I find that when I disagree with or disapprove of my brother (who in many ways is very much like me), I mentally characterize him as a "typical male." That is, I attribute his offending attitudes to an accident of birth. Other times, I must more effortfully resort to a lower level category, "conservative," and the more complex excuse that, in some families, the only available path of rebellion is to become conventional. At such moments, I deny all similarity and focus on the differences between us. Again, making a categorical attribution relieves him of responsibility for his behavior, but, more importantly, it is easier for me to cope with my negative affect towards him from a categorical distance.

I think such categorical attribution is different from the case Brewer describes, in which an aspect of one's friend Janet is that she is a nurse; the category is subordinate to the individual. Instead, the category seems to be overwhelming the individual in one's perception. Reference to the category is not motivated merely by its utility in summarizing the other, but by the affective need to recategorize the other as an outgroup member. Consequently, in the heat of one's anger any other confirming behaviors (and not disconfirming behaviors) that support the categorization will come to mind. Such attention to confirming, rather than to disconfirming, traits is a characteristic of category-based processing. At such moments, one believes the other's behavior is truly produced by their membership in the outgroup category.

Outcome dependency and category-based processing: Reciprocity and attribution in tenure decisions. The second route to person-based processing is through self-involving goals. An encounter with a physician to learn about the outcome of a diagnostic test (e.g., for AIDS) would be self-involving, but would not lead to person-based processing, because attention would be self-focused. We must assume, therefore, that achievement of the goal depends on a personal judgment about ourselves by the other for person-based processing to take place. It may be that such self-involving goals in which attention is focused on the other always carry the risk of rejection.

Not only will one be motivated to process the person's behavior very carefully and effortfully, the person's primary identification may typically be irrelevant in such cases. Although one might approach such a person slightly differently depending on whether she is of the same or other sex, and depending on her age category, these factors are much less material to the success of the encounter than the degree to which the individual is shy or outgoing, paranoid, cooperative, status-conscious, or open-minded. Such judgments will also be a matter of degree (person-based traits are points on continua of dimensions, rather than features), and discrepant behavior will contribute as much as confirming behavior to the overall impression. Also, important categorical information is given by the context in most cases of outcome-dependency (e.g., profession, and evaluator role).

Let's suppose that the target person is the department chair, and you are up for tenure. Suppose that his recommendation is positive, he presents a strong case for you, and you are successful. You will still process him in a person-based way, and will credit him with processing you in a person-based way: He decided your case on your merits. (Others may not see it that way. In my own recent experience, a colleague of a woman who is up for tenure said that she didn't deserve it but would be tenured because there are not and never have been any tenured women in that department: He made a category-based attribution for her predicted success. She also felt that her success was assured, but on the grounds of her recent accomplishments, which she listed—a person-based attribution.)

If your chair makes a negative recommendation, however, your processing of him may change—especially if you clearly feel the outcome was unjustified. You will need to make ego-defensive attributions, and these will typically involve attributing the negative decision to category-based processing of yourself, if you have any basis for it at all. According to the reciprocity-of-processing rule that I am advocating, such perceived category-based processing should provoke retaliatory category-based processing. Srull and Wyer (1986) point out that negative feedback instigates "an active attempt to discredit the source of the affect" (p. 541). Some forms this discrediting may take are noticing consistencies and ignoring inconsistencies in his character with a negatively valenced category; and freely making category-based inferences, even when they are exaggerations and inconsistent with other information you have about the person.

In other words, one way of effecting a self-serving bias in the face of failure is to attribute the negative judgment of oneself not to one's own traits and behaviors, but to the others' judgment biases. Such biases are assumed to be due to the other's outgroup membership (at some level; one may have to go quite far down in the hierarchy to locate the outgroup, if one is also white male, for example) and inability to process oneself in a person-based way. It should be noted, as well, that the negative judgment of oneself eliminates the motivation for person-based processing.

Summary: Affectively Motivated and Reciprocating Mode Switching

For both sources of person-based processing (outcome dependency and close relationships), the switch to category-based processing is due to the arousal of negative affect and a need to attribute the source of this affect to the other's membership in some (outgroup) category. With affection-motivated person-based processing, one wants to achieve emotional distance from the other's behavior, but with outcome-dependent person-based processing, one wants to create distance between oneself and the judgment the other has passed. In the first case, one wants to distance the other from his behavior; in the second, one wants to obliterate distinctions between the other and his category.

Switching from person-based processing to category-based processing and the converse are mirror images. Positive affect leads one into person-based processing, and negative affect leads one into category-based processing. Also, when one feels one is being processed in a person-based way (which promotes a positive response), one is prone to reciprocate; and when one feels one is being processed in a category-based manner (which promotes a negative response), one is inclined to reciprocate. With affection-motivated person-based processing, we may either initiate or reciprocate the switch to category-based processing.

CONTEXT DEPENDENCY OF INGROUP DEFINITION

In her discussion of the role of similarity in promoting person-based processing, Brewer cites evidence that such effects are limited to ingroups defined at the level of the subtype. Yet we also know that people tend to define themselves in contradistinction to any group they are in, i.e., contextually (cf. McGuire, McGuire, Child, & Fujioka, 1978). What is salient in any setting is our difference, and the social context determines how low in the hierarchy one has to go to define oneself. In some settings, of course, self-identification may be at the level of primary identification.

If self-definition is contextually determined, then identification of similars (ingroup members) must be also. A friend tells me that at her job (she works for a state agency), she identified the only other lesbian on staff. She claims that she processes this woman in a person-based way: She seeks her out, is very interested in her, and feels a bond of similarity. (She also believes there is some outcome-dependency involved and that she must maintain positive relations with the woman.) She certainly won't make any category-based inferences about the woman on the basis of this ingroup identification, because she has none for her own group. Yet in the context of a lesbian gathering, she maintains that she would not pay particular attention to this woman, but would seek out other psychologists, or, if there were none, other academics. Simple identification of others as lesbians is insufficient in this context for her to perceive similarity and to feel the consequent positive affect. If one tends to process ingroup members in a person-based way (effortfully, bottom-up, and utilizing a complex, propositional representation), then whether one processes a particular individual in a person-based way depends on whether the context promotes perception of the person as an ingroup member.

There are even contexts in which distinctiveness per se is the basis of perceived similarity. For instance, the only white female and the only black male in a group of white males may gravitate toward each other, at least to explore similarities in perception of the group.

ATYPICALITY AND CATEGORY-MATCHING: THE WOMAN ENGINEER, BLACK PHYSICIST, LADY PROFESSOR, AND OTHER ANOMALIES

Identity/Category Conflicts

One area in which further work is needed is how we categorize people who do not match the prototype for the category to which they ostensibly belong. Brewer maintains that we first perform a primary identification, and that, if there is no existing representation for the category within this primary bifurcation, we subtype. Thus the representation of a female doctor is not a conjunction of ''woman'' + ''doctor'' but is a subtype of female, separate from the representation of ''(male) doctor.'' Rothbart and John (1985), on the other hand, suggest that we categorize on the basis of prototype-matching: A highly educated black biochemist is not a good fit for the category (here, primary identification) ''black'' so we categorize him with (white) scientists instead.

It could be, though, that the female doctor and the black biochemist are actually two different cases, not that these are alternative predictions about the same case. Brewer acknowledges that treatment of anomalies is affected by prior experience with similar nonprototypical cases. Other factors may also determine what one does with anomalies. Predictions may have to account for the influence of (1) prior experience with such anomalies; (2) familiarity with the available categories (richness of knowledge); (3) whether there is affective inconsistency between the primary identification and the category; and (4) degree of prejudice (strength of stereotypes associated with the primary identification).

First, consider the case in which there is no prior experience, and in which familiarity with the category is also poor. For me, a female engineer would be such a case, because not only do I lack familiarity with female engineers (1), my representation of the category of male engineers is impoverished (2). According to Brewer, because I have no prior experience with female engineers, I would individuate. I believe, however, that because I don't have any close female subtype to draw on in this case, I would have to start by modifying the male category, drawing on whatever inferences are attached to my pictoliteral representation of male engineers, but discarding those implications that are affectively inconsistent with female (3).

Brewer's example of the female doctor does not present the same problem. One's representation of male doctor is quite rich, and, because there are quite a few female doctors around, most of us have had the opportunity to develop a subtype of female doctors. I agree, in this case, that the representation of female doctor is separate from the representation of male doctor. Research on expectations and evaluations of female professors, a case similar to the female doctor, supports Brewer's contention that this sort of familiar but atypical subtype constitutes a separate representation within the primary partition. The point of contention is how such subtypes are derived. We agree that individuation is involved, but disagree whether it is individuation of the nearest subtype within the primary partition, or whether initially one finds the closest case across primary partitions.

Rothbart and John's (1985) black biochemist presents a third sort of categorization dilemma. According to Rothbart and John, this man would not necessarily be categorized as a black. The probable reason is that there are no aspects of one's representation of black men that are informative as to what this man is like: The primary identification has no predictive or explanatory value. One's representation of scientists is much more useful. For example, I would expect this man to have more in common with Linus Pauling than with Eddie Murphy or O. J. Simpson. Brewer would predict that one would individuate him, and eventually create a subtype of blacks who are scientists. But I think that most of us have had some experience with blacks whom we did not categorize as black. A striking, middle-class black graduate student in our department reports that she is often asked where she is from. She feels that people want her to identify herself as something other (more exotic? more acceptable?) than a black American, because she is not a good fit with the category.

The strength of one's prejudice may also determine whether it is the primary identification that dominates, or the more appropriate but nonprototypical subcategory. For example, when Ted Koppel interviewed Sally Ride before her first trip into space, he had only one question for her which he pursued with the dogged irascibility he might apply to getting a politician to admit to carrying on a covert war. The question was whether, as a woman, her descriptions of outer space wouldn't be more poetic than the "Oh, wow!" type evocations of her male predecessors. Her response, equally repetitive and insistent, was that she was an astrophysicist, not a poet: She categorically denied that her gender would significantly alter her experience of space travel or her ability to articulate the experience. Similarly, someone afflicted with superstitious beliefs about blacks might find the black biochemist problematic; I think she would be more likely to draw on her stereotype of blacks than her stereotype of (white) scientists.

In sum, the utility of the primary identification vs. the utility of identity-inconsistent categories may determine where one initially situates the anomalous person and begins the individuation or subtyping process.

Category/Category Conflicts

Another point about nonprototypicality and subtyping is suggested by Brewer's concluding recommendation that decision-makers be trained to recognize the difference between person- and category-based inferences. Note that, in the example of outcome dependency described above, tenure decisions, the person about whom the judgment is being made is motivated to engage in person-based processing, but the person performing the judgment is not so motivated (unless he should be disqualified for affective involvement). Assuming that the judge (prototypical male department chair) is at some point doing category-based processing, he should, according to Brewer's description, descend through the hierarchy until he finds a good match with a pictoliterally represented prototype. In the best case, the woman will match the prototype for successful female professional. That is, her attributes and salient behavior will match the image the judge holds of such women. The popular media image is a confident, assertive young woman who wears a suit and carries a leather attache case; she tends to be tall, bespectacled, and sleek.

What happens, though, if the candidate is a better match for some other subtype? For example, if she is an excellent match with the judge's image of the perfect wife and mother? Physically, a zaftig earth mother in peasant dress; interpersonally, soothing, softspoken, and nurturing? When he looks at her vita, will he look for confirmation of this category, ignoring disconfirming evidence? Moreover, will he fail to focus on the features that are consistent with the successful woman prototype and emphasize too much her maternal attributes in his representation of her?

Brewer maintains that we move downward through the hierarchy when there is a mismatch, rather than horizontally. On the other hand, one goes only as far down in the hierarchy of categories as is necessary to find a match. The question, then, is whether the good pictoliteral match would draw him toward the (inappropriate) earth mother category, or whether the task would orient him to the category more relevant to the judgment. In the long run, the result might be comparable. If he originally categorized her as an earth mother, he might individuate and ultimately create a tenurable subtype of earth mothers. If he originally categorized her as a professional, the judge might individuate her under the professional woman category, and eventually create an earth mother subtype of professional women. It would seem that the first such anomaly the judge encountered would benefit more from being individuated under professional types than under earth mothers. In either case, the woman who was a good match with the successful professional prototype (at the highest possible level) would present an easier and more favorable case. She would require less extensive processing and could be the unequivocal beneficiary of category-based inferences.

CONCLUSIONS

The gist of my comments is that the affective and social context will influence one's perception of others (as similar or dissimilar, or as an ingroup or outgroup member) and affect the processing mode. A strength of Brewer's model is that it so easily accommodates interactive considerations. For example, Brewer suggests, with what strikes me as excessive optimism, that social judges be trained to distinguish between person- and category-based processing. A more fruitful approach might be to find ways to motivate judges to adopt a person-based mode, e.g., through reciprocal evaluations.

It is somewhat troubling that there is linguistic overlap between my construals of Brewer's model and Fiske and Pavelchak's (1986) model of piecemeal vs. schema-triggered affect, yet I have made no conceptual connections. There need not be any: The role I am describing for affect is as motivation to adopt one or the other processing mode; Fiske and Pavelchak described how affect is linked to person representations. The proposals can be integrated, however. For instance, I have suggested that positive affect tends to promote person-based processing and negative affect tends to promote category-based processing. It has also been found that careful, bottom-up processing of the sort found in the person-based mode produces more liking than category-based processing (Lassiter & Stone, 1984). Perhaps this effect is due to the way that the general evaluation is arrived at, according to Fiske and Pavelchak's model. That is, perhaps the weighted average of traits (as in piecemeal processing) is usually more positive than the affective tags on categories (schema-triggered affect). One factor that might support this tendency is that whenever someone is processed as a category member, they are processed as an outgroup member, with all the attendant affective consequences. Thus categorization may often breed contempt.

REFERENCES

Feinberg, R. A., Miller, F. G., & Ross, G. A. (1981). Perceived and actual locus of control similarity among friends. *Personality and Social Psychology Bulletin, 7,* 85–89.

Fiske, S. T., & Pavelchak, M. A. (1986). Category-based vs. piecemeal-based affective responses: Developments in schema-triggered affect. In R. M. Sorrentino & E. T. Higgins (Eds.), *Handbook of motivation and cognition* (pp. 167–203). New York: Guilford.

Lassiter, G. D., & Stone, J. I. (1984). Affective consequences of variation in behavior perception: When liking is in the level of analysis. *Personality and Social Psychology Bulletin, 10,* 253–259.

McGuire, W. J., McGuire, C. V., Child, P., & Fujioka, T. (1978). Salience of ethnicity in the spontaneous self-concept as a function of one's distinctiveness in the social environment. *Journal of Personality and Social Psychology, 36,* 511–520.

Rothbart, M., & John, O. P. (1985). Social categorization and behavioral episodes: A cognitive analysis of the effects of intergroup contact. *Journal of Social Issues, 41,* 81–104.

Srull, T. K., & Wyer, R. S., Jr. (1986). The role of chronic and temporary goals in social information processing. In R. M. Sorrentino & E. T. Higgins (Eds.), *Handbook of motivation and cognition* (pp. 503–549). New York: Guilford.

12 Categorization and Impression Formation: Capturing the Mind's Flexibility

Myron Rothbart
University of Oregon

It is always a great pleasure to read a paper by Marilynn Brewer, as one is assured of a cogent and thoughtful analysis of an important problem. This paper is no exception. Admiration is not equivalent to agreement, however, and there are a number of central assumptions of the present model that can be questioned. In the spirit of this new series, I offer these comments in the hope of clarifying or expanding the ideas put forth by Brewer. If these concerns represent a misreading of the model, I am confident of edification by Brewer's response, and if these represent a legitimate challenge to the model, they may help to stimulate thought that may clarify the process of impression formation.

As I understand it, Brewer is attempting to map the relation between the distal and proximal social stimulus. Just as theorists in the domain of visual perception found it useful to distinguish between the stimulus as it exists in the world and the stimulus as encoded, Brewer wants to understand the relation between the social object and its mental representation. Because of the complexity of social stimuli, and because they can be represented by so many attributes, it is important to be able to specify which attributes, dimensions, or features of a person are being attended to when making judgments about, or interacting with, that person. As a major contributor to the study of intergroup relations, Brewer is aware (more accurately, has experimentally demonstrated) that category membership is an important determinant of perception and action, and that the attributes of the category, rather than the attributes of the person (when personal attributes are at variance with category attributes), may dominate perception. We can perceive individuals in terms of their unique attributes or we can perceive them as exemplars of social categories, and it is this difference that Brewer wishes to explain in her dual process model.

Brewer makes the radical assumption that for a given episode in the impression-formation process, the decision is made to represent the person *either* as a member of a social category *or* in a personalized manner. Referring to her Fig. 1.1, this decision comes after the process of *identification,* and depends on whether or not the perceiver is involved, in some nontrivial way, with the stimulus person. Involvement leads to personalization, and noninvolvement leads to categorization. Leaving aside the problem that involvement may better be conceptualized as a continuous rather than dichotomous variable, the model as depicted in Fig. 1.1 clearly implies a unidirectional sequence, with no connections between the left-hand categorization branch and the right-hand personalization branch.

At this point I must express some confusion about temporal aspects of the model. On the basis of comments on p. 4, the model appears to pertain only to initial impressions, and is mute regarding the issue of integrating that first impression with later information (episodes) regarding the same person. Integrating multiple representations is not a trivial problem, given the critical importance assigned to the difference between categorical and personalized representations. Since, for a given person, some episodes may be represented categorically, and others personally, the question of how these representations are unified becomes paramount.

However, even if this model is restricted to the initial impression only, concerns about temporal relations persist. What exactly is the nature and duration of an episode? Is an interaction with a stranger on a cross-country flight a single episode? If so, would it allow for the possibility of a categorical representation early in the episode, but a personalized representation later in the episode as involvement and information increase? I understand the model's answer to be no, since once a representation starts down the path of categorization it can never become personalized.

It may be useful to consider the following three cases. In Case I we meet Joe, a fraternity member, with whom we are minimally involved, and later learn that he is a dedicated scholar. The most differentiated view of Joe that is possible is that he is, say, a member of the subtyped category *serious fraternity member,* but Joe will never have his own node with the associated attributes of serious, sensitive, musical, gentle, etc. In Case II we interact with a new neighbor, with whom we have some involvement, assign him his own person node with the attributes friendly, generous, helpful, and later discover that he is a member of the American Nazi Party. Presumably, his membership in the Nazi Party would be represented either by a set of traits associated with the person node (for example, *bigoted, fascistic,* etc.), or the category "Nazi" would simply be attached as another attribute to the person node, but he would never be represented as an exemplar of the category "Nazi."

In the previous two cases, we have examples in which it seems reasonable to expect a shift either from a categorical representation to a personal one, or vice-versa, but this does not seem possible given the model depicted in Fig. 1.1. Moreover, the temporal flow of the model is from lesser to greater differentiation (more obvious on the categorical than the personal side), and it would not allow for the possibility that movement could occur from highly differentiated to more global, undifferentiated categories.

Imagine now a Modified Case I in which Joe, who has already been categorized as a *serious fraternity member,* is observed at a boisterous party quaffing beer and urinating off of the balcony onto the guests below. One would think that this new behavior would render the overall impression of Joe as closer to the superordinate category of *fraternity member* than the subordinate category of *serious fraternity member.* But that implies "upward" movement on the categorization branch of the model, in which new information leads to a less differentiated categorical representation, which does not appear to be allowed by the model. We have argued alsewhere (Rothbart & John, 1985) that new information about a stimulus person may either decrease *or* increase the overall goodness-of-fit of that individual to an associated social category, and it cannot be assumed that new information can only move the representation to a more, rather than a less, differentiated state.

Finally, consider a Case III example where we meet Tom, who is an excellent fit to the category *fraternity member.* According to the model, processing of information about Tom comes to an end. Is there a mechanism in the model to start up the process when we later learn that Tom has attributes that require a more differentiated representation of him?

The dual process assumption creates a necessary dilemma, in that it is impossible to imagine the representation of any human being without reference to at least *some* social categories. Brewer argues, for example, that gender and age in particular are encoded automatically for all stimulus persons, with the assumption that "those dimensions of information about persons that are used so frequently and consistently" (p. 6) will be automatically encoded.[1] This would play havoc with the either/or dual process model, because it allows for the virtual certainty that categorical representation of some sort is present for all stimulus persons. The dilemma is handled by Brewer by labeling this primitive form of categorization as *identification,* and separating it from the later process of categorization by two decision processes: (a) the relevance of the stimulus person to the perceiver's goals, and (b) the aforementioned judgment of self-involvement.

The solution Brewer provides is not completely satisfying, for two reasons.

---

[1]Brewer's examples of automatically encoded categories, such as gender, age, and race, appear to be restricted to physiognomic attributes. By attributing such automatic encoding to frequency and consistency, problems may be created for the theory. For example, in Northern Ireland, where residents are infinitely sensitive to evidence of a person's identification as a Catholic or Protestant, religion would be encoded automatically. Is this case better described in the model at the level of identification or at the level of categorization/typing, where self-involvement in ingroup-outgroup identification becomes so important?

First, whether it is called identification or categorization, it still seems that all stimulus persons will be represented in part as exemplars of social categories; as such they will be represented in the left panel of her Fig. 1.4. But clearly they may later be personalized, which means they will also be represented in the right panel of that Figure. All of which implies that everyone may well be represented as both an individual node as well as an exemplar of a category, which seems to us to question the either/or character of the dual process model. Second, the distinction between relevance and involvement seemed quite arbitrary, but it was a necessary addition if identification was to be isolated as a separate process.

The basic disagreement with this model can now be stated: The postulation of two qualitatively separate processes is unconvincing at best, and troublesome at worst. On a priori grounds, it is not clear why the mind should be so concerned about whether an attribute or feature is represented as a noun category or as an adjective trait. It is certainly *possible* that Joe, represented as an instance of the category *fraternity member,* is psychologically very different from Joe, represented as a node, one of whose attributes is fraternity member. But it seems to us more parsimonious to view Joe as being associated with a number of attributes, some being noun categories and some being adjective traits, with the relative weights given to one attribute over another determined by a number of factors, including the perceiver's needs as well as situational context. But that is a different model, in which the distinction between categorical and trait information is considered unimportant, and it is *the relative strength* of the categorical and personalized information, at a particular point in time, that influences judgment.

More basically, it is not clear that there are meaningful differences between a stimulus person who is represented as a highly differentiated category member and one who is personalized. Consider the example used by Brewer on p. 12, in which the following subtype of the category *businessmen* is described: "an uptight authoritarian boss who is a tightwad and a stickler for detail." Note that "uptight" and "authoritarian" are actually adjectival in this context (they describe "boss"), and tightwad and stickler are nouns that could be easily be replaced by the adjectives "stingy" and "compulsive," respectively. It simply is not clear to us whether this subtype leads to psychologically different consequences than a personalized representation in which there is a node for the stimulus person, with "boss," "stingy," and "stickler" as attributes attached to the node.

The difficulty created by the either/or dual process model, is that it is not sufficiently flexible either to permit the possibility that categories *and* traits can be simultaneously associated with a stimulus person, or that new information can lead to *less differentiated* as well as more differentiated representations.

There are two aspects of the model I am in total agreement with, but wonder if there is not a more compelling metaphor for thinking about these phenomenon. First, there is strong agreement that the representation of a person can vary in degree of generality-specificity, although I suspect this is true for both categories and traits.[2] And second, there is agreement that one of the most important determinants of the degree of specificity is the perceiver's goals and/or involvement vis-à-vis the stimulus person. The points of disagreement are in distinguishing between noun categories and adjective traits as describing different modes of representations. Attributes are attributes, and I suspect that the mind, unlike our elementary school teachers, could care less whether the attributes are nouns or adjectives. There is strong agreement that judgments about a stimulus person may, at any point, be more heavily weighted by categorical than trait information (or vice-versa), but that is a question of differences in weight, and does not require a dual process model.

I would like to offer an alternative metaphor for thinking about the generality-specificity issue. Imagine that obtaining information about a person has an analogue in learning about a specimen under a microscope. Under conditions of weak magnification, it is possible to make gross distinctions and differentiations, but it requires increasingly stronger levels of magnification to learn the detailed attributes about the object under investigation. Now add another assumption that allows emulation of Brewer's principle that "processing proceeds from global to specific . . . and is expected to stop at the highest level of abstraction that will suffice" (p. 6).[3] That assumption is that increasingly greater amounts of effort are required to achieve increasingly greater amounts of magnification/information. In other words, the perceiver is motivated to stop at the lowest (i.e., weakest) level of magnification sufficient to satisfy his or her goals and objectives.

It is assumed, then, that broad social categories (e.g., gender) are analogous to the weakest levels of magnification, and that, in general, trait attributes are analogous to higher levels of magnification. More specifically, broad social categories can be thought of as labels for constellations of attributes (including trait attributes), each of which is only loosely associated with the category. Thus, information about relevant personality traits (e.g., knowing whether a person is assertive or passive) is much more informative in predicting relevant social behavior than category membership (e.g., male or female). Since traits are only probabilistically linked to social categories, it is not surprising that trait information may lead to more precise predictions than category information.[4]

The microscope analogy also implies that movement can go from stronger to

---

[2]Note that specifity can be increased either by categorizing in more narrowly defined person-type categories (e.g., salesman rather than Extrovert), or by the attribution of more narrowly defined adjective traits (e.g., talkative rather than extroverted). Indeed, both noun (or type) categories (see Cantor & Mischel, 1979) and adjective trait concepts (see Hampson, John, & Goldberg, 1986) can be organized in the form of hierarchies, such that a few broad superordinate categories subsume narrower subordinate ones.

[3]Brewer made this statement with regard to category based processing, but as already stated, the principle may be general to all attributes, categorical or otherwise.

[4]For a recent discussion of trait concepts and the tradeoff between bandwidth and precision see Hampson, John, and Goldberg (1986).

weaker levels of magnification as well as in the direction of greater magnification. In social perception, there are occasions in which the setting, in combination with the perceiver's objectives, leads to the use of more *super*ordinate and less differentiated constructs even though more differentiated attributes are available (and encoded).

In summary, I see the value of Brewer's model as (a) emphasizing the interdependence of the perceiver's goals with the generality or specificity of the constructs used to encode the characteristics of the stimulus person, and (b) attempting to distinguish the conditions under which categorical or individuating information is most salient. However, there are difficulties with the dual process assumption. Its lack of flexibility in being able to shift between category and personalized representations, and in only being able to form increasingly differentiated representations does not, in this author's view, capture the mind's flexibility in representing an individual both categorically and personally, as well as perceiving that person in a differentiated *or* undifferentiated manner.

ACKNOWLEDGMENT

The generosity of the Oregon Tuesday Evening Social/Personality Research Group in allowing me to plagiarize their ideas is gratefully acknowledged. This manuscript benefited greatly from the astute comments of Lewis Goldberg, Hill Goldsmith, Susan Green, Oliver John, Robert Mauro, and Mary Rothbart.

REFERENCES

Cantor, N., & Mischel, W. (1979). Prototypes in person perception. In L. Berkowitz (Ed.), *Advances in experimental social psychology* (Vol. 12). New York: Academic Press.

Hampson, S. E., John, O. P., & Goldberg, L. R. (1986). Category breadth and hierarchical structure in personality: Studies of asymmetries in judgments of trait implications. *Journal of Personality and Social Psychology, 51*, 37–54.

Rothbart, M., & John, O. P. (1985). Social categorization and behavioral episodes: A cognitive analysis of the effects of intergroup contact. *Journal of Social Issues, 41*, 81–104.

13 On Greeks and Horses: Impression Formation with Social and Nonsocial Objects

Yaacov Schul
The Hebrew University of Jerusalem

Eugene Burnstein
The University of Michigan

Brewer chose to present a model of impression formation that deemphasizes differences between perception of social and nonsocial objects. In particular she assumes that ". . . (1) in the majority of the time perception of social objects do not differ from nonsocial perception either in structure or process. (2) When it does differ, it is determined by the perceiver's purposes and processing goals, not by the characteristics of the target of perception." (p. 4). Her model further postulates (cf. Fig. 1.1) that processing can take one of two routes following identification: either top-down (i.e., categorical processing) or bottom-up (i.e., personalistic processing).

This chapter takes the opposite perspective. It explores how characteristics that distinguish social from nonsocial objects influence the operations carried out during impression formation. In other words, we shall argue that even though perception of social objects is similar in many respects to that of nonsocial objects, important differences (which must reflect properties of these objects) do exist. These differences appear not only during the identification of objects, but also during later stages of the impression formation process. At the same time, however, it is difficult to imagine any impression that is not influenced by top-down processes, that is, by the perceiver's goals, purposes, past knowledge, and expectations. Thus, we contend, the distinction drawn by Brewer between categorical (or top-down) and personalistic (or bottom-up) impressions is too sharp to be useful.

It has been said that all of human experience is reflected in the saga of Troy. The story begins following 9 years of bitter and inconclusive battle on the plains surrounding the city. At that point Odysseus has the idea of building a wooden horse large enough to conceal a score of people inside. His hope is that while the

145

Greek army pretended to sail home, the Trojans would bring the horse to Athena's temple within the city. This well-known tale is instructive for our purposes.

Let us put ourselves in place of the Trojan king, Priam. What was his impression of the wooden horse? His first step must have been to identify the object—to separate this horse-like entity as a figure from the mist and fog and ground. Correct identification under the conditions faced by Priam, we shall see, is neither automatic nor trivial. In fact, he failed to attend to several features that, were they identified and categorized appropriately, could have completely changed the fate of the city.

Identification involves at least two types of operations: top-down and bottom-up. The perceiver might be more sensitive to the presence of a particular object because of the momentary accessibility of its representation (see Bargh, 1984; Higgins & King, 1981, for recent reviews of the factors influencing construct accessibility). Thus, if Priam expects to see a horse, he will be more sensitive to the contours of horse-like objects. The influence of the top-down processes on the determination of the perceptual unit is illustrated by studies that compare chunking in experts and in novices. Expert chess players relative to novices, for example, attend to larger units that contain more relational information (Chase & Simon, 1973; see also Reitman, 1976). Markus, Smith, and Morland (1985) have recently extended these findings to the domain of categories referring to the self. They have shown that subjects with a highly elaborated and accessible self-category utilized different units, either more refined or more global, depending on their goals, than those with an unelaborated and less accessible self-category.

Identification, however, does not require that the observer access an appropriate category to represent the object. Indeed, it may not require categorization at all. One can look at a meaningless shape, focus on a particular patch within it and define the patch as the object of interest. Such an entity need not have any meaning, nor need it correspond to a particular category (except, of course, the category of things that are bounded but for the moment not understood). The patch is identified in the sense that it lies within a well-defined boundary. Identification, in this case, corresponds to a bottom-up process whereby the boundaries are recognized because they have a salient feature. Newtson and associates (Newtson, 1973; Newtson & Engquist, 1976) demonstrated that segments at the boundaries of behavioral units, the breakpoints, are different from the nonboundary segments in that they contain more information about change. In some sense, the boundaries leap to the foreground as one observes the stream of behavior (cf. Triesman, 1986). Taylor and Fiske (1978, Taylor et al., 1979) report that group members are seen as influential in discussions to the extent that they are salient, even though the basis for their salience is logically unrelated to influence. What these individuals do is define an important social boundary or "patch" in the group (e.g., the solo black in an otherwise all white group). Thus, despite their irrelevance, features that attract attention, say, because of their boundary-setting function, are likely to affect future processing of the stimulus.

The balance between top-down and bottom-up influences during identification will vary as a function of category strength (i.e., strength of expectations) and the clarity of the to-be-encoded events. Compare the encoding of a stream of activity with encoding a still-shot of that activity. Whereas, the boundaries of the perceptual units in the still-shot are relatively well defined, those of the stream are not. Indeed, in analyses of dyadic interaction psychologists have used very different types of units such as specific speech acts (e.g., Kraut & Higgins, 1984), characteristics of the participants (e.g., their goals or motives, Jones & Pittman, 1982), and characteristics of the dyad as a unit (e.g., congruence of expectations, Abramovitz, Berger, & Weary, 1982).

The saga of Troy would have ended quite differently if the sea mists had masked the horse sufficiently long. Unfortunately, Priam did identify an object. At first, most likely, he could not categorize it meaningfully. As he approached the horse, however, its "true" significance must have begun to unfold. At that point, Priam probably recognized several potential identities: It was certainly horse-like, wooden, quite large, and rather beautiful. Next, Priam may have attempted to categorize it as either man-made or god-made. A man-made artifact, would have a completely different meaning than a god-made one, even though their physical features were identical. Once this was decided, it might then be possible to classify the object further according to the intentions of the creator. If the Greeks had made it, is it truly a gift to Athena (as an inscription on it said), or is it some trick to undermine Troy? Here again, categorization in no way depends on the proximal features of the object but rather on much more distal characteristics, namely, how in this context it fits in with Priam's knowledge about Greek trickery.

By now the reader may object to the different characterizations of the horse-like object. Are not "wooden" and "made by Greeks" really attributes of the object rather than categorizations? More generally, you may say, we should decide whether attributes and categories refer to different or to the same concept (Lingle, Altom, & Medin, 1984). On the one hand, "being in category X" can serve as an attribute, suggesting that the set of categories includes the set of attributes. Obversely, the class of all objects with attribute X can function as a category, suggesting that the set of attributes includes the set of categories. As such, the two appear to be interchangeable. One might argue that attributes, unlike categories, need not be binary. Instead of characterizing John as "honest" one can attribute "honesty" to John *to a certain degree*. Indeed, according to the classical view of categorization (Bruner, Goodnow, & Austin, 1956) category membership is an either-or relationship; an instance can be either a member of a category or not a member, but not a member to a degree. Recent advances in cognitive psychology (most notably Rosch's research e.g., 1975,

1977), however, have shown that objects vary in their fit (or degree of inclusion) with a category. Thus, the semihonesty of John may be rephrased in terms of John's fit to the category prototype of an "honest person."

It might be that, while categories and attributes are equivalent logically, they are different psychologically. That is to say, although people in principle are capable of using categories and attributes interchangably, they in fact do not. The "minimal group" paradigm has taught us that people will allow themselves to utilize the most arbitrary and insignificant attributes (e.g., those who overestimate dots versus those who underestimate them) to distinguish ingroup from outgroup. The literature on stereotypes suggests that any partition of two groups with no real differences between the members of the two groups may itself serve as an attribute and serve to recruit still other attributes in order to make the category boundaries more distinctive. Comparable effects can be observed in the behavior of groups in competition (Sherif et al., 1961), particularly those that have an initial disadvantage (see Lemaine, Kastersztein, & Personnaz, 1979).

The distinction between categories and attributes, therefore, seems to reflect the focus of attention. At any given point, the observer may chose to consider particular attributes of the object. One or more of these attributes become a category, a salient identity of the object, while the remaining become subattributes of that identity or are dropped from working memory. Therefore, I may think of myself right now as a Professor who is also incidentally male, and a parent. The next minute, however, (say, upon hearing my son call for help), I may shift attention to my Parent identity and the professorship reverts to the status of an attribute. Similarly, I may think of a person as a nurse and tag this identity with an attribute "Janet"; later I can just as well shift to the identity "Janet" and tag it with the attribute "nurse."

Some ways of categorization appear more natural than others. Once you know Janet, her identity as "Janet" is likely to dominate that of being "female," a "nurse," or a "baseball player." Still, this dominance is far from being absolute. One may focus on Janet's "nurse" identity if it becomes relevant for a particular goal. Under such conditions, the "Janet" identity may serve as an attribute, or may disappear altogether. The possibility of interchanging attributes and categories makes it still less likely that different representational formats are utilized for what Brewer terms category-type and person-type judgments.

The categorization of an object, that is, its identity, need not be expressed in terms of its physical appearance. The Trojan horse is not merely a wooden artifact. It is also an object that carries the intentions of its creators (as well as 20 Greeks). In other words, the identity of an object can be influenced by its purpose. Here, another distinction between "social" and "nonsocial" entities may be considered. The purposes of nonsocial entities are relatively stable and usually can be inferred with confidence from their appearance. In contrast, the purposes of social entities are often hidden. The meaning of such objects is determined not only by how they look but also by how they were intended to be seen. Thus, categorization may involve putting yourself in the place of the actor trying to comprehend what led to act in this manner. For example, when I tell a joke does the other person's laughter indicate pure enjoyment, politeness, or ingratiation? In short, as we all know, the same act is likely to be categorized quite differently depending on the intentions of the actor. This suggests that not only are people especially tuned to object information that signals intention, but also that once such information is detected it may radically influence further processing of the object.

One of the main problems Priam faced in categorizing the horse was to determine its purpose. Taking the words that the Greeks inscribed at face value, many of the elders suggested that it is a true gift to Athena. Others, and especially Laocoon, a priest of Appllo's temple, warned Priam that the Greeks in general, and Odysseus in particular, are known for their subterfuge and, thus, not to bring the horse inside the city walls. Just as Laocoon was about to win his case, an ostensibly terrified Greek was discovered and brought to the king. The Greek, Sinon, told the Trojans that the horse was indeed meant as a present to Athena. While Priam was considering Laocoon's arguments and Sinon's testimony, two serpents rose from the sea and killed Laocoon as well as his two sons. This vivid event convinced Priam that the wooden horse was intended as a gift to Athena. The story goes on to tell that the sounds of the Greek soldiers inside the horse could be heard several times as the horse was moved toward the city. The Trojans, however, paid no attention to these sounds; because they made no sense in terms of the perceived purpose of the horse, they were not processed any further and thereby not identified. Notice the difficulties the Trojans had in arriving at a categorization. Determination of the nature of the horse-like object was in fact quite laborious; Priam labored mightily to negotiate among numerous opposing pieces of information. This, again, may be more characteristic of "social" than "nonsocial" perception because the former is more concerned with properties that are inherently ambiguous and readily hidden—namely, purpose and intention.

Recent research has demonstrated that much of the cognitive work during impression formation is concered with attempts to negotiate among the conflicting pieces of information, that is, to reduce inconsistencies (see Hastie, Park, & Weber, 1984 for a review). It has been shown that under certain specifable conditions individuals attempt to reduce ambiguity and conflict by integrating the information. Integration will occur when the pertinent object is unified (e.g., a person or a homogeneous group, Burnstein & Schul, 1983; Srull, 1981; Srull, Lichtenschtein, & Rothbart, 1985), the information given is relevant (Schul, Burnstein, & Martinez, 1983), and represents dispositional features of the object (Crocker, Hannah, & Weber, 1983). In short, the integration of information depends on an initial categorization of the object that implies that the object has integrity and coherence.

Once the integrity of an object has been established, integration can take one of two forms: The individual may focus on one identity of the object and attempt to reconcile the other characterizations of the object with that identity. In this case integration occurs under the specification of a particular categorization (cf. inference testing in Carlston, 1980). However, if there is conflicting information with no established category, each conflicting piece of information may activate a different category, and integration occurs at the level of categories rather than through inferences, which link the information with a given category. Thus, one may have to reconcile a "Professor" identity with a "Parent" identity, or an "Extrovert" identity with a "Librarian" identity. Integration of categories may involve complete domination by one category over another; or a merger of categories and creation of a new category that may serve (but need not always be) as a subcategory of one of the originals (cf. the concept of subtyping discussed by Brewer). Note, however, that with or without an early categorization, integration involves consideration of the entire set of relevant properties of the object.

One final effect of the stimulus information on impression formation can occur through its impact on the judgment scale. Impressions are often expressed on subjective scales such as attractive/unattractive, positive/negative, interesting/uninteresting, etc. In order to be able to specify the location of an object on a continuum of this kind, one must anchor the scale. That is, the individual making the judgment must have a sense of what the end points of the scale (or for that matter, any other point on the scale) denote. An object is not interesting in absolute terms, it is interesting *relative* to a standard. Nor can life be said to be really good or bad. Its perceived quality depends on the standard with which it is compared (Brickman, Coats, & Janoff-Bulman, 1978). Because the scales that are used almost never have an objective or inherent anchor (e.g., an absolute zero point) social judgments are highly susceptible to the vicissitudes of subjective anchoring. As a result, the nature of the stimulus object as well as the context of comparison can have impact on the scale of judgment that is *independent* of its influences on categorization (Higgins & Luria, 1983). Even if the categorization of an object is based solely on one of its attributes, the magnitude of the judgment might be influenced by the other attributes via their impact on the standard used for comparison. Japan, for instance, would be readily categorized as a modern nation. *How* modern, however, would depend on whether observers allowed the attribute of geography or that of technology to determine their standard of comparison, that is, whether they compared Japan to other countries in Asia or to other countries with advanced technology.

So far we have argued that characteristics of the object, relevant as well as irrelevant to the actual judgments, can exert influence at several stages in impression formation, namely, during identification, categorization, and response-selection. This suggests that bottom-up processes are likely to operate in forming most impressions. At the same time, however, the seemingly opposite claim can be made, namely, that once an observer is appropriately primed, person perception, even at a very concrete level, involves comparisons with prototypes, if only the prototypes of classes of purposive acts or intentions. It is, therefore, top-down and categorical by nature. This is so even when the object is a single individual who is quite relevant to the observer's purposes and the observer is highly involved in the matter, that is, even when all the conditions specified by Brewer for noncategorical or personalized processing are met.

Even at a very concrete level we still perceive intention or purpose, and chunk activity accordingly. Although these chunks may be quite small, except in special circumstances (e.g., an orthopedic examination), they are, needless to say, never at the level of the responding muscle or limb. Indeed, given the discriminative capacity of our sensory system, the natural units of person perception, whatever else their nature, are amazingly abstract and prototypic before any higher level categorization occurs. Trait descriptions (e.g., the child is self-sufficient), which are often taken as the basic data in examples of bottom-up processing are themselves categorical and reflect underlying knowledge that could not have been encoded without the use of other only slightly less abstract categories (e.g., he dresses himself, makes his own breakfast, etc.). Thus, in impression formation it is more a matter of how abstract the category is than whether or not categorization occurs. Hence, a model that assumes that these judgments must be either categorical or noncategorical may not be useful.

Brewer attributes the choice between category-based processing and personalistic processing to the involvement of the processor. The role of the observer's involvement in categorizing, however, can be quite complex and cannot be separated from his prior categorizations. To illustrate, suppose I am asked to evaluate a candidate for a job. I may feel very involved or not at all involved in the process; also I may or may not have made a similar judgment about this candidate in the past. Note that the past categorization (e.g., How good an administrator is she?) might be rather irrelevant to the present one (e.g., How good a mathematician is she?). Nonetheless a past categorization, rather than present (or past) information, may be utilized in making the current judgment. Schematically, we are dealing with the traditional 2 × 2 design: high versus low involvement in the task, and absence versus existence of past categorization.

The role of involvement in this example can be multifaceted. First, it functions to increase the cost and benefits associated with the task. As such, individuals are likely to spend more time and energy to arrive at the "correct" evaluation under high involvement. In this sense, they will use content-relevant attributes rather than superficial attributes (Chaiken, 1980; also see the distinction between *central* and *peripheral* routes to attitude change in Petty & Cacioppo, 1984).

When one is knowledgeable about the issue, involvement may have still another influence. Commitment to prior categorizations is likely to grow with involvement. Therefore, as involvement increases, one is likely to interpret new information in terms of past categorizations. The Trojan saga contained numerous instances, one of which we have already noted: Once the horse-like object was categorized as a gift to Athena, the people failed to understand the significance of the noises from within it. The correct interpretation was simply not compatible with their prior categorization of the object. Janis' (1982) analysis of GroupThink in the Bay of Pigs decision illustrates the same process in more recent times. In Kennedy's advisory group the search for information or as well as its interpretation was doubtlessly influenced by many factors. Among them was the fact that the participants were highly involved; their motivation to succeed was strong. And at the same time, prior categorization was pronounced. That is, to say, they had powerful preconceptions about the Soviet intentions, the Castro regime, etc. By holding fast to their preconceptions, they failed to recognize evidence to the contrary. In short, when one has not already categorized the object, self-involvement may induce a more extensive search for information, or bottom-up processing. Whereas, when the object has been previously categorized self-involvement may promote reliance on the past judgment and lead to top-down processing.

Finally, let us return to the distinction between social and nonsocial objects. Social categories are rather fuzzy. For this reason it might be more useful to focus on specific attributes associated with a category. To illustrate, consider whether the Trojan horse was really a social or a nonsocial entity? Simply as a wooden artifact, it might be considered nonsocial. But this can be done only if one ignores the context in which it is deployed. From this perspective, the horse in question is part of a social transaction, a tactical move in the great game between Trojan and Greek. Indeed, virtually any object can be viewed as "social" in the right context. Hence, when we know enough to say what this context is, at that time the conceptual distinction between social and nonsocial objects will disappear. Until then we must live with these ideas even though they make us uncomfortable.

CONCLUSION

Perhaps the most important issue raised by Brewer has to do with the differences between top-down and bottom-up processes in the context of impression formation: When do we encode others in terms of relatively general, abstract classes (i.e., categorically or top-down) and when, in terms of relatively idiosyncratic, concrete ones (i.e., personalistically or bottom-up)? Which aspects of the object determines how we encode it? At what level are persons typically or most usefully represented? Or most generally, what are the natural categories of person perception?

The dangers of premature specificity is well known. At this stage of theorizing, therefore, being vague may not only be the better part of valor but also more fruitful. Partly, this may stem from our relative lack of knowledge about the natural categories of person perception. We do not think that much more can be said at present about this issue than the general assertion that individuals will encode others according to these categories unless there is incentive to do otherwise. Whatever *the* natural categories are remains to be discovered. Therefore, rather than looking at impression formation as a single process, it might be more fruitful to examine the different operations carried out in the making of an impression and to explore how each of these operations is influenced by top-down or bottom-up processes.

ACKNOWLEDGMENT

Preparation of this chapter was supported in part by grants from the United States-Israel Binational Science Foundation and the National Science Foundation (BNS 85-4236)

REFERENCES

Abramovitz, S. I., Berger, A., & Weary, G. (1982). Similarity between clinician and client: Its influence on the helping relationship. In T. A. Wills (Ed.), *Basic processes in helping relationships* (pp. 357–376). NY: Academic Press.

Bargh, J. A. (1984). Automatic and conscious processing of social information. In R. S. Wyer & T. K. Srull (Eds.), *Handbook of social cognition* (Vol. 3, pp. 1–43). Hillsdale, NJ: Lawrence Erlbaum Associates.

Brickman, P., Coats, D., & Janoff-Bulman, R. (1978). Lottery winners and accidents victims: Is happiness relative? *Journal of Personality and Social Psychology, 36,* 917–927.

Bruner, J. S., Goodnow, J. J., & Austin, G. A. (1956). *A study of thinking.* New York: Wiley.

Burnstein, E., & Schul, Y. (1983). The informational basis of social judgements: Memory for integrated and non-integrated trait descriptions. *Journal of Experimental Social Psychology, 19,* 49–57.

Carlston, D. E. (1980). Events, inferences, and impression formation. In R. Hastie, T. Ostrome, E. Ebbesen, R. Wyer, D. Hamilton, & D. Carlston (Eds.), *Person memory* (pp. 89–177). Hillsdale, NJ: Lawrence Earlbaum Associates.

Chaiken, S. (1980). Heuristic versus systematic information processing and the use of the source versus the message cues in persuasion. *Journal of Personality and Social Psychology, 39,* 752–766.

Chase, W. G., & Simon, H. A. (1973). Perception and chess. *Cognitive Psychology, 4,* 55–81.

Crocker, J., Hannah, D. B., & Weber, R. (1983). Person memory and causal attribution. *Journal of Personality and Social Psychology, 44,* 55–66.

Hastie, R., Park, B., & Weber, R. (1984). Social memory. In R. S. Wyer & T. K. Srull (Eds.), *Handbook of social cognition* (vol. 2, pp. 151–212).

Higgins, T. E., & King, G. (1981). Accessibility of social constructs: Information processing consequences of individual and contextual variability. In N. Cantor & J. Kihlstrom (Eds.), *Personality cognition and social interaction.* Hillsdale, NJ: Lawrence Erlbaum Associates.

Higgins, T. E., & Luria, L. (1983). Context, categorization, and recall: The "change of standard" effect. *Cognitive Psychology, 15,* 525–547.

Janis, I. L. (1982). *Groupthink.* (Second Edition). Boston: Houghton Mifflin.

Jones, E. E., & Pittman, T. S. (1982). Toward a general theory of strategic self presentation. In J. Suls (Ed.), *Psychological perspectives on the self* (vol. 1). Hillsdale, NJ: Lawrence Erlbaum Associates.

Kraut, R. E., & Higgins, T. E. (1984). Communication and social cognition. In R. S. Wyer & T. K. Srull (Eds.) *Handbook of social cognition* (Vol. 3, pp. 87–127). Hillsdale, NJ: Lawrence Erlbaum Associates.

Lemaine, G., Kastersztein, J., & Personnaz, B. (1979). Social differentiation. In H. Tajfel (Ed.), *Differentiation between social groups*. New York: Academic Press.

Lingle, J. H., Altom, M. W., & Medin, D. L. (1984). Of cabbages and kings: Assessing the extendibility of natural object concept models to social things. In R. S. Wyer & T. K. Srull (Eds.), *Handbook of social cognition* (Vol. 1, pp. 71–160). Hillsdale, NJ: Lawrence Erlbaum Associates.

Markus, H., Smith, J., & Moreland, R. L. (1985). Role of the self-concept in the perception of others. *Journal of Personality and Social Psychology, 49,* 1494–1512.

Newtson, D. (1973). Attribution and the unit of perception of ongoing behavior. *Journal of Personality and Social Psychology, 28,* 28–38.

Newston, D., & Engquist, G. (1976). The perceptual organization of ongoing behavior. *Journal of Experimental Social Psychology, 12,* 847–862.

Petty, R. E., & Cacioppo, J. T. (1984). The effect of involvement on responses to argument quantity and quality: Central and peripheral routes to persuasion. *Journal of Personality and Social Psychology, 46,* 69–81.

Reitman, J. (1976). Skilled perception in GO: Deducing memory structures from inter-response times. *Cognitive Psychology, 8,* 336–356.

Rosch, E. (1975). Cognitive representations of semantic categories. *Journal of Experimental Psychology: General, 104,* 192–233.

Rosch, E. (1977). Principles of categorization. In E. Rosch & Lloyd (Eds.), *Cognition and categorization*. Hillsdale, NJ: Lawrence Erlbaum Associates.

Schul, Y., Burnstein, E., & Martinez, J. (1983). The informational basis of social judgements: Under what conditions are inconsistent trait descriptions processed as easily as consistent ones? *European Journal of Social Psychology, 13,* 143–151.

Sherif, M., Harvey, O. J., White, B. J., Hood, W. R., & Sherif, C. (1961). *Intergroup conflict and cooperation: The Robbers Cave Experiment*. University of Oklahoma Book Exchange.

Srull, T. K. (1981). Person memory: Some tests of associative storage and retrieval models. *Journal of Experimental Psychology: Human Learning and Memory, 7,* 440–463.

Srull, T. K., Lichtenstein, M., & Rothbart, M. (1985). Associative storage and retrieval processes in person memory. *Journal of Experimental Psychology: Learning Memory and Cognition, 11,* 316–345.

Taylor, S. E., & Fiske, S. T. (1978). Salience, attention, and attribution: Top of the head phenomenon. In L. Berkowitz (Ed.), *Advances of experimental social psychology*. New York: Academic Press.

Taylor, S. E., Crocker, J., Fiske, S. T., Sprinzen, M., & Winkler, J. D. (1979). The generalizability of salience effect. *Journal of Personality and Social Psychology, 37,* 357–368.

Treisman, A. (1986). Features and objects in visual processing. *Scientific American, 255,* 106–115.

14 Are Two Modes Better Than One? A Critique of Brewer's Dual Process Model

Richard C. Sherman
Miami University

The area of social cognition has grown rapidly over the past 10–15 years, with an attendant increase in both the range of processes studied and the sophistication with which topics are approached. Until recently, there has been little attempt to integrate the diverse models and findings that have emerged from this work, although the ultimate benefit of social cognition for advancing our understanding of social behavior may well depend on the development of such integrations.

Brewer's dual process model of impression formation is clearly meant to be an integrative framework, and therein lies its potential contribution. As Brewer notes, however, the model is not intended to be as comprehensive or general as others that have been recently proposed, such as the formulation of Wyer and Srull (1986). Indeed, the Wyer and Srull model represents a remarkably ambitious attempt to integrate nearly all aspects of social cognition into a single set of processing and structural principles. Brewer's focus is much narrower, though her model still covers considerable theoretical and empirical ground. Specifically, her model is meant to represent ". . . that portion of social information processing in which incoming information about a new stimulus person (or set of persons) is integrated with prior knowledge drawn from long term memory" (p. 4). Brewer correctly recognizes, however, that a truly useful model of impression formation must also consider processing of additional information pertaining to persons about whom the perceiver already has some knowledge, and much of her discussion deals with questions concerning such processing.

In the remarks that follow, I will not attempt a thorough critique of all aspects of the dual process model. Rather, I will focus on four characteristics which I regard as both strengths and weaknesses of Brewer's framework: (1) the distinction between Identification and Categorization stages of processing; (2) the pictoliteral and hierarchical nature of categorical representations; (3) the determinants of categorical versus person-based processing and the level at which branching occurs; (4) the transition or evolution from one type of representation to the other.

THE DISTINCTION BETWEEN IDENTIFICATION
AND CATEGORIZATION

Brewer proposes that impression formation progresses sequentially through a series of processing modes, or stages. The first of these, the identification stage, is postulated to involve the automatic classification of the stimulus person along a small set of dimensions, such as age, sex, skin color. The process is automatic in the sense that it is ". . . stimulus controlled and not attentionally mediated" (p. 6). It also includes a global judgment of relevance to the perceiver's immediate needs and goals, and may include classification along primary affective dimensions such as hostile–friendly and strong–weak. The outcome of this stage is a crucial aspect of the model: a decision as to whether further processing is necessary, and if so, whether that processing will be category-based or person-based.

Recognition of the fact that impression formation often begins at a superficial level and procedes without much conscious intervention is a positive feature of Brewer's model. Indeed, it is hard to imagine that a perceiver could intentionally ignore the primary dimensions of age, sex, or race in an initial encounter with a target, providing that appropriate cues were available. Thus, the identification process may indeed be automatic in the additional sense that it is unavoidable under certain circumstances.

However, there are several issues that can be raised here, many of which are concerned with the sufficiency and separability of the processes that are proposed to take place in the Identification and Categorization stages. First, Brewer proposes that primary identification is sufficient for making the decisions that determine whether further processing is necessary and the form it will take. Specifically, the model postulates that classification of the target along age, sex, or race dimensions is enough to allow the perceiver to judge (a) the target's relevance to the perceiver's goals, and (b) the level of "self-involvement" the perceiver has with the target. Brewer's own examples imply, however, that additional processing must take place, at least in some situations. For instance, Brewer suggests that a traveler lost in a foreign city will make a judgment as to whether a stranger is a "local" as opposed to another foreigner before any further information seeking. It is doubtful that this judgment could be made simply on the basis of primary dimensions such as age or sex—although race might provide a sufficient cue at times. Rather, some processing (probably intentional and controlled rather than automatic) of other physical or behavioral features of the stimulus person would be required. Further, under conditions where a particular person category is relevant to the perceiver's goals (or is highly available in memory), it would seem that a target whose visible features provide a close match to that category would be automatically processed beyond the identification stage.

In short, it might be proposed that initial identification is automatic and primary, but processing continues until it produces an adequate basis for the relevance and self-involvement decisions. This possibility poses problems for the model as currently structured, however, since it would mean that not all decisions about further processing occur during the identification stage.

A second, related question involves the possibility that other automatic processes may influence the outcome of the identification stage. For example, recognizing a stranger as being physically similar to a friend generally occurs quite automatically and without conscious effort. In other situations, a person may seem familiar to us, though we cannot immediately say why that is so. In both of these instances the processing of stimulus information goes beyond primary classification or identification, and may influence the perceiver's decision of relevance and self-involvement. For example, stimulus persons who seem familiar or who are recognized as similar to a past acquaintance may be more likely to be judged by the perceiver as relevant and self-involving. If so, the model predicts that further processing of such targets will be person-based rather than category-based.

THE PICTOLITERAL AND HIERARCHICAL CHARACTER
OF PERSON CATEGORIES

According to the dual process model, one of types of processing that may result from the identification stage is category-based, i.e., incoming information is encoded and interpreted according to preexisting social categories, or person types. These categories are represented hierarchically, with the primary partitionings corresponding to the dimensions used in the identification stage. More specific or concrete subcategories are nested with these partitionings and are defined by combinations of social roles and other features.

The most intriguing aspect of this part of the model is the assumption that person types are represented as "pictoliteral" images in memory. These images are analogue representations, unmediated by verbal description. Traits and other semantic features are inferred from these pictoliteral representations at the time judgments are made, rather than represented directly in the mental image. Target information is categorized by a "template matching" operation which begins at the most general level and progresses to more specific categories until an adequate fit is attained. If information is inconsistent with the category prototypes, or if more information is available than can be fit into a single category, the individual may be encoded as a special instance of a category, a process called "individuation."

This emphasis on visual representation is, as Brewer points out, unique among models of social memory. Several models recognize the potential impact that visual information may have on impression formation, and some include the possibility that person information may be represented in imaginal form (Lord, 1980; Swann & Miller, 1982; Wyer & Srull, 1986). None of these, however, place visual representation in such a central role as it occupies in Brewer's model.

Despite the centrality of the pictoliteral assumption, Brewer has left many questions unanswered about how imaginal representations are involved in the impression formation process. For example, if person types are analogue images from which prototypic traits and behaviors must be inferred, then the categorization process must be more complex than Brewer has described. Specifically, if the initial information about a target includes nonvisual information from which a perceiver may infer traits, attitudes, etc., then the template matching operation would presumably involve examination of the fit between the target inferences and the pictoliteral inferences, in addition to the matching of visual images. That is, the pictoliteral representation *by itself* seems to be inadequate for the categorization process to be completed in this type of instance. A related question concerns the nature of the template. Is there one template that includes both imaginal and inferred semantic features or two separate templates, one for each type of information?

Similarly, the model proposes that once a satisfactory categorization of the stimulus person is achieved, further information processing will be organized around that category. Again, however, the additional information presumably may include semantic or nonvisual information which would be in a different format than the pictoliteral image, and thus the mechanism of comparison is not clear. One possibility is that trait and propositional concepts are derived from the prototypic image and then compared to a semantic or propositional representation of the incoming information. Another possibility is that the representation of a category prototype is not purely analogue, as Brewer proposes, but contains both pictoliteral and semantic components, as has been proposed in dual-code imagery models (cf. Kosslyn & Shwartz, 1977). Such a representation would be maximally efficient for processing information that is both visual and semantic, as is the case in many impression formation situations.

Aside from the questions of format and process noted above, the hierarchical organization of social categories raises some interesting questions of its own. The model proposes that a particular category can be differentiated into subtypes of increasingly greater detail and specificity as additional features are included in the classification process. "Young women," is a fairly general category, for example, while "young women newscasters" and "young women athletes" are more specific instances of the general category "young women."

A particular woman might be classified as a member of either of these sub-categories. The most interesting situation, however, arises when the target fits both subcategories. This is not the same type of situation discussed at length by Brewer, in which information is encountered that is inconsistent with an otherwise appropriate category. Here, information consistent with one of the categories is not inconsistent with the other. The model might propose that two representations of the stimulus person would be generated in this instance, one corresponding to membership in each of the categories. A second possibility, perhaps more in keeping with other aspects of Brewer's discussion, is that the target will be represented as an individuated instance of just one of the categories. Which category is chosen as the superordinate presumably might depend on such factors as primacy, salience, and level of activation of the two categories. The choice is important, because the model proposes that in the individuation process, information that is consistent with the main category is not incorporated into the individuated representation, whereas information about the secondary category is attached directly to the individual.

To take the issue of multiple categories a step further, Brewer seems to suggest that a new category may be formed from a combination of old ones if enough instances of the combined features are encountered. In the example being considered, this would involve the combination of young women newscasters and young women athletes. There are a number of possibilities concerning the hierarchical relationship between the old and new categories, and these different possibilities have correspondingly different implications for how the target may be represented in memory. Specifically, the new category in this example might be (1) young women newscasters who are also athletes, (2) young women athletes who are also newscasters, or (3) young women who are both newscasters and athletes. The first two possibilities would involve further differentiation of the existing subcategories, thus deepening the level of hierarchy, whereas the third possibility involves the creation of an entirely new subcategory at the same level. The trait inferences drawn from the first two categories would presumably differ with respect to their constituent qualities, whereas this would not be the case in the third. Thus, the addition of some mechanism to the model that would specify the nature of the hierarchical elaboration and the conditions under which it takes place would seem to be necessary.

THE DETERMINANTS OF CATEGORICAL VS. PERSON-BASED PROCESSING

According to the model, the choice between category and person-based processing depends upon whether the situation or characteristics of the target engage "self-involvement" at the time of identification. Brewer defines self-involvement as a feeling on the part of the perceiver of being closely related to or interdependent with the target, or being ego-involved in the judgment task. Self-involvement leads to person-based processing, while its absence leads to category-based processing.

This aspect of the model, despite its importance, is unfortunately one of the least developed. Brewer proposes that the major element of self-involvement that leads to the activation of person-based processing is the perceiver's affective investment in the process. The level of investment is postulated to be a function of the target's relationship to the perceiver's personal or social identity, and the target's relevance to the perceiver's personal needs and goals. Investment is proposed to be high under two conditions: (a) similarity of category membership between perceiver and target; (b) outcome interdependence between perceiver and target. Although it is not clearly articulated, the mechanism underlying personalized processing appears to be the greater attention paid to individuating information, particularly that which is expectancy-inconsistent.

The nature of self-involvement as described by Brewer is not precise enough to rule out a number of situations that blur the distinction between category-based and person-based processing. For example, it can be argued that in many situations a perceiver may have highly salient personal needs that make categorization, not personalization, the most appropriate processing goal. The lost traveler in a foreign city, for instance, might presumably have a very high level of affective involvement in processing information about strangers. Being in need of help from a friendly local resident, it is likely that incoming information would be matched against trait and category prototypes that would be relevant for satisfying that need. As defined by the model this would be category-based processing.

Conversely, the establishment of a person-based representation may occur in the absence of ostensibly high self-involvement. Conditions under which this happens include simply instructing perceivers to form an impression of individuals under high memory load (Srull, 1983), group situations of low memory load (Rothbart, Fulero, Jensen, Howard, & Birrell, 1978), and instances where visible characteristics of the target are distinctive given the group context (McCann, Ostrom, Tyner, & Mitchell, 1985; Taylor, Fiske, Etcoff, & Ruderman, 1978). In short, the determination of person-based processing may reside as much in the processing demands of the context in which information is encountered as it does in the self-involvement of the perceiver.

Granting for the moment that self-involvement *is* a necessary precondition for person-based processing, there are still some difficulties with the model in terms of specifying the point at which branching occurs. This was discussed earlier in considering the adequacy of the identification stage for assessing relevance and self-involvement, in which it was argued that categorization beyond the primary level may, at times, be necessary before such assessments can be made. In the present context this possibility can be carried further to suggest that in the course of category-based processing certain features of the target may be detected (or inferred) that stimulate self-involvement and heighten affective investment, and therebye produce a shift to person-based processing. This may have been the case, for example, in the Brewer and Lui (1985) study, where similarity between perceivers and targets at the subtype level of categorization, but not the superordinate level, resulted in greater differentiation and complexity of judgments.

In short, there seems to be no simple or clear relationship between the affective involvement of the perceiver and the mode of processing social information. Each may influence the other in ways that have not yet been fully specified by any model, including Brewer's. Perhaps the best characterization at the present time is that processing mode is determined by a complex interaction between (a) the perceiver's momentary and long-term personal goals, (b) the processing goals of the perceiver, (c) the structure, amount, and content of incoming information, and (d) current and anticipated task demands. Understanding how these factors exert their mutual influence is one of the major challenges facing cognitive social psychologists (cf. Wyer & Srull, 1986).

THE TRANSITION FROM ONE TYPE OF REPRESENTATION TO THE OTHER

One of the areas of social cognition that has been relatively unexplored is how the format and structure of a perceiver's representation of another person changes over time. Within the context of the dual process model, such changes would be from pictoliteral categorical representations to propositional networks organized around specific individual identities or vice versa.

As the model is presently formulated, it does not accommodate these transitions. For example, Brewer seems to argue that a category-based representation can only become more "individuated" with additional information and greater experience with the target. Information that is inconsistent with or goes beyond category expectations is attached to the individual, not the category as a whole. Thus, although the category representation of a person may become more differentiated, its essential character is not altered. This is a rather strong assumption, and appears to be contradicted by evidence of shifts in memory organization to person-based patterns with increasing familiarity (e.g., Pryor & Ostrom, 1981; Srull, 1983).

Brewer does allow for the possibility that information about a particular individual may be coded in memory in both a category-based and person-based representation simultaneously (p. 25). She does not specify, however, the conditions under which this might occur, though the evidence she cites appears to have been obtained under low self-involvement and in a situation where some information referred to the target by name and some by category label (Wyer & Martin, 1986). Thus, dual representations might be quite common. There are two implications of this that are not adequately addressed. First, if dual codes can be generated from the same input stream of information, then the branching assumptions of the model are either inaccurate or incomplete. Second, new information might plausibly be relevant to both representations, yet the model seems to suggest that it will be incorporated into just one, resulting in greater individuation *or* greater personalization. One model of social cognition that seems to hold promise for handling the multiple-code problem is that proposed by Wyer and Srull (1986), which specifies not only the nature of multiple codes in memory but also the relationship between information contained in different representations. In principle, at least, there seems to be no reason why certain features of the Wyer-Srull model might not be incorporated into the dual process formulation.

SUMMARY

Brewer's dual process model has considerable heuristic value for contributing to our understanding of impression formation processes. Among its positive features are (1) the emphasis on the role of visual information and imaginal representations in impression formation, (2) the depiction of initial processes as automatic and stimulus-controlled, and (3) the focus given to affect and emotion as potential determinants of processing mode and representation format.

However, there are also several shortcomings of the model as it is now formulated that limit its contribution. Most of these center in the lack of specification of the mechanisms that control processing and determine the organization and format of the representation of information. The immediate challenge faced by proponents of the model is therefore to detail these mechanisms and the principles that govern them so that the potential of model can be more clearly assessed.

REFERENCES

Brewer, M. B., & Lui, L. (1985). Categorization of the elderly by the elderly: Effects of perceiver category membership. *Personality and Social Psychology Bulletin, 10,* 585–595.

Kosslyn, S. M., & Shwartz, S. P. (1977). A simulation of visual imagery. *Cognitive Science, 1,* 265–295.

Lord, C. G. (1980). Schemas and images as memory aids: Two modes of processing social information. *Journal of Personality and Social Psychology, 38,* 257–269.

McCann, C. D., Ostrom, T. M., Tyner, L. K., & Mitchell, M. L. (1985). Person perception in heterogeneous groups. *Journal of Personality and Social Psychology, 49,* 1449–1459.

Pryor, J. B., & Ostrom, T. M. (1981). The cognitive organization of social information: A converging operations approach. *Journal of Personality and Social Psychology, 41,* 628–641.

Rothbart, M., Fulero, S., Jensen, C., Howard, J., & Birrell, P. (1978). From individual to group impressions: Availability heuristics in stereotype formation. *Journal of Experimental Social Psychology, 14,* 237–255.

Srull, T. K. (1983). Organizational and retrieval processes in person memory: An examination of processing objectives, presentation format, and the possible role of self-generated retrieval cues. *Journal of Personality and Social Psychology, 44,* 1157–1170.

Swann, W. E., & Miller, L. C. (1982). Why never forgetting a face matters: Visual imagery and social memory. *Journal of Personality and Social Psychology, 43,* 475–480.

Taylor, S. E., Fiske, S. T., Etcoff, N. L., & Ruderman, A. J. (1978). Categorical and contextual bases of person memory and stereotyping. *Journal of Personality and Social Psychology, 36,* 778–793.

Wyer, R. S., & Martin, L. L. (1986). Person memory: The role of traits, group stereotypes, and specific behaviors in the cognitive representation of persons. *Journal of Personality and Social Psychology, 50,* 661–675.

Wyer, R. S., & Srull, T. K. (1986). Human cognition in its social context. *Psychological Review, 93,* 322–359.

15 Impression Formation in a General Framework of Social and Nonsocial Cognition

Eliot R. Smith
Purdue University

Researchers and theorists in social cognition are increasingly turning to complex models involving both postulated memory structures (e.g., schemas, categories) and processes. This trend stems from a growing recognition that hypotheses concerning cognitive structures cannot be adequately formulated or tested in the absence of assumptions about processes, and vice versa (Locksley et al., 1984; Wyer & Srull, 1986). Brewer's person memory model is a welcome step forward along these lines.

My own theoretical preference (Smith, 1984) is for models that lean more toward the pole of explanatory adequacy than toward parsimony. I have advocated the adoption of J. R. Anderson's ACT* model (1983) of memory and cognitive processes as a base which can be extended with constructs that are essential in accounting for *social* cognition (e.g., affect, the self, attitudes, attributional inferences, person impressions). Characteristic features of ACT*, and thus of the sort of encompassing theory of social cognition that I envision, are the following:

(a) it is a global model that integrates cognitive structure and process;

(b) procedurally, it includes both automatic and controlled processing modes;

(c) structurally, it possesses multiple representational formats (for propositions, images, etc.) but no absolute distinction between semantic and episodic memory; and

(d) it emphasizes the role of goals in directing processing.[1]

---

[1]Many of these global features are shared by Wyer and Srull's (1986) model, but there are many detailed differences, whose discussion is not essential to the purpose of this Commentary.

Thus, from my perspective the positive aspects of Brewer's model include its emphasis on the interaction of structure and processes, on the distinct roles of automatic and controlled processing, and on the importance of the perceiver's goals.

In this Commentary, I examine the extent to which Brewer's insights regarding impression formation can be related to more general issues in social and nonsocial cognition. I focus on three: the notion of primitive categorizations (by gender, race, or other highly salient distinctions), the structure and use of person categories, and the nature and use of person-based representations.

AUTOMATIC ("PRIMITIVE") CATEGORIZATION

Brewer holds that automatic or preattentive processes not only categorize people as people, but also classify them along a few highly salient dimensions (age, race, or gender). Evidence for automatic processing can come from Stroop interference, where a dimension that is putatively processed automatically interferes with controlled processing that is intended to focus on a different dimension.

The Stroop-type study that Brewer cites is unconvincing, however. Subjects made same/different judgments on pairs of pictures with respect to either gender or occupation. The pictures' match or mismatch on gender significantly influenced RTs to the occupation question, while the reverse did not hold. However, there are at least two problems with drawing the conclusion from this evidence that gender must be processed automatically. First, as Brewer later notes, people may hold different representations of social roles (such as occupations) for role occupants differing in gender—even when both genders can hold the same role. That is, female doctor may not be represented as the same occupation as male doctor (p. 12). Thus a gender mismatch in the pictures may cause subjects to access different occupational representations and therefore to take a relatively long time to decide that the occupations are actually the same. In effect, Brewer's claim is that gender is an attribute of all social roles, including occupations.

A broader argument is that occupation and gender are correlated in the real world. Subjects obviously know these covariations and may use them in the occupation-judgment task. Thus one would expect people to use gender information in the occupation judgment, because they have found gender to be a useful cue to people's occupations in the past. Better evidence of Stroop interference requires that the automatically processed dimension and the other dimension used in the task have an arbitrary relationship where subjects do not have non-laboratory experience with particular covariations between the dimensions (for example, the color of ink in which words are printed and the content of the words).

A recent study (Zarate & Smith, 1986) obtained results suggesting Stroop interference in a study without these interpretive problems. Subjects read a category label (a racial or gender label or any of several attributes used as controls) and were then shown a head-and-shoulders photograph of a person. They pressed a key as quickly as possible to indicate whether or not the label described the pictured person. The response times to verify different categorizations for photos of different types were the main variable of interest. An informative pattern emerged on the categorization times for race and sex. Black photos were categorized by sex more slowly than white photos. Conversely, female photos were categorized by race more slowly than male photos. This pattern suggests that attributes (being black or female) that depart from a cultural "standard" (white, male) are processed automatically and can interfere with processing on other dimensions. This accords with Brewer's prediction, except that white male may serve as a default categorization that does *not* require special processing. Further research based on this type of method may provide fuller evidence on what attributes are processed automatically by what types of subjects in what contexts and conditions.

Of course, the specific dimensions that are classified automatically will depend on people's learning history as well as on context. Practice making particular categorizations or other types of social judgment can lead to automaticity of processing (Anderson, 1982; Smith & Lerner, 1986). Thus, there can be no fixed line between dimensions that are processed automatically and those that are not. A new-car salesman who (because of occupational demands) classifies hundreds of people daily as potential customers versus mere "lookers" may eventually make distinctions along that dimension automatically. In our society race, gender, age, and (I would add) socioeconomic status are highly salient determinants of many significant social roles, so they are probably processed automatically by most adults. But this might not hold true in other cultures, while other dimensions (e.g., clan membership) might attain automatic status.

STRUCTURE AND USE OF PERSON CATEGORIES

Brewer's views on the nature and use of person categories are difficult to characterize exactly. For example, I was unable to identify her position with any of the three classes of prototype-based categorization models discussed by Smith and Medin (1981); featural, dimensional, or holistic. This ambiguity makes it difficult to evaluate Brewer's proposals definitively. However, some comments can still be made.

Structure of Categories

Brewer clearly believes that person categories constitute discrete types rather than points on continuous-valued dimensions (p. 9). She also holds that the underlying attributes of categories, the stimulus features that underlie similarity judgments and are cues to category membership, are generally binary-valued features rather than continuous dimensions (pp. 9, 12). The evidence she cites (cf. Dull, 1982; Tversky, 1977) pertains to the nature of attributes rather than categories themselves. (These two issues are not identical, because either discrete types or continuous dimensions as a final category structure could be underlaid by a similarity metric based on either discrete features or continuous attributes.)

Brewer goes on to describe person categories as "fuzzy sets" (p. 10), naming an approach which has major problems as a theory of category structure (Osherson & Smith, 1981). However, Brewer does not actually seem to be invoking the assumptions of fuzzy-set theory in this paper.

Finally, Brewer states that person types are represented by *images*, which are described as "specific," "configural," "analogue," and continuous (p. 13). This idea contrasts confusingly with the claims that categories are discrete types defined by discrete attributes. Images that are analogue and continuous are the very opposite of discrete; for example, such facial-appearance variables as "babyishness," eye size, and forehead height are intrinsically continuous. Therefore categories represented by visual templates or images necessarily fall along continuous-valued dimensions rather than constituting discrete types. It is unclear how Brewer intends to reconcile these divergent implications of her ideas. Thus, in terms of postulated category structure, it is not clear to me whether Brewer's model is featural or dimensional (Medin & Smith, 1984; Smith & Medin, 1981). Are the attributes across which category-to-instance similarity is defined discrete features or continuous dimensions?

Brewer's other principal claim on category structure is that all categories are nested within partitions of the "primitive," automatically processed dimensions—that is, that those dimensions are attributes of all categories. This implies that subject-identified person types will be nested within these partitions. However, Brewer's data (p. 16) support this idea only weakly. Relatively few of the types cross primary dimension boundaries, but some above-chance nesting of types within *any* dimension (e.g., eye color, hair length) is to be expected since all dimensions contribute to the perceptual similarity of stimuli. We need to empirically differentiate Brewer's claim that the primitive dimensions enclose *all* person types from the weaker and self-evident idea that socially significant dimensions (like gender and age) influence similarity judgments, leading to a strong tendency for types to be nested within these dimensions. To support Brewer's stronger hypothesis, the logic of the situation seems to call for nearly exceptionless nesting, which is not observed.

Categorization Processes

Given a set of categories represented in memory, how are they used to categorize new instances? The standard assumption for a featural or dimensional model of categorization is that the similarity of the new person to candidate categories would be computed, and the category with the most similarity to the new person would be used to encode the person. The nature of the similarity metric would, of course, differ depending on whether the category attributes are featural or dimensional (Smith & Medin, 1981, chaps. 4–5). The metric could also involve independent cues or relational coding (Medin & Schaffer, 1978), depending on whether stimulus-prototype similarities on different features (or dimensions) are weighted and summed or are combined by a multiplicative or more complex rule. Prototype models have typically been assumed to be independent-cue models, although this is not necessary. A number of tests have compared independent cue and relational coding models, with consistent support for the latter (Medin, Altom, & Murphy, 1984, p. 350).

However, Brewer does not follow any of the above assumptions on these issues. Instead, she invokes a template-matching process (pp. 14–16). Her reason seems to be the "strength and rapidity" with which social categorizations can be made. However, template matching or holistic categorization processes have serious problems (Smith & Medin, 1981, ch. 6). Everyday circumstances can easily cause such extreme changes in visual appearance that stored templates will fail to match the stimulus. A person who is viewed from a different distance or a different angle (head-on, three-quarters right or left, etc.) will form a very different image on the retina, and even these transformations will pose insuperable problems for simple template-matching processes. Even if an image normalization process is assumed to allow for such transformations, losing weight, getting a sun-tan, or growing a beard could cause such major overall changes in facial appearance that a template may fail to match, while recognition processes based on invariant facial features or dimensional values would have little problem.

In summary, from this paper I was unable to determine Brewer's exact assumptions about category structure and categorization processes. Except for the in-passing reference to fuzzy sets, which I believe is not intended to invoke the full set of assumptions of that theory, Brewer does not adopt any of the recent models of categorization (e.g., Elio & Anderson, 1981; Hintzman, 1986; Medin & Schaffer, 1978), either whole or as a basis for modification. Since her own model cannot easily be defined from the material in this paper, there is little basis for the explicit and careful derivation of testable hypotheses that would allow the validation of Brewer's insights. In general, closer theoretical contact between models of social and nonsocial categorization might improve both the precision of social cognition models and the breadth and realism of nonsocial models.

NATURE AND USE OF PERSON-BASED REPRESENTATIONS

Perhaps the most novel hypothesis in Brewer's model is that under some conditions person-based rather than category-based impressions are formed. Person-based impressions are (a) driven by bottom-up processing, dependent on the person's actual observed characteristics rather than on a priori expectations. (b) They are represented propositionally rather than as images. Finally, (c) the person's attributes including category memberships (e.g., occupation) are represented as subordinate to the person node, rather than the reverse.

Of course, it is difficult empirically to discriminate propositional from image-based or other types of representations (cf. Anderson, 1978). The basic reasons Brewer gives for preferring images to represent person types (pp. 13–14) are that images can represent configurations of information, going beyond discrete features or attributes, and that categorizing people by visual appearance and drawing inferences can be done with great "strength and rapidity" (p. 14). Are these reasons less true for familiar persons (for whom person-based representations are used) than for unfamiliar ones? It seems likely that well-known individuals can be visually recognized with even more strength and rapidity than can others. In general, more attention is needed toward the derivation of specific empirical hypotheses that will allow the testing of image versus propositional representation models. Lord's (1980) study along these lines stands essentially alone to date.

The issue on which I wish to focus in this section, however, is the meaning of the "mental flip-flop" (p. 22) which differentiates category-based from person-based representations in Brewer's model. In a category-based representation, for instance, the information "Janet is a nurse" would be represented (presumably propositionally) with Janet being one member of the category of nurses. The person node is "subordinate" to the category. In a person-based representation, however, the same information would be represented with nurse subordinate to the Janet node. Her occupation is one of many attributes known about Janet and she is not just one of many nurses known to the perceiver. This mental flip-flop is intuitively appealing but the exact distinction between the two postulated representations is unclear.

Like many theorists in social cognition, Brewer does not spell out her general assumptions regarding memory and cognitive processes in any detail; this is one of the reasons that I believe social cognition models might profitably be built within the context of a general, well-specified cognitive theory. Let us fill in some reasonable assumptions and see whether they allow any way to fulfill Brewer's requirements. In one model of propositional memory (Anderson's ACT*, 1983) links between concepts are represented by proposition nodes whose arguments are other nodes in memory. That is, the proposition "Janet is a nurse" would be represented by a proposition node with three links emanating from it: an S (subject) link to a node for Janet, an R (relation) link to a node representing the relation of category membership, and a P (predicate) link to a node representing the concept of nurse. This representation is symmetrical in that neither node (Janet or nurse) is "subordinate" to the other, giving no basis for transformation into a distinct "flipped" representation. This single representation can be used both to name Janet as an example of a nurse and to retrieve being a nurse as an attribute of Janet.

An asymmetry could be introduced by one aspect of ACT*'s memory model: differential fan. Fan refers to the number of facts known about a concept in memory (i.e., the number of links spreading from a given node). A larger fan makes the retrieval of any given link harder (slower and less probable). The concepts of Janet and nurse might have different fan. For example, the perceiver might know 20 nurses but only know 5 attributes of Janet. It would then be easier to retrieve Janet's occupation than to retrieve Janet as an example of a nurse. Conversely, if only 5 nurses are known but 20 facts about Janet are known, it would be relatively easy to name Janet as an example of a nurse but harder to retrieve nurse as her occupation.[2] Note that the direction of these trends caused by fan effects in memory is *opposite* to what Brewer's model might predict, if one assumes that person-based representations of well-known individuals generally incorporate more information than do category-based ones. Brewer might predict that a person represented in a category-based manner would be readily cited as an example of the occupation, while it would be more difficult to come up with attributes of the person directly. Similarly, Brewer might predict that someone represented in a person-based manner in memory would be less likely to be cited as an example of the occupation but could have his or her attributes retrieved quickly.

In summary, propositional representations as usually conceived in cognitive models[3] do not allow asymmetry of the sort Brewer postulates, and introducing asymmetry via differential fan generates predictions which seem to go in the wrong direction (though this is my inference; Brewer herself does not spell out retrieval predictions of this sort). Thus, overall it is not clear how Brewer's distinction can be expressed within a propositional memory model.

Why Aren't Person Representations Used to Classify Others?

As noted above, the core idea in Brewer's model is that two types of representations are stored in memory, categorical and person-based. Only categories (person types), and not person-based representations, are used in the process of comprehending and making inferences about newly encountered persons. Moreover, the categories are used as prototypes: the most similar type or subtype from memory is used to categorize the new person. We end up with a dual-representa-

---

[2]This example deals only with the effects of fan. One could make the additional assumption that information about Janet in the latter case is organized in such a way that increasing fan does not materially slow the retrieval of any one fact (Reder & Anderson, 1980). However, the point of the example stands: fan effects cannot generate an asymmetric representation with the properties required by Brewer's model.

[3]Alternative models might generate different predictions. However, as noted, Brewer does not commit herself to a particular general framework of assumptions regarding memory and cognitive processes, and her specification that the representation is propositional appears to rule out some (nonpropositional) alternatives like Wyer and Srull's (1986) Storage Bin model.

tion model in which more abstract (categorical) representations are used as prototypes to make classification decisions, and more concrete (person-based) representations are output from person perception and inference processes but are not used in further classification decisions.

Though this sort of prototype-based model of categorization has been common in social cognition (e.g., Brewer, Dull, & Lui, 1981; Cantor & Mischel, 1979), it has difficulty in accounting for several types of observations. A theoretical alternative, an exemplar-based model of categorization, can do better in many cases by assuming that previously encountered *person* (in addition to category) representations can be accessed from memory and used to classify and make inferences about newly encountered persons. Some observations that weigh in favor of an exemplar model of social categorization are the following (cf. Kahneman & Miller, 1986; Medin & Smith, 1984; Smith & Medin, 1981).

1. A prototype-based category cannot represent within-category variability in a natural way. People can make judgments about the amount of variation within social groups, and in fact such judgments are systematically influenced by the perceiver's group membership: Ingroups are judged to be more diverse than outgroups (Quattrone, 1986). Yet a prototype image of a category does not represent the category's variability at all, and must be supplemented by some other representation (Smith & Medin, 1981, p. 87). If category representations include remembered exemplars of the category, then it becomes natural to postulate a process of retrieving a sample of exemplars and computing their variability along a target attribute (Linville, Fischer, & Salovey, 1987).

2. Prototype representations (at least with independent-cue similarity metrics) cannot represent correlated attributes within a category. The usual example is the correlation of size and singing within the category of birds. People know that small birds are more likely to sing than are large birds, and can use such knowledge of attribute correlations in categorization, finding it easier to classify new instances that maintain learned correlations than instances that violate them (Medin & Schaffer, 1978). However, a prototype cannot represent correlations among attributes. For example, if the prototype bird is a small bird that sings, like a robin, then birds that differ on two features (large, nonsinging birds) would be predicted to be *more* dissimilar to the prototype and hence harder to classify than birds that differ on only one feature (large, singing birds or small, nonsinging birds). This is contrary to the evidence. A set of stored exemplars, most of which are either small and singing or large and nonsinging, could be used to classify new exemplars in a way that would be sensitive to correlations among attributes (Smith & Medin, 1981, p. 157).

3. Prototype models have trouble accounting for category learning: It's hard to know when and how to update the prototype or to form new subtypes as experience with the category accumulates. If the typical attributes of category

members that one encounters change over time, then a prototype formed on the basis of early experience needs to be modified to more accurately reflect more recent experiences. (Alternatively, one could predict that prototypes never change once they are formed, leading to obvious but yet-untested predictions concerning classification errors.) But how much should it be changed? Presumably the prototype should have a weight equal to the number of exemplars that contributed to its formation, and each new exemplar should have weight 1, in computing the new prototype. However, the prototype does not contain information about how many cases it was based on; like variability information, this would have to be represented separately. If the category is represented in memory as a set of exemplars, the addition of new ones which (along with old ones) will affect future processing becomes a natural operation. In fact, one might predict that recent experiences (because they are more accessible in memory) might be overweighted in making new categorization decisions.

4. Priming and context influence categorization judgments (Barsalou, 1982; Kahneman & Miller, 1986; Roth & Shoben, 1983; Smith & Medin, 1981, pp. 93–96). For example, a robin is ordinarily more easily categorized as a bird than a chicken is, but in the sentence "The bird walked across the barnyard" the reverse is the case (Roth & Shoben, 1983). Prototype models have particular difficulty with these observations. Do we have a separate prototype for each possible context? In that case the model loses its claim to parsimony, and in the limit comes close to an exemplar model. Context, priming, and "availability" effects are easy to account for by an exemplar model, as the particular set of exemplars that is retrieved from memory and used to process new experiences may depend on contextual factors as well as on the specific instance that is being processed (Barsalou, 1987; Kahneman & Miller, 1986).

5. As Kahneman and Miller (1986) have observed, people can use ad hoc categories just as easily as familiar ones. That is, people don't seem to have much trouble using categories like "things that might fall on your head" (Barsalou, 1987) for which it is implausible that they have formed and stored a prototype. Retrieval of specific exemplars seems to be the only reasonable mechanism by which people can make judgments about ad hoc categories. Thus, a model that says people use prototypes for familiar categories seems to require a prediction that ad hoc categories should be considerably more difficult to deal with.

6. Finally, prototype models have problems accounting for long-lasting effects of single experiences with category members. A single experience might have a minor impact on the prototype (e.g., a prototype that was based on 100 cases may be moved 1% of the way from its original values toward the new exemplar's attribute values). Unless one assumes that information about the specific experience is also stored and used in the future, however, a repetition of that experience or a new one similar to it will not be processed specially. That is, prototype models assume that similarity to the prototype, not similarity to old

exemplars, determines how a new instance will be processed. Exemplar models, in contrast, predict that the treatment of a new exemplar that is identical or similar to one previously encountered may be influenced by the attributes of the old one.

Lewicki (1986) has demonstrated this phenomenon in the social realm. In one study, subjects who encountered an experimenter who insulted them later avoided a different person who had hair of a similar length; control subjects who were not insulted by the experimenter showed no tendency to avoid the person with the similar attribute. In another study, Lewicki showed subjects three photographs of females paired with verbal descriptions which emphasized a specific ability (e.g., math, languages) in each case. The person described as high in math ability had a different type of hair style than the other pictured women. Subjects were then asked in an ostensibly separate experiment to rate six new photos on a number of dimensions including math ability. With other dimensions of facial similarity controlled, the test photo with hair arranged similarly to the high-math-ability person was also rated significantly higher in math ability. In these and other studies, it is implausible to argue that one's prototypic representation of a unfriendly person or of a person with strong math abilities is changed in a lasting manner by a single experience. Instead, the results seem to call for the assumption that information about the specific experience is stored and can influence judgment and inferences in the future.

In summary, Brewer is probably correct in postulating that perceivers store information about both social categories and individual persons in memory. However, information about specific, known persons or category exemplars as well as category-level information may be used to categorize, make inferences, and form representations of newly encountered individuals. The advantages of exemplar-based representations of social categories are strong, in the areas mentioned above and potentially in other areas as well (Linville et al., 1987; Smith, 1988).

CONCLUSIONS

Social cognition may be moving closer to claiming its "sovereign" status (Ostrom, 1984) among the related fields of social, cognitive, developmental, and personality psychology. The progress in this direction to date reflects the power of emerging theoretical paradigms but is limited by the difficulty of several major issues that remain. One significant issue that has run through this Commentary is how impression formation can be fit within general models of social and non-social cognition. Brewer's model takes a step toward such integration in its recognition of the importance of goals, the contributions of automatic and controlled processes, the interaction of structure and process, and the fact that persons are not always perceived and represented in the same way.

However, impression formation models ultimately need more theoretical explicitness. The value of Brewer's insights would be increased by the provision of more detail on the structure and processing of representations in this model (e.g., how categories are represented, how category-to-instance similarity is computed, what the "mental flip-flop" means). Finally, we should explore models of person perception and person memory that supplement the storage of category-level and person-level information with processes that can use exemplars (not just category prototypes) to categorize and make inferences about people. The potential for theoretical and empirical gains from contact between the literatures on person memory and categorization processes is great (Kahneman & Miller, 1986; Linville et al., 1987; Rothbart & John, 1985; Smith, 1988).

ACKNOWLEDGMENT

Preparation of this article was facilitated by Office of Naval Research Contract N00014-84-K-0288. Correspondence regarding this article should be sent to Eliot R. Smith, Department of Psychological Sciences, Purdue University, West Lafayette, Indiana 47907.

REFERENCES

Anderson, J. R. (1978). Arguments concerning representations for mental imagery. *Psychological Review, 85,* 249–277.

Anderson, J. R. (1982). Acquisition of cognitive skill. *Psychological Review, 89,* 369–406.

Anderson, J. R. (1983). *The architecture of cognition.* Cambridge, MA: Harvard University Press.

Barsalou, L. W. (1982). Context-independent and context-dependent information in concepts. *Memory and Cognition, 10,* 82–93.

Barsalou, L. W. (1987). The instability of graded structure: Implications for the nature of concepts. In U. Neisser (Ed.), *Concepts and conceptual development.* Cambridge, England: Cambridge University Press.

Brewer, M. B., Dull, V. T., & Lui, L. (1981). Perceptions of the elderly: Stereotypes as prototypes. *Journal of Personality and Social Psychology, 41,* 656–670.

Cantor, N., & Mischel, W. (1979). Prototypes in person perception. In L. Berkowitz (Ed.), *Advances in experimental social psychology* (Vol. 12, pp. 3–52). New York: Academic Press.

Dull, V. T. (1982). *Two strategies of social classification.* Unpublished dissertation, University of California, Santa Barbara.

Elio, R., & Anderson, J. R. (1981). The effects of category generalizations and instance similarity on schema abstraction. *Journal of Experimental Psychology: Human Learning and Memory, 7,* 397–417.

Hintzman, D. L. (1986). "Schema abstraction" in a multiple-trace memory model. *Psychological Review, 93,* 411–428.

Kahneman, D., & Miller, D. T. (1986). Norm theory: Comparing reality to its alternatives. *Psychological Review, 93,* 136–153.

Lewicki, P. (1986). *Nonconscious social information processing.* Hillsdale, NJ: Lawrence Erlbaum Associates.

Linville, P. W., Fischer, G. W., & Salovey, P. (1987). *Perceived distributions of the characteristics of ingroup and outgroup members.* Unpublished paper, Yale University.

Locksley, A., Stangor, C., Hepburn, C., Grosovsky, E., & Hochstrasser, M. (1984). The ambiguity of recognition memory tests of schema theories. *Cognitive Psychology, 16,* 421–448.

Lord, C. G. (1980). Schemas and images as memory aids: Two modes of processing social information. *Journal of Personality and Social Psychology, 38,* 257–269.

Medin, D. L., Altom, M. W., & Murphy, T. D. (1984). Given versus induced category representations: Use of prototype and exemplar information in classification. *Journal of Experimental Psychology: Learning, Memory, and Cognition, 10,* 333–352.

Medin, D. L., & Schaffer, M. M. (1978). A context theory of classification learning. *Psychological Review, 85,* 207–238.

Medin, D. L., & Smith, E. E. (1984). Concepts and concept formation. *Annual Review of Psychology, 35,* 113–138.

Osherson, D. N., & Smith, E. E. (1981). On the adequacy of prototype theory as a theory of concepts. *Cognition, 9,* 35–58.

Ostrom, T. M. (1984). The sovereignty of social cognition. In R. S. Wyer & T. K. Srull (Eds.), *Handbook of social cognition* (vol. 1, pp. 1–38). Hillsdale, NJ: Lawrence Erlbaum Associates.

Quattrone, G. A. (1986). On the perception of a group's variability. In S. Worchel & W. Austin (Eds.), *The psychology of intergroup relations* (Vol. 2, pp. 25–48). Chicago: Nelson-Hall.

Reder, L. M., & Anderson, J. R. (1980). A partial resolution of the paradox of interference: The role of integrating knowledge. *Cognitive Psychology, 12,* 447–472.

Roth, E. M., & Shoben, E. J. (1983). The effect of context on the structure of categories. *Cognitive Psychology, 15,* 346–378.

Rothbart, M., & John, O. P. (1985). Social categorization and behavioral episodes: A cognitive analysis of the effects of intergroup contact. *Journal of Social Issues, 41*(3), 81–104.

Smith, E. E., & Medin, D. L. (1981). *Categories and concepts.* Cambridge, MA: Harvard University Press.

Smith, E. R. (1984). Model of social inference processes. *Psychological Review, 91,* 392–413.

Smith, E. R. (1988). Category accessibility effects in a simulated exemplar-based memory. *Journal of Experimental Social Psychology, 24.*

Smith, E. R., & Lerner, M. (1986). Development of automatism of social judgments. *Journal of Personality and Social Psychology, 50,* 246–259.

Tversky, A. (1977). Features of similarity. *Psychological Review, 93,* 3–22.

Wyer, R. S., & Srull, T. K. (1986). Human cognition in its social context. *Psychological Review, 93,* 322–359.

Zarate, M. A., & Smith, E. R. (1986). *Categorization processes in person perception.* Unpublished manuscript, Purdue University.

16 Reply to Commentaries

Marilynn B. Brewer
University of California, Los Angeles

The reader has by now a virtual smorgasbord of social cognition facts, concepts, and models from which to choose a stimulating (and filling) intellectual feast. I am very impressed with the calibre of constructive criticism represented in all of the commentaries that were written for this volume. Each of the commenters took the dual process model seriously as a point of departure, and then brought in their own points of view to challenge basic tenets of the model, elaborate components where the model is currently imprecise, or expand on points that are not addressed adequately within the constraints of the model. The result is a much richer set of ideas with considerably more heuristic value than could have been derived from the original theory paper alone.

I do not think it is either possible or appropriate to reply to each of the commentaries in turn or to address all of the points raised by the various authors. Instead, I will limit my final comments to a defense (and clarification where needed) of those basic distinctions in the dual process model that stimulated the most active debate.

A defense of sharp dichotomies is always difficult because such distinctions are inevitably oversimplifications—referring to differences that are actually multifaceted continua rather than distinct phenomena. To state aspects of any theoretical model in terms of dichotomies is justified only as a device to call attention to distinctions that have functional significance. On these grounds, I think that the ultimate impact of the many commentaries on the dual process model is to reinforce the basic distinctions represented in that model.

Two Processes or One?
The dual process aspect of the original model certainly received the most critical attention. Most of the commenters challenge the branching feature of the model

that separates category-based (top-down) from person-based (bottom-up) processing at an early stage. The critics differ, however, in the alternative models that they propose in place of this assumption. Some prefer a single levels-of-processing model that begins with top-down processing (e.g., Fiske, McCauley); others advocate a single-process model that is either all bottom-up (e.g., Hampson) or bidirectional (e.g., O'Sullivan, Rothbart, Schul & Bernstein, Sherman). Still others opt for a multiform model in which different processing modes operate simultaneously or in parallel (e.g., Anderson, Feldman). Preferences among these alternative representations tend to be correlated to some degree with beliefs about whether social and nonsocial cognition should be treated as distinct or as essentially the same.

The disagreements over appropriate alternatives to the dual process assumption suggest that the basic distinction between the processes and outcomes associated with top-down vs. bottom-up processing has functional significance. The history of my own thinking on this issue is illustrative. As Fiske points out in her commentary, an earlier version of my model was presented in a presidential address to the Western Psychological Association annual convention (Brewer, 1985). At that time the model took the form of a single levels-of-processing continuum, beginning with top-down, category-based processing and progressing to personalization as the final stage of "deep" processing at the individual level.

Working within that earlier framework gave me two problems. First, the stage model implied that perceivers had to progress through earlier stages before reaching later ones. Thus, a personalized impression of a target individual would not be achieved until the individual had first been typed and individuated with respect to some category placement. Second, the progression from "individuation" to "personalization" required a major reorganization of information that had already been stored and structured in memory in a different form—an assumption that did not seem consistent with much of the research on memory-based judgments (e.g., Schul, 1986). Ultimately, the inconsistencies in my own conceptualization led me to abandon a single process approach in favor of the dual process model. (It is of some interest to note that Susan Fiske and I seem to have reversed positions here. At the time I was developing the earlier levels-of-processing model, the Fiske and Pavelchak (1986) model had a branching feature similar to the one I now advocate.)

In the current version of the model, person- and category-based processing differ in how new information is incorporated into an existing impression and the way that information is organized hierarchically. An analogy may be provided by thinking of two different ways in which a physical structure (such as a scale-model building or a piece of sculpture) can be constructed from component elements. In one mode, the constructor starts with a mold or a frame and inserts new component materials into the existing framework, filling in some parts here, and adding some new elements there, but the final product is constrained by the structural features of the original mold. In the second mode, the constructor starts with the individual component elements, piecing them together in novel ways, constrained only by the possible structural relationships between new elements and those that have already been incorporated in the construction. We would agree that these two modes of construction are not entirely dissimilar. Both are limited by some common structural constraints, and even the piecemeal construction project is guided by some prior model of the structure to be produced. But I think we would also agree that the products of the two construction modes are likely to differ significantly in content and structural properties.

The distinction drawn in the dual process model between individuated and personalized representations of individuals is analogous to these two types of constructions. Personalized impressions differ both in the level of abstraction at which information is represented and in the idiosyncratic configuration of component elements contained in the representation. Most of the commenters on the model challenged the meaningfulness of this distinction, but I was delighted to learn of some supportive evidence in the research reported by Klatzky and Andersen. Results from a new paradigm for studying impression formation under naturalistic conditions (Park, 1986) also indicate that impressions formed of real people over time (under conditions conducive to personalized impression formation) tend to be trait dominated in the way that Klatzky and Andersen report to be characteristic of high intimate as compared to low intimate person representations.

To hold that personalized and category-based impressions are distinct and separate representations does not mean that they are mutually exclusive. Both types of representation may be formed of the same individual. O'Sullivan's comments are particularly interesting on this point because they place dual processing in an interactive context, suggesting that during the course of a single social exchange, processing may switch from one mode to another depending on arousal of affect and reciprocity.

In the original paper, evidence in support of dual representations is cited from a study by Wyer and Martin (1986). What the dual process model implies is that such representations are very different ways of viewing the same individual that are not easily reconciled, and are *not* interchangeable in the manner suggested by Feldman and Schul and Bernstein, nor different gradations of the same representation as suggested by Rothbart. Further, personalized impressions are not expected to become category exemplars, as suggested by Smith.

Representation Format: Visual or Propositional?

Probably the most controversial aspect of the dual process model is its tying of process and form in the creation of different person representations. Some commenters site this aspect as a major strength of the model (e.g., Medin), while others regard it as a significant flaw (e.g., Fiske). Much of the argument in favor of different representational formats is implicit in the discussion of the distinction between personalized and individuated representations. The issue of difference in format is probably less essential than that of difference in structure, though the former serves to accentuate the latter.

I was distressed that Klatzky and Andersen did not accept my emphasis on pictoliteral representations of social categories, since I had intended that conceptualization to included *inferences about* nonvisual attributes, roles, behaviors, etc. (as suggested in the comments by Sherman). However, Klatzky implies that her use of the term is more strictly limited to visual representation, so I have apparently overextended the concept in my useage. The distinction that Klatzky and Andersen draw between social stereotypes and "trait types" seems to me consistent with the dual process model assumptions if one takes into account different types of categories as discussed in the following section.

Identification Versus Categorization

One of the implicit points (though apparently not well articulated) of the dual process model is that there are different kinds of social categories that enter the person perception process at different stages. This point is made more explicit by the classification provided in Feldman's comment (Table 3.1). In my model, feature-based categories (or in Feldman's terms, "taxonomic categories") characterize the identification stage of processing; person types (represented by pictoliteral *prototypes*) characterize category-based processing; and trait dimensions are used to organize person-based impressions. Thus, multiple representations (as emphasized in the comments by Anderson, as well as Klatzky and Andersen) are allowed for in the model but as products of different representational processes.

Several of the commenters challenge in particular the distinction drawn in the model between identification (as a precategorization process) and person typing (e.g., Feldman, McArthur, Schul & Bernstein, Smith), seeing these as continuations of the same categorization (or stimulus-driven) process differing only in attention to detail. In my model, identification is simply feature recognition, which has no particular stereotyping content. Person categories (types), on the other hand, are feature *configurations* that are rich in stereotypic implications. If forced to make inferences based on taxonomic classifications alone (e.g., knowing only that the target person is male or female), the perceiver will draw on particularly salient person types within that taxonomic category as "default" options, but if provided with more concrete information will readily abandon the standard stereotype in favor of more differentiated subtypings. A number of recent studies (e.g., Pratto, Bargh, & Fisher, 1986; Pryor, McDaniel, & Kott-Russo, 1986) support the contention that global, abstract attributes (such as "masculine" and "feminine") function very differently in person memory than do more concrete social stereotypes.

RELEVANCE VERSUS SELF-INVOLVEMENT

Closely related to criticisms of the identification-categorization distinction in the dual process model are criticisms of the distinction between relevance (as the primary determinant of processing beyond the identification stage) and self-involvement (as the primary determinant of person-based versus category-based processing). In my view, relevance refers to somewhat distal judgments of the stimulus with respect to task demands and situational goals whereas self-involvement was intended to refer to more proximal judgments with respect to enduring personal needs and self identity. Most critics see these as two different sources of motivational or attentional factors that determine level of processing.

Self-involvement is, admittedly, one of the least clearly articulated aspects of the dual process model at this stage of development. In retrospect, a better term to have used in this connection might be "self-referencing" rather than self-involvement, since that more clearly distinguishes it from "importance" in a more general sense. Perhaps an example will also help to clarify the distinction.

When members of the social psychology faculty in my department are evaluating applicants for admission to our doctoral program, there are really two potential judgments to be made. One is to determine whether the applicant is a suitable candidate for the PhD degree in our program, and the other is whether the applicant is to be accepted as one's own advisee and a future member of one's research team. For me, both are personally involving judgment tasks in the sense that they are important and I am motivated to make a good, carefully considered decision on the basis of the information I have available. However, I am aware that I use that information differently and employ different judgment rules when I find myself making the former decision rather the latter.

Usually, some piece of information encountered early in reviewing the applicant's file (such as the expressed field of interest or the mention of my name versus some other faculty member's name in the applicant's goal statement) cues one decisional set or the other. If I adopt the objective graduate admission set, I am likely to compare the information about the candidate to various prototypic conceptions that I have about successful and unsuccessful doctoral students, increasing my ratings to the extent that his or her features match those of some successful model. If, on the other hand, I find myself evaluating the applicant as a personal advisee, I am more likely to use myself as the important reference point, seeking information relevant to social comparison needs, complementarity of interests and abilities (I don't want my students to match my computer skills; I want them to exceed mine), and compatability of interpersonal style. Interestingly, if I find reason to reject the applicant on such personalized bases, I also find it very difficult to revert to the other judgment mode in order to make a final decision about suitability for admission to the program in general. That is because the change in self-reference requires that I go back to the original information and reorganize it in a different representational framework.

O'Sullivan's comments on the social context of person perception raise the possibility that interactants in a social exchange may come to the situation with different goals and perspectives that lead to different processing modes. The effects of such asymmetries on the course of interaction and the impressions of the interacting parties that are ultimately formed would make an interesting focus for research on the interrelationships between social cognition and social interaction.

Where is Behavior?

One final point of debate about the dual process model is the criticism—made most emphatically by Jones and Hampson—that it does not effectively incorporate the extensive theory and research literature on attributional processes, and I agree that this is a major weakness of the model. The original purpose of the dual process model was to reconcile the largely independent literatures on social category stereotypes and impression formation at the person level, and this did not adequately address person perception processes in which behavior rather than the person is the unit of analysis. While we may disagree as to the relative distribution of category-based, person-based, and behavior-based processing in everyday social cognition, I think most researchers would agree that a complete theory of social perception would incorporate all three. Recent models of attributional processes (e.g., Green, Lightfoot, Bandy, & Buchanan, 1985; Jones & McGillis, 1976; Trope, 1986) recognize that attributional outcomes are greatly affected by the context provided by expectancies associated with individual persons, with social categories, and with situations (scripts). This point of contact between attributional processes and social categorization should be much more fully elaborated, and I hope that the dual process model provides a framework for such further development.

REFERENCES

Brewer, M. B. (1985). *Forming impressions of others: From social object to person.* Presidential address to annual meeting of the Western Psychological Association, San Jose, CA.

Fiske, S. T., & Pavelchak, M. A. (1986). Category-based versus piecemeal-based affective responses: Developments in schema-triggered affect. In R. M. Sorrentino & E. T. Higgins (Eds.), *The handbook of motivation and cognition: Foundations of social behavior* (pp. 167–203). New York: Guilford Press.

Green, S., Lightfoot, M., Bandy, C., & Buchanan, D. (1985). A general model of the attribution process. *Basic and Applied Social Psychology, 6,* 159–179.

Jones, E. E., & McGillis, D. (1976). Correspondent inferences and the attribution cube: A comparative reappraisal. In J. Harvey, W. Ickes, & R. Kidd (Eds.), *New directions in attribution research* (Vol. 1, pp. 389–420). Hillsdale, NJ: Lawrence Erlbaum Associates.

Park, B. (1986). A method for studying the development of impressions of real people. *Journal of Personality and Social Psychology, 51,* 907–917.

Pratto, F., Bargh, J., & Fisher, J. (1986). *When do stereotypes of groups influence judgments of individuals? The independence of global and trait-level components of sex stereotypes.* Unpublished manuscript. New York University.

Pryor, J., McDaniel, M., & Kott-Russo, T. (1986). The influence of the level of schema abstractness upon the processing of social information. *Journal of Experimental Social Psychology, 22,* 312–327.

Schul, Y. (1986). The effect of the amount of information and its relevance on memory-based and stimulus-based judgments. *Journal of Experimental Social Psychology, 22,* 355–373.

Trope, Y. (1986). Identification and inferential processes in dispositional attribution. *Psychological Review, 93,* 239–257.

Wyer, R. S., & Martin, L. L. (1986). Person memory: The role of traits, group stereotypes, and specific behaviors in the cognitive representation of persons. *Journal of Personality and Social Psychology, 50,* 661–675.

Author Index

Numbers in *italics* denote pages with bibliographic information.

Subject Index